WHO WAS EDGAR CAYCE?

EDGAR CAYCE, unwitting seer and clairvoyant, touched millions of lives with his innate spiritual wisdom and his uncanny healing visions.

Born in 1877 in Hopkinsville, Kentucky, Edgar Cayce had a seventh-grade education, yet was able to repeat complex and technical medical jargon when under a trance. In this state, he was said to heal many of the people who came seeking his counsel with his recommendations for medical treatment. Cayce soon began to talk about spiritual notions such as Atlantis, reincarnation, dreams, astrology, and more. He would also predict some of the more astounding events of the twentieth century, such as World Wars and the Great Depression.

The Washington Post wrote: "His words have inspired faith in spirituality, which for many people is more powerful than science." Called the "sleeping prophet" and "America's greatest psychic," Cayce, who died in 1945, may have been the first to usher in what is now known as the New Age Movement. More than fifty years after his death, his work continues to influence our lives in powerful new ways.

D1453369

BOOKS IN THE EDGAR CAYCE SERIES
FROM ST. MARTIN'S PAPERBACKS

PASSAGE TO THE MILLENNIUM

Edgar Cayce and the Age of Aquarius

MARY ELLEN CARTER

St. Martin's Paperbacks

For my grandchildren, Jon, Julia, and Sean

PASSAGE TO THE MILLENNIUM

Copyright © 1998 by Mary Ellen Carter.

Edgar Cayce Readings Copyright © 1971 by Edgar Cayce Foundation. Used by permission.

ISBN: 0-312-96743-8

Printed in the United States of America

St. Martin's Paperbacks edition / November 1998

10 9 8 7 6 5 4 3 2 1

CONTENTS

ACKNOWLEDGMENTS

To my daughter Joanna and my son Jim for their loving support for me while I wrote this book, I owe my greatest gratitude. I am especially grateful to Jim for reading the manuscript in its early phases and for giving me good helpful advice throughout.

I look back to 1991 when I acquired better understanding and concern for the Russians than I had before, thanks to Grigori Polunov, a Russian literary agent living in the United States. He had become interested in the Edgar Cayce readings. I appreciate that Jeanette Thomas, Administrator of Records for the Edgar Cayce Foundation, put him in touch with me. I never met him in person, but at his request I sent him a copy of *Passage to the Millennium*. His reaction was: "Russia needs this book!" I think it was, in part, because it includes Edgar Cayce's amazing predictions that Russia was being "born again." Because he was living in America and had seen how freedom and democracy really do work, he yearned to bring to his native land Cayce's message that could help heal his people. But, sadly, he died before he could see it happen. I treasure the enthusiasm he had for this book and the valuable and revealing perspective he brought to bear.

I have drawn on many sources covering the events of the century's last two decades. Throughout the writing of the book, I was fortunate to hear speakers appearing before audiences in Virginia Beach and Norfolk with diverse points of view yet on the same wavelength: an American who is teaching young democracies to work; a Russian professor who spoke of glasnost; an American professor of Russian history;

an American authority on the United Nations; a German professor speaking on the fall of the Berlin Wall. And there were from throughout the world a number of outstanding journalists and writers, historians, religious leaders, and spokesmen and -women who made their statements at various times in the recent past, without which Cayce's prophecies would not have been validated. I thank them for their contributions to this project.

1

"A New Order"

*It is also understood, comprehended by some, that
a new order of conditions is to arise; that there must
be the greater consideration of each individual, each
soul being his brother's keeper. (3976-18)*

THE CAYCE READINGS, CENTRAL to this book, predicted
the fall of the Soviet Union. Subsequently, we saw communism fall in the majority of nations. Since 1932, other major
political, social, and economic conditions were addressed by
Cayce, referring to deeds of consciousness of world leaders
and of ordinary men and women, to truth or error that motivated them, as well as astrological influences. It was only in
the last decade of the twentieth century that we could evaluate
how accurate were his predictions, or how his words could
be of help today.

Changes Cayce previewed are not only political but also
religious in character. Throughout time, in fact, all political
and social change has grown out of understanding in the
hearts of a few leaders of what our familiar religious values
and concepts represent. In the past, this occurred seldom, as
history recounts just a few enlightened groups such as the
Essenes two thousand years ago ushering in and nurturing the
advent of the birth of Jesus Christ. Another major period was
the seventeenth and eighteenth centuries when Western civilization broke from monarchy to independence. It was a natural outgrowth from biblical teachings about man's freedom

under God. In the 1990s, we have seen many nations free from oligarchy and communism.

Events that brought great changes in the twentieth century in hindsight can be seen as passage into the new millennium. Many people born ninety years ago have lived through two world wars and the Great Depression in the early years to see the rise and fall of communism in much of the world; friendship between the United States and Russia; slavery give way to freedom; improvement in race relations; progress toward peace in the Middle East and other nations, all evincing growth in consciousness by masses of people. Can we look forward to the continuation of that work of the human heart and mind as we go into the twenty-first century?

In 1938 Cayce spoke of "a new order of conditions to arise." He described it as based on Christian principles and standards in the interests of all people.

However, by the 1920s there was, according to irrefutable historic documentation, already in place a "new order" that was not in the interests of anyone but a few wealthy and powerful men while their fellowman suffered through two world wars and the Great Depression of the 1930s. That new order was created by a ruthless "invisible government" reported to have been in existence since 1910, controlling all banking institutions and thus all financial conditions. Unbelievable as it seems, the group is said to this day to orchestrate wars and financial booms and busts for the benefit of the power elite.

"Outwardly we have a Constitutional government," states James Perloff in his book *Shadows of Power*. But regardless of who is in the White House, Perloff states, "Within our government we have another body . . . a bureaucratic elite is sure our Constitution is outmoded . . . all strange foreign policy agreements may be traced to this group who are going to make us over to suit *them*." He calls it "a legitimate mafia" and says this secret government promotes the idea of "globalism" in order to build a new international order serving only those elite factions.[1]

According to a growing number of authors, this "new

world order" is instigated and operated by various agencies based on humanistic notions that have impeded spiritual progress since Adam. Its aim, say these authors, is "one world" under socialism, which will cut down America's sovereignty and that of all other democracies and lead ultimately to a world dictatorship. It was characterized in 1913 as "the invisible government by the money power" by Congressman Charles Lindbergh, Sr., one of the foremost opponents of the Federal Reserve Act.[2]

Belief in God inspires people to seek freedom to worship and to create their own destinies. It is inherent in the teachings of Jesus Christ. Democracy is inherent in its tenets. So, not surprisingly, those "one world" folks never mention any religious concepts as its basis. In the old Marxist mind-set, it seeks in fact to do away with religion, according to these critics. In his book *None Dare Call It Treason*, John Stormer states that the Protestant Christian doctrine was corrupted more than seventy years ago when several influential socialist professors in the theological seminaries attacked the virgin birth of Mary and the risen Christ. Later, that apostasy was preached from the pulpits, paving the way for a secular society. It served to empower those of like minds who want to create a socialist world state.[3] Reportedly, facilitating this goal are the Federal Reserve Board, the Council on Foreign Relations, and the Trilateral Commission.

According to several authors, through behind-the-scenes political manipulation, membership in these organizations has provided entree into the highest offices of the land and includes presidents since Woodrow Wilson.

States Bill Still in *On the Horns of the Beast*, the Federal Reserve became law in 1913 yet not a part of the federal government. Because of "the Fed," ". . . the American people have lost the power to control their own money. Congress granted it away in 1913 to a stockholder-owned corporation—the Federal Reserve. It's not Constitutional. It's not legal. . . ." He goes on, "America is on the horns of a beast—an economic beast—that threatens to destroy our nation as we know it, and drastically alter the lives of all who live here."[4]

How did it happen in this nation protected by laws governing the commonwealth?

In 1913, after a few days of swiftly manipulated pressure in the Senate and House, the Federal Reserve Act was passed before Congress had had time to discuss it fully, Still explains. Until 1913, banks were owned privately. The nation was financially strong. But when the "Federal Reserve System" was created, "the new bank now had total control over how much money was made available in the U.S., by control of its lending policies with power to issue U.S. currency, lend the government money at interest, and then convert that federal debt into money to be loaned out by its member banks ten times over, or more, to their customers. What a deal!' The new bank would be owned privately by banks around the country but dominated by the New York Federal Reserve Bank, which itself was dominated by . . . the Rockefellers, the Morgans, . . . the Rothschilds.''⁵

The system of credit was now in the hands of a few men who within only ten years allowed the national debt to rise sharply from about $1 billion to $25 billion!

A debt-based money system now required more money. So President Wilson was persuaded to sign the new income tax bill. In 1916 he wrote in his book *The New Freedom*: "We have come to be one of the worst ruled, one of the most completely controlled governments in the civilized world . . . a government by the opinion and duress of a small group of dominant men."⁶ In 1924, "On his deathbed, Wilson is reported to have said, 'I have unwittingly ruined my government.' '' ⁷

Until then, there had been no income tax, because there had been enough revenue from tariffs and excise taxes. Now began the taxation of America's hard-earned income to pay the banker-originated federal debt.

Although we trustingly believe that the rise and fall of interest rates are to protect us from inflation, Still declares: "The Federal Reserve System has not been a source of economic stability. It has not held inflation in check. It causes inflation for its own benefit. The Fed hasn't prevented depressions. It has intentionally caused them in order to fleece

America's middle-class flock. . . . throughout its history, the Fed has been directly responsible for empowering America's enemies financially, so they could better make war on American citizens. This is treason against American national sovereignty!"[8] He reminds us that the Federal Reserve lent millions to the communist dictatorship in Russia after World War I. Plans were to create a "one world" that included communism, neatly socialized for our children and grandchildren.

Why haven't we been told about the invisible government? The answer is: The world has been kept ignorant of it by secrecy and deception during the entire twentieth century.

I would not pay attention to these frightening reports if they had not been thoroughly documented by the authors with names, places, dates, and historic events as irrefutable proofs. It is a background with sinister significance. Among the betrayers, however, as the authors tell us, there are reported good men in government who were the deceived and the betrayed who looked back in regret for their part in helping to carry out the scheme.

Which brings us to what the good people around Edgar Cayce were asking him as he lay on his couch in his self-induced psychic sleep.

"WHO CONTROLS THE FINANCIAL WORLD?"

Passage to the Millennium is about international events as they transpired during the twentieth century and interpreted by the Edgar Cayce readings. They bear witness that Cayce clearly must have seen these groups and their high-handed plan for a "one world" under socialist control. *This* "new world order" is *not* the "new order" described by Edgar Cayce.

Edgar Cayce predicted sixty-five years ago the major political, social, and economic events in the years since his time. *Passage to the Millennium* is an account of how those predictions came about. His words were poised for consideration only in the last decade of the twentieth century because, until now, his prophecies of world affairs had not yet been fulfilled.

As we approached the Age of Aquarius, the times were indeed changing at an accelerated rate. But even in his day, his words were urgent because, as a prominent economist later declared, the world was at a crossroads.

In Cayce's time, when Russia was of opposite ideology to both religious and democratic nations and her people had suffered for seventy years because of it, he indicated that the *new order* was based on religious principles. It was in sharp contrast to the ideas that led to socialism under Stalin. He warned against greed and selfishness in any country, including the United States, that made for hardships for its citizens.

Happily, great unprecedented changes are taking place not envisioned by anyone but Cayce. We touch on world events from 1913 to the present, however sketchily, when we were still caught in old world nationalism and isolationism. But there has been developing a new vision on the part of many to look out for the other guy, an evolving metamorphosis by reform of old ways to more enlightened ways, a world renewed, if not yet fully reborn, by the same benevolent forces that have shaped our destinies in the past. But there is another, age-old, opposing force at work—those "principalities" of darkness that are, in our time, the outgrowth from that same sinister origin: the claim that man alone moves his destiny, and that some of us can bully the rest of us with impunity. It was the same mind-set that brought Russia and her satellite nations to ruin by the "invisible government." This is an organization of secrecy that today is warned against by journalists who see specific evidence of such manipulation of the economy. Now, as in the past, many people in the third world who still live under economic and political tyranny cannot speak out for fear of death to themselves or their families. Only "the new order" under God's law can work for all people, Cayce indicated. Many agree. God's "invisible government," inclusive of all faiths, is invisible because it is of our hearts and minds, and we see the results manifested only in social, economic, and political reform. Parallels are drawn between that true invisible government and Freemasonry, as both point out to us America's spiritual role in leadership and the transcendency of all mankind. For man is designed to strive for peace and soul victory—and win—in the face of all odds. The peace and plenty we seek are not yet won. A lot depends on our everyday lives and whether we live selfishly or for others. It was a recurring theme in the readings of Edgar Cayce.

In his trance state, in tune with his higher mind, he was able both to prophesy about and advise with authority on issues of his time and ours. He has over the years had an amazing record of prophecy fulfillment and reliability, both on the personal level for many people and on the world level.

During the 1930s, one of the major subjects on which Cayce was asked for advice was the economy. The crash of 1929 was still fresh in everyone's minds during those troubled years. In 1932 he was asked by his alert friends for "financial and political advice for establishing peace on earth and good will among men." On the subject of world economics he had much to say, throwing light on that dark side of finance of which we have become aware. He cited the cause behind the financial crash of 1929 that led to the Great Depression. It was a revelation of the truth:

"The most serious point in the present civilization has been the fall of '29 when there was given into the hands of two—yea, three—individuals—the financial conditions and situations in the world."

"Who controls the financial world?" he was then asked.

"Warburg, Mellon, Morgan," he replied. (3976-10)

These were Paul Warburg, member of the Council on Foreign Relations and member and architect of the Federal Reserve; John P. Morgan, closely associated with the CFR founders; and Andrew Mellon, U.S. secretary of the treasury.

In my book *Edgar Cayce on Prophecy*, I offered several readings given on the economy. Among them were these: "Edgar Cayce attributed the division in this country to 'fear on the part of those who control capital investment' and a lack of universal oneness of purpose."[9]

"The causes of the Great Depression . . . were the 'combination of wrath, oppression and sin.'"[10] Here again he seems to describe the activities of the "legitimate mafia," especially the Federal Reserve.

How did the Fed cause the crash of 1929? According to Bill Still, in August 1929, the Fed began to tighten money, raising interest rates. The Bank of England did the same. "At the same time the Fed began to sell government securities, another money contracting move. This was the final signal to get out of the stock market and put all their assets in cash or gold bullion. And that's what they did. . . . The effects of the Fed, says this author, can take up to a year to be felt," but in 1929 "the system began to sink about six weeks later."[11]

Throughout the 1930s and 1940s, Cayce continued to speak out against the greed and selfishness of what was unmistakably that of the invisible government. Today, that oppressive system is reported to prevail, implying new leaders of like mind who would seek to do away with nationhood and impose a world government based on manipulation and deceit—a conspiracy among the major powers.

In 1997, manipulation against the economic well-being of the American people was again evident. Since the beginning of 1997, the nation's credit unions that provide small loans for working people became the target of the big banking industry. Whereas throughout the past several decades, banks have lost half their former market share in deposits, the credit unions have remained strong. They were intended to serve the working people who wanted small loans from an institution in their own area, where they could help control it with a democratic system and by vote. They are non-profit, and thus tax-exempt. In early 1997, the American Bankers Association sued the United States credit union industry on the grounds the competition was unfair. On July 28, 1998, I talked to Ron Burniske, president and CEO of Chartway Federal Credit Union. The decision would affect many members of its ten branches in Norfolk and Chesapeake, Virginia and five more in Houston and Rhode Island. He said that although the lower court said the banks overstepped the rights of the credit unions, the Supreme Court favored the banks. But he said the House voted 400 to 45 for credit unions. The Senate made victory complete with the score 93 to 6. I asked what it meant to him. "Free choice!" he replied happily, "for people who want to join credit unions."

In January 1997, UN Secretary General Kofi Annan declared to President Clinton his resolve to reform the UN. Journalist Cliff Kincaid referred to the UN's demand of the United States to pay up a "debt" of more than $1 billion. But, he says, during 1992–1995 we supported the UN-backed peacekeeping operations with $6.6 billion, $4.8 billion of which was never counted as a gift.

However, most controversial is the UN's push for global taxation, which former Secretary General Boutros Boutros-Ghali endorsed. The U.S. Senate voted against that, and global taxes decreased by a 70–28 margin. "Nevertheless," states Kincaid, "officials at the UN Development Programme have edited a 300-page book, titled 'The Tobin Tax,' . . . on how to implement a global tax on international currency. . . . This tax could affect IRAs, pension funds, mutual funds, and other investments of ordinary Americans. Will Annan make sure that work on these schemes stops immediately?"[13]

We wonder what is behind such a "global" tax, if not the busy and voracious "legitimate mafia"?

During the twentieth century, all nations have entered a time of testing the will for, and adherance to, principle. We are not always successful. We still have the laggards who would cling to power over the rest of mankind. For forty-five years since the UN was formed, the organization was not effective until the Gulf War against Saddam Hussein.

GOD'S NEW ORDER

The Presbyterian Sunday school teacher spoke of principles, ideas, and ideals. These applied to nations, to groups, and also to individuals. His World Affairs readings, which were both national and international in scope, particularly related Christian principles to the conduct of nations. This was consistent with Cayce's central theme running throughout his readings: the sovereignty of Jesus the Christ in both the saving of individuals and of nations.

This series of twenty-nine readings was given beginning in

1927 at the request of individual members of A.R.E.; and later by the group called the Glad Helpers; Study Group One, led by Cayce himself; and the Norfolk Study Group. From 1939 until his death, readings were given as well for the Seventh through the Thirteenth Annual Congresses, 1938–1944.

Prophecy of great world changes was stated over the years in various readings, but particularly in the collection termed "World Affairs," later published as a *Circulating File*. It was in context with current events taking place but looking beyond to a time Cayce called "the new order." They were given in compliance with topics requested for the times: the Great Depression, World War II, when they were needed perhaps more than in any other time in history because of the magnitude of world suffering. Principles, standards, and ideals of Christ were to be those on which the new order would be created, a blueprint for rebuilding on the ruins of the old order.

As we have seen, Cayce had a markedly different one-world vision from that of the "legitimate mafia." The causes of economic failure and political instability of the time, he said, were greed and selfishness. His strong words for the evils of his day sound amazingly appropriate for our times as well: "There is arising in the affairs and the experiences of man everywhere the necessity of there being not so much the consideration of a land as of all lands as a unit. For *Mankind* is his brother, and thou *art* thy brother's keeper." This is hardly interpreted to mean the "one world" of financial overlords. Certainly the financiers did not consider themselves their brothers' keepers! Only Cayce conveyed a world united in the power of true brotherhood.

In another reading he harked back to a few years before when the fate of mankind was at stake: the Versailles Peace Conference in June 1919 ending World War I.

"The closest there has come the laying of an *ideal* was when those nations, those representatives of many nations, sat as in counsel. And yet man's greed, man's fear of his own self, so entered in that it became as a stumblingblock for the world. And there has arisen from those same influences, those forces, that have become crystallized in the minds of individuals that have gathered about themselves, and crystallized into activity, such an influence that soon there must be a reckoning. For again has the Prince of Peace been *crucified* upon the altar, the cross of greed!'' (3976-16) There's no doubt he meant the invisible government in place then. It's interesting that the first of Wilson's Fourteen Points for world peace was: no secret international understandings. Next came absolute freedom of the seas in peace and war, followed by removal of economic barriers and reduction of armaments.

All nations signed the treaties except America. Instead of finding support, when Wilson returned home he found American political leaders in acrimonious debate on the hard treaty of peace with Germany. Both Republican and Democratic parties opposed it; the Senate rejected it. President Wilson staunchly defended it throughout his term, which led to a physical breakdown from which he never recovered. Congress later made separate peace treaties with Germany and Austria.[14]

Then followed the Roaring Twenties, a time of ''easy money,'' and suddenly the crash of 1929.

Influences Cayce refers to here were those he said destroyed in 1918 what could have been a new order benevolent for everybody under the League of Nations, reducing the chances of another war. It had been suggested by Wilson in his Fourteen Points, but when the United States refused to join, other nations declined and the League was dissolved.

During the 1930s, Cayce emphasized many times that there must be the return to a standard in the top levels of the financial and political affairs of the world. It had been exemplified, he said, in the spirit ''directing those influences in the peace at Versailles . . .''

It was ''a peace without victory,'' without revenge; he wanted terms of open covenants of peace, removal of economic barriers, freedom for the various European nations to regain sovereignty and autonomy, restoration of lands to their former owners.

Without the backing he had hoped from Congress, Wilson went to Paris to try at the peace conference to win support for his plan. Europeans, too, rejected it. Was such massive opposition to Wilson due to the invisible world government? Cayce stated that Wilson's Peace of Versailles was "damned by those of other thought that would make capital of same" (3976-12). Yet, he said, "in the *soul* of the representative of the United States sat the Prince of Peace; yet many would have you believe, in the economical world, the financial world, that had *that* man never left his home . . . that the *world* would be better today. Not so; for 'Ye shall pay every whit.' For 'the heavens and earth may pass away, but *My Word* shall not' are the words of him Who *made* the world" (3976-8).

"THE LEVELING"

Millions of people were caught in the Great Depression. When this reading was given on April 18, 1936, the times were black with despair in a world suffering under tyranny, war, and economic hardship. Small wars had continued in Europe based on old problems. By 1936 World War II was already beginning.

Cayce now advised: ". . . it behooves all of those who have an ideal as individuals, as well as groups or societies or organizations, to be practising, applying same in their experience—and their relationships as one to another. For unless these are up and doing, then there must indeed be a new order in THEIR relationships and their activities."

The ideals in Wilson's Fourteen Points have influenced world leaders since then, especially in ending the cold war with Russia, a "peace without victory, without revenge," which of course we all cheered. They were the foundation for today's summits.

Wilson's Fourteen Points for overcoming war and world suffering can be seen as a giant step toward the third millennium and what it could mean for us. It was only a few years after World War I that Cayce declared there was to be a "leveling" in the political, the economic, and "the whole relationships" in the world. He urged that we pray to be guided in all our ways. Change in those concerns could include institutions and governments designed to serve all people alike through prayer by those who believe in a God who knows our dire needs. As Mahatma Gandhi showed, as Nelson Mandela and Martin Luther King have shown, the most effective means of bringing about a benevolent leveling is the power of prayer. He ascribed the ending of World War I in 1918 to that invincible power: "What do you think caused that meeting between the democratic countries and the totalitarian states? Was it because of the wisdom of the men that met? Rather *it was the prayers of the mothers and the fathers* of each nation represented there that there might not be any more destruction of life!" (3976-23)

This reinforces Cayce's advice that we "Pray that peace may be in the minds and hearts of those who direct the destiny of the many throughout the world. For they are NOT in power of themselves . . ." (3976-21). Today, we would do well to pray that not only peace but also wisdom be in the minds and hearts who lead against those who seek to destroy our freedom through economic bondage: the invisible government. Cayce advised a return to a standard, in whatever endeavor we address, to implement reform for the highest good. At that time, as now, the realization of peace on earth, good will toward men depended on standards set before those who led.

RETURN TO A STANDARD

In the 1930s the "period of aggression" by Germany, Italy, and Japan had prompted appeasement by Britain and France. In 1932 Cayce stated in reading 3976-10: "There must be first the return to a *standard* by which peace on earth and good will might be achieved on the political and economic level, by which it is to be judged, and then there may be gradually worked out a plausible, equitable, applicable situation in the affairs of the world." They must be considered, he said, "as a unit only and not as a whole, for there are conditions and developments in the present that are of the unit-making conditions in the financial and political arena." By the phrase "not as a whole," he seems to reject the idea of a "one world" or "whole world" government, but rather one made up of the many distinct nations cooperating in groups for mutual benefit. Did he foresee the danger of one world under the control of powerful banking institutions? Today, we are aware of banks and savings and loans that have brought about hardships for many, the growing gap between business profit and the workers' pay, reports of slave labor in some countries. We can almost hear Cayce's words resounding for us, as well, because the age-old greed of the money changers that angered Jesus Christ hasn't gone away.

In 1938, as the Depression deepened, Cayce told the A.R.E. Congress: "It is also understood, comprehended by some, that a new order of conditions is to arise; that there must be the greater consideration of each individual, each soul being his brother's keeper" (3976-18). Sadly, when that reading was given, the world had fallen deep into the worst period of man's history, when such a "new order" under God seemed to be more remote than ever. In this reading, again, he favored the World Court: "That which has been presented in the World Court in the present is the better basis for the *final* relief, that will make for the working out of the financial and political powers that be." He was evidently drawing attention to a meeting of the World Court in Geneva to which President Herbert Hoover had sent a delegation just days before. It was a typical case in which he was "in tune" with events taking place anywhere in the world, especially as they had to do with the question he was addressing at the time.

In June 1938, Cayce warned that

> . . . there must be many a purging in high places as well as low; the greater consideration of each individual, each soul being his brother's keeper . . . For His ways will carry through. For as He gave, "Though the heavens and the earth may pass away, My Word will not pass away." All too often has this message been forgotten in the pulpits and in the organizations, not only in the national relationships but in the international relationships. . . .
> And as the dealings are as one to another, unless these

are in keeping with those tenets they must fail; for all power in heaven and earth hath been given into His hands. . . .

And ONLY those who have set their ideal in Him and practised it in their dealings with their fellow man may expect to survive the wrath of the Lord. . . ."

(3976-18)

WORLD WAR II BEGINS

At that terrible juncture, the beginning of World War II, Cayce declared that we have forgotten God. The core of his message was our daily lives and how we live them, individually and collectively. God's standards of love and harmony as expressed in all major religions must be adhered to by the nations if there is to be lasting peace and prosperity. But at this worst point in modern history, Cayce's kind of "new order" seemed to be more remote than ever. In the 1930s the period of aggression by Germany, Italy, and Japan had prompted appeasement by Britain and France. By 1938 Stalin had punished millions who opposed his methods of collectivization with death by enforced famine.

More than ever, at this low moment, A.R.E. members sought from the readings answers "in keeping with the ideal and purposes of the work." Preparing for the Seventh Annual Congress, Hugh Lynn Cayce, son of Edgar Cayce and manager of the A.R.E., requested a reading on national and international affairs to be given in the presence of congress members. It was the first such for congress and was to continue to be the high point of subsequent congresses until Cayce's final one in 1944. These special readings were given as guidance in the work as it pertained to current issues facing the world.

As world depression and then World War II progressed, questions about the outcome and details of involvement by each nation, including America, were uppermost. By June 1944, the world was still in the last throes of war. Cayce was ailing and would die six months later. The last World Affairs reading, Number 29, was given at the Thirteenth Annual Congress.

"AN ENLIGHTENING"

The Cayce readings advisedly should be seen as a blueprint for the new order of which he spoke in the 1930s and 1940s and today's leaders speak in the last decade of the twentieth century. Dealing with the basic problems of mankind—political, social, religious—principles he suggested for practical solutions to those problems can be used today toward a better world, because they contain the wisdom of the ages, timeless and universal. They are found in the tenets of Freemasonry, which are known to be based on Christian principles as the apex of all great world religions from antiquity.

Although this book is a statement about Cayce's prophecies leading us into the millennium, prophecy was secondary to our spiritual needs. It was important only as it enlightened us to those needs. Foretold events, he indicated consistently, hinged on our deeds of consciousness, our motives and desires, the quality of our relationships, personal or group, extending to national and international concerns. The future was qualified by such phrases as those beginning with "if" or "unless." So as Americans feared being drawn into World War II, the message was: "If there is still kept that attitude of peace and harmony . . . ; If there are the considerations of the rights of others . . ." This implies that we might have been spared had we practiced those precepts.

In April 1941, eight months before Pearl Harbor, Cayce stated:

What is coming to pass? And how may ye as individuals help? As indicated in that given, to each it will become a personal thing, a personal condition. Thus it will require—yea, demand—that there be an expression on the part of each as to that given thirty-two hundred years ago: "Declare ye today WHOM you will serve! As for me and my house, we will serve the living God."

If there be sufficient, then, of those that will not only

declare this in mind and in purpose but by deed and word of mouth, there may come then *an enlightening* through that which has been promised of old: that the young shall dream dreams, the old men shall have visions, the daughters or maidens may know the spirit of truth—yea, that all may come to the greater knowledge of the indwelling of the Prince of Peace.

(3976-26)

A REPORT CARD FOR THE NATIONS

Reflecting Cayce's extensive knowledge of the Bible, the readings were couched in his consciousness of its message. They brought it anew to a world that had no longer considered its teachings believable against empirical science. He related our desperate trials to the Old Testament situation in which God promised He would save a city if only ten good people prayed. But he also explained the events of war, depression, and social unrest as the result of greed and selfishness on the part of many: "those (sins) that have sent and made the conditions are greed, selfishness that have been practiced in the minds, in the lives, in the experience of the nation . . ."

The spiritual laws Cayce referred to were based on the command: "Thou shalt love the Lord thy God with all thine heart, and thy neighbor as thyself. . . . There is no experience of man that has not its inception or purpose in the spirit of those injunctions but what *must* fail, unless it is founded in the spirit of truth" (3976-14).

The final World Affairs reading was a summing up, a look back to the origin of nations, a solemn charge to sons and daughters of God as to their missions on earth today, and a report card for the nations. It was an exhortation to "love thy neighbor as thyself," indigenous to Cayce's theme that everything depends on the way we treat one another. By 1944, Cayce's supporters were well aware of the spiritual challenges he had consistently thrown down for them: in essence, to *live* the teachings of Christ. They were rank-and-file church members—Sunday school teachers, laymen in many Catholic and Protestant churches—drawn to the Cayce fold because of the teachings they found compatible with their own beliefs. Going against the modern tide, they found instead even a deeper challenge that Jesus Christ had taught: to "seek the kingdom within." They became a people set apart, and those who remained with the "Work," as the readings called it, were able to speak to others attracted as *they* had been because, as Cayce said, it was for them if it rang true.

On June 22, 1944, in the presence of the Thirteenth Annual Congress, Cayce presented the last reading on World Affairs. As she had done many times before, Gertrude, his wife, conducted the procedure. As Edgar settled down on the couch, she had before her the questions to be asked on behalf of congress members.

She began to read aloud: "It has been indicated through this channel that much might be given regarding what the vibrations of nations, as individuals, might mean. You will give such information of the various nations, particularly in connection with the seven sins and twelve virtues in the human family, which will be helpful to us as an organization and as individuals in our attempt to be channels of blessing to our fellow man."

There followed a dissertation on the relationship of God's purpose to the nations of the earth. As we find, today's panorama of many nations sweeping away their old political bondage was foretold explicitly in this reading. The great changes that President Bush called the "new era" have taken us by surprise, in a mere five years, but building up long before as the cold war lingered. Cayce presaged for the 1990s the friendship of the United States and Russia. It is one of the most important predictions Cayce made, yet it has not made much sense until now.

To help us understand our relationship to higher laws, Cayce gave us insight into the work of the spirit, or the "vibrations" of the major nations. Those vibrations, or spirit of nations, have been built up over centuries by the collective thoughts and desires, the goals and purposes agreed on by leaders, by the good or bad influences expressed by the people themselves. Nations create their karma—the law of cause and efect—just as do individuals, he said. Thus, nations have the option either to exist for material gain and power at the expense of their people and other nations or to be a blessing to them. It is the effects of these attitudes and actions that characterize the vibrations.

"When there came about the periods of man's evolution in the earth, what was given then as to why man must be separated into tongues, into nations, into groups? 'Lest they in their foolish wisdom defy God.' [See Genesis 11: 1-9]. What is here then intimated? That man, seeking his own gratification of the lusts of the flesh, might even in the earth defy God. With what, then, has man been endowed by his Creator? All that would be necessary for each individual soul-entity to be a companion with God. And that is God's desire toward man.

"Thus, when man began to defy God in the earth and the confusion arose which is represented in the Tower of Babel, these are representations of what was then the basis, the beginnings, of nations. Nations were set up then in various portions of the land, and each group, one stronger than another, set about to seek their gratifications. . . ." That is, man put material success first. "It isn't that God chose to reserve or save anything that was good from man, so long as man was, is, and will be one who uses that living soul as a companion with God. That's God's purpose. That should be man's purpose.

"In the application of this principle, then, in the present day, what has come about? Each nation has set some standard of some activity of man as its idea", either in self-interest or in the manner of "preparation for that companionship with God. For remember, there are unchangeable laws. For God is law. Law is God. Love is law. Love is God. There are then in the hearts, the minds of man, various concepts of these laws and as to where and to what they are applicable. Then, just as in the days of old, the nature of the flesh, human flesh and its natures, has not changed, but the spirit maketh alive. The truth makes one free. Just as man has done throughout the ages, so in the present": various nations "have seen the light. They have, through one form or another, sought to es-

tablish as the ideal of that nation, of that people, some word
some symbol that has and does represent those peoples i
those days of the fathers of the present land called America

"What is the spirit of America? Most individuals proudl*
boast 'freedom.' Freedom of what? When ye bind men'
hearts and minds through various ways and manners, does i
give them freedom of speech? Freedom from want? Not un
less those basic principles are applicable throughout the tenets
and lines as has been set, but with that principle freedom. For
God meant man to be free and thus gave man will, a wil
even to defy God. God hath not willed that any soul should
perish, but hath with every trial or temptation prepared a way
of escape."

He pointed out that many teachers have claimed that their
way to spiritual knowledge is best; "and yet in the Teacher
of teachers is found the way, He Who even in Himself fulfilled the law. For when God said, 'Let there be light,' there
came Light into that which He had created, that was without
form and was void and it became the Word, and the Word
dwelt among men and men perceived it not. The Word today
dwells among men and many men perceive it not."

Here he defined the sins of the major nations. America's
sin is that she has forgotten the principles upon which she
was founded. They are summed up in the motto "In God We
Trust," but that principle is forgotten when we do not practice
it. "Do ye use that in thine own heart when you pay your
just debts? Do ye use that in thy prayer when ye send thy
missionaries to other lands? I give it for in God we trust? Not
for the other 50 cents, either!"

Russia "will be guided by that friendship with the nation
that hath even set on its present monetary unit 'In God We
Trust.' "In the application of those principles, in those forms
and manners in which the nations of the earth have and do
measure to those in their activities, yea, to be sure, America
may boast; but rather is that principle being forgotten" when
it is not adhered to . . . "and that is the sin of America."

He identified the sins of other countries: England's sin is
the idea, not the ideal, of "being just a little bit better than

the other fellow." The sin of France is the "gratifying of the desires of the body."

What caused the fall of Rome? "The same as at Babel. The dissentions, the activities that would enforce upon these, in this or that sphere, servitude; that a few might just agree, that a few might even declare their oneness with the higher forces. For theirs was the way that seemeth right to a man but the end is death. That is the sin of Italy."

It was, we recall, the Caesars who demanded that they be worshiped as gods in order to maintain power over their subjects, "declaring their oneness with the higher forces" (3976-29).

"The sin of China? Yea, there is the quietude that will not be turned aside, saving itself by the slow growth. There has been a growth, a stream through the land in ages which asks to be left alone to be just satisfied with that within itself. It awoke one day and cut its hair off! And it began to think and to do something with its thinking! This, here, will be one day the cradle of Christianity, as applied in the lives of men. Yea, it is far off as man counts time, but only a day in the heart of God—for tomorrow China will awake. Let each and every soul as they come to those understandings, do something, then, in his or her own heart. Just as in India, the cradle of knowledge not applied, except within self. What is the sin of India? SELF, and left the 'ish' off—just 'self.' " (3976-29).

Certain years seem to have special significance. Edgar Cayce died in 1945, his work on earth completed. It was that year that the UN was formed, the year oil was first produced in the Gulf countries, the first time the atomic bomb was used to end a war, the beginning of the cold war. Cayce's prophecies were given in the context of events of the 1930s and 1940s, but the destiny of nations of which he spoke was his message for our times, the end of an old era, the beginning of a new one.

Said Cayce, Russia would be "guided by what? That friendship" with America. (3976-29) That prophecy echoed across the world and down the years in a moment of history on September 30, 1990. In an interview with Tom Brokaw on NBC's *Meet the Press,* Minister Eduard A. Shevardnadze said he believed the basis of the new world order was the new relationship between the USSR and the U.S.[15] But it went much farther than that: Gary Allen's book in 1972 put that "relationship" in the context of years of conspiracy for world government and the push for American acceptance of communism.[16]

On May 31, 1990, President George Bush and President Mikhail Gorbachev met in Washington in a four-day summit resolving to increase the pace of summitry and to conclude in 1990 a treaty cutting conventional arms in Europe. Gorbachev called it "a new phase of cooperation." Bush said, "We've moved a long way from the depths of the Cold War."[17]

That cooperation among leaders today heralds this new cycle, Aquarius, as a time when nations are growing up. Many wise people are striving to work *with* God and not against Him. Will the Tower of Babel finally come down? It is a symbol of materialism and selfishness that no longer seems to characterize our New Age mind-set. "It isn't that God chose to reserve or save anything that was good from man," states this reading, "so long as man is, and will be, one who uses that living soul as a companion with God. That's God's purpose. That should be man's purpose" (3976-29).

Ever since the UN was formed, such strength had not been seen. Rather, it has proved to be ineffective. Successes of that institution to which Bush could allude so reassuringly are, we hope, precursors of a time that will indeed be based on the highest ideals of which man is aware. We hope the leaders act solely upon those ideals, a foundation based on belief in the First Cause, the Creative Principle, God. In the 1990s we have seen slaughter in Bosnia, Yugoslavia; longtime repression in Somalia, Zaire, and Haiti; unrest in Albania, with varied success in solving deep-set problems. Once again, it's a time of testing the will for, and adhering to, principle. It appears to be the time at the end of the old millennium when we are alerted to admit that there are those who work with the dark forces to bring about great human misery, threatening our very existence.

When in August 1991 we found that, once again, we were sending troops and ships, ammunition and guns to defend peace and freedom—in this case of Kuwait—we were brought up short to know the realities of living in a world where war has always been possible. And just as did many in wars past, we were brought up short to turn to prayer.

2

THE AWAKENING

*The awakening of the individual to the truth of
the divine heritage in each individual that may respond to that creative energy in the universal forces.
(254-48)*

"IT'S ME, O, LORD!"

THERE'S AN OLD SPIRITUAL Americans have sung for
years: "It's me, it's me, O Lord/Standin' in the need of
prayer." Cayce reminds us that it is not our brother or our
sister who is necessarily at fault, but ourselves, and that our
individual responsibility for creating a better world is by the
tenet, "Others, Lord, Others!" Nations do not bear the responsibility alone for man's progress, for a nation can act
only collectively. It is the individual who is the ultimate hope
of a better world.

"Beware," stated the seer, "lest ye as an individual soul,
a son, a daughter of God, fail in thy mission in the earth
today! That those ye know, those ye contact shall know the
truth of God, not by thy word, bombastic words, but in longsuffering, in patience, in harmony, that ye create in thine own
lives, for it must begin with thee. God hath shown ye the
pattern, even one Jesus, who became the Christ, that ye may
have an advocate with the Father . . ."(3976-29).

He insisted that it was indeed the individual who was of
ultimate influence for good or ill to his brother, his sister, as
well as large groups. "Then, today, we are to answer within

our individual consciousness, 'Am I my brother's keeper?' Not, 'What does the world owe me?' But 'What contribution can I, as an individual soul seeking God, seeking to know His face, make that may hasten the day of the Lord?' " (3976-22, June 13, 1939).

Here Cayce declares that there are three natural laws of man's material existence: survival of his species, self-expression of one's own concept of life, and recognition ("to be heard, to be noticed") in his own activity.

"Out of this individual purpose grows . . . nationalism, patriotism, and the ability to rule—or force his concept upon others." The conditions in the world today, Cayce said, are a challenge to every thinking person

> that ye are not only to pray for peace but are to PURSUE peace—by LIVING the second phase of the divine injunction, "thy neighbor as thyself."
> We realize that selfishness, jealousies, those things that make people afraid must gradually be put away.
> First, then, as an individual, self must be conquered . . .
> (376-22)

As scholars have observed communist and fascist ideologies controlling millions of people's lives for seventy years past, we have seen the results: a collapse of the very foundations of those forms of government. The individual has been submerged for "the good of the many." The ideologues have refused to recognize that nations are made up of living, breathing human beings in whom lives the God-given spirit of freedom.

The exact opposite is to be found in the religions of people who, as Cayce held, "worship the one God." It is the individual who is precious, under a government of, for, and by the people that characterized the forming of the United States.

Talented, diverse leaders sharing a belief in God spurred the American Revolution, wrote the Constitution. That document was to be hailed as the work of political genius. "Writing in December, 1787, John Adams said that 'the deliberate union of so great and various a people in such a place is, if not the greatest exertion of human understanding, the greatest single effort of a national deliberation that the world has ever seen.' ''[1]

Heroes of the new order—such as Walesa, Havel, Mandela, and countless others—are individuals who had lived with the idea of freedom long before they saw it come about. As we have observed, their lives were a series of steps toward the day of their leadership, whether in the trade unions, arts and letters, or politics.

Poets, playwrights, and musicians all have the advantage of knowing freedom of expression from within, regardlesss of the imposed tyranny from without. That is, just as is one's faith, art is a secret, hidden gift from the Creative Forces, as Cayce called the mystic Source of man's inspiration. It serves its practitioners well, nourishing them and those who share it in times of imprisonment or liberty.

Havel, Lindesberger, playwright and musician, respectively, joined those poets, novelists, and composers of the Soviet Union who have prevailed in spite of communist blackout of intellect and expression. They, as the American revolutionists, come close to the ideal of the philosopher king!

How has it happened that, instead of seasoned politicians, it was writers and musicians who have taken on the role of leaders in that modern-day revolution—peaceful in intent, as was the American? From the ranks of Polish working people came such as Walesa. When he and Havel visited America, they referred warmly to America's struggle for independence more than two hundred years ago. We saw in them the same spirit of freedom in which our forefathers declared their independence.

As has Mikhail Gorbachev, they made friendship between their nations—Czechoslovakia and Poland—and the United States highly visible. This underscores, however, that Cayce predicted that it would be that friendship between the USSR and the U.S. that would lead the world.

Cayce urged that we not only look forward to know the future but also look back so as to assess the conditions that have brought us to the present. He told a small group in April 1933 to "consider . . . the form of government [of America] and the policies of those who formed it, and how the people in their various walks of life have adhered to them, or how those principles [of the founding fathers] have been fostered or furthered in their application . . ." (3976-11). The American revolutionaries were lawyers, farmers, philosophers, educated men, practical and prudent. They have been the inspiration for the world, admired for their genius by British prime minister William Gladstone who called the Constitution "the most wonderful work ever struck off at a given time by the brain and purpose of man."[2]

CAYCE AND FREEMASONRY

And for the world's victims of tyranny it has been hope.

It would seem that we live in the time Cayce predicted when the "leveling" would occur:

> Though there may come those periods when there will be great stress, as brother rises against brother, as group or sect or race rises against race—yet the leveling must come.
>
> And only those who have set their ideal in Him and practiced it in their dealings with their fellow man may expect to survive the wrath of the Lord.
>
> And in thy dealings, then, whether at home, in thy dealings with state or the national situations, or the international affairs—there must come *all* under that purpose, that desire.
>
> And then there should be, there *will* be those rising to power that are able to meet the needs. For none are in power but that have been given the opportunity by the will of the Father—from which all power emanates.
>
> Hence those will be leveled with the purpose, "My word shall *not* fail!"
>
> (3976-18)

"No country is stronger than its greatest weakness in any section . . . For it must be a COOPERATIVE, COORDINAT-

ING activity as a unit of government" in its legislation and administration (3976-17).

Major tenets in the Edgar Cayce readings are found in Freemasonry. In them both, "the ideals of the ages" are held up before us as our spiritual heritage of the far past. Ritual and ancient wisdom had as their purpose to inspire and lift the individual neophyte. In Masonry, it has been preserved as a secret fraternity. In the Edgar Cayce readings, presented to the world in the first half of the twentieth century, the ideals of the ages were revived in cosmic perspective of where we have been in history and where we are going.

Just as Cayce emphasized the important role of the individual in world affairs, so does Freemasonry. Both of these proponents of undying truth hold that it is "mankind" that is responsible for what happens in the world arena—man collectively; but nothing happens unless individuals make decisions and act.

The world population is made up of "you and me," and each one is important. This is expressed in Jesus Christ as the Good Shepherd, seeking not only for the good of the flock, though that is important, but for the good of one lonely, lost sheep. It is the opposite of the philosophy of a slave state that somehow convinces its members to think they are expendable.

We grow as we learn to base our lives on ideals. Cayce had much to say about ideals. "Ideas," he said, "are worthy of man's consideration—but *ideals* are something more! They must be *lived* each day, each hour of each day . . ." (3976-7).

Throughout these pages there are a number of Cayce's references to ideals and principles held in Freemasonry as well. Given in each time and again are the phrases "the brotherhood of man, the Fatherhood of God," "the New Order," "the ideals of the ages." Still another beautiful phrase that seems to describe the roles of both philosophies is "the invisible empire in the hearts of men." I have quoted in the chapter "Freedom! Freedom!" from this 1927 reading that set before us the pattern of the Christ as the basis for the invisible empire of spiritual consciousness and the new world order of which Cayce spoke.

Ideals for the new order were to be found "Only in Him in whom there was found no guile, and though He were buffeted by man—though He was ridiculed by those in power, though He suffered among those convicted of crime in the flesh, and railings against their fellow man—yet those tenets as were proclaimed by that as the man, making self as the son of man, and through those conditions became the Son of the Living God—in these tenets, in these ways and manners, may such conditions be brought to the realization of those that would build an invisible empire within the hearts of men . . ." (3976-4).

Although the tenets Cayce spoke of are of the Christian faith, Cayce said that all religions that teach worship of the One God are of the Christ. These include Judaism, Buddhism, Hinduism, and Islam.

Freemasonry includes these religions in the same way.

This ancient fellowship had its beginnings in ancient Egypt. However, according to its teachings, they are timeless as truth is timeless. "In its highest sense it is neither historical nor archeological," says Manly P. Hall. Instead, it is "a divine symbolic language perpetuating under certain concrete symbols the sacred mysteries of the ancients."[3]

Freemasonry is a "science of the soul," Hall says. "It is not a creed or doctrine but a universal expression of the Divine Wisdom. Only those who see in it a cosmic study, a life work, a divine inspiration to better thinking, better feeling, and better living, with the spiritual attainment of enlightenment as the end, and with the daily life of the true Mason as the means, have gained even the slightest insight into the true mysteries of the ancient rites."[4]

This description of Freemasonry can be applied in its entirety to the Edgar Cayce readings. Both emphasize not the ritual in religious practice but what it represents: the spiritual attainment of enlightenment, of understanding the meaning of life. It's not surprising that the name of the organization carrying the same divine message is the Association for Research and Enlightenment!

Another major factor in Freemasonry is its eighteenth-century role in the establishment of America as a free and democratic nation. Cayce, as well, held up to us the magnificent vision of America as having set the goal of freedom for the rest of the world. To a woman seeking information as to how she could use her abilities as a speaker and writer was given this: "For, with those changes that will be wrought, Americanism—the ism—with the universal thought that is expressed and manifested in the brotherhood of man into group thought, as expressed by the Masonic Order, will be the eventual rule in the settlement of affairs in the world . . . Not that the world is to become a Masonic Order, but the principles that are embraced in same will be the basis upon which the new order of peace is to be established in '44 and '45. When these things are considered, then, it is self-evident that individuals should be up and doing. Especially the entity [this woman] with its abilities, has definite work to do in the present." She was told that she had the ability to work with groups, bringing people together, unifying those who hold Christian principles. Her reading was given at a time when communism was being promulgated—in the 1930s and 1940s—in America. She was warned not to join groups that were questionable, for a great number of people would be questioned as to their ideals. It was a time of conflict between communism and the American way.

As this woman was told, "Not as a church, not as an ism or cult, but in that every soul does the best he can where he is—and all with one ideal: I *am* my brother's keeper—Christ the Lord is my brother!"

Many leaders of the American Revolution were Masons. Among the signers of the Declaration of Independence who were known to belong to the mystic order were Benjamin Franklin, John Hancock, John Witherspoon, and twelve others. Since that time, at least thirteen presidents, starting with George Washington, were Masons, and fifteen vice presidents.[5] Masonic ideals were major influences in forming the new nation, having been carried over from England and Europe. Those ideals, of political and religious freedom, found their natural expression in the Constitution's Bill of Rights.

Franklin D. Roosevelt was a Mason. During his presidency, which was marked by some very difficult times, Cayce was asked, "Is Roosevelt right?" Cayce answered that "He, Roosevelt, has been raised for a privilege . . . As to what will be done, as it was with him who sat at the peace table and proclaimed a way, yet was rejected among men, even in his own land, when he stood in the position as Roosevelt does to his people. What will the people do with the spirit of truth that is being proclaimed by him (Roosevelt), is rather the question. He has been called. What will ye do with this man?" (3976-15)

Yet Cayce warned that social justice and social order "shall be ever NOT as of ANY individual, but that . . . all are free, all are equal before God. The social order, the religious order, the economic order must all be for ONE God. For, know that the Lord thy God is ONE!" (3976-24)

Some groups now still seek change by means of war and revolution: In the beautiful hills and valleys of tortured nations today, it is has been sought with guns; warring factions around the world are responsible for the death and injury of thousands of innocent victims by terrorism that has made the world unsafe anywhere, including America.

But Cayce spoke of the "awakening" for our times. It actually began in the nineteenth century with such persons as Madame Blavatsky and has only in recent decades become associated with what is popularly called the New Age. Freemasonry, as well, has looked long to this age, preparing, as Heline says, developing an awakening for "the new race."[6]

Now there are those everywhere who see the changes taking place. As we approach the Age of Enlightenment, another kind of revolution is taking place in the *consciousness* of much of the Western world. Since Cayce foresaw in 1934 "the awakening," changes take place by what Harman says are "signs of respiritualization of Western society." They include self-realization, transcendent meaning, inner growth, Christian evangelical fundamentalism, and metaphysical perception. Harman cites our growing recognition of, and emphasis on, the metaphysical meaning of life: "from radicalization to changing consciousness."[7]

Cayce seems to refer also to political change of great shock to those who have continued to ignore the signs. He refers to the rise in power by the powerless, the fall of despots: ". . . for these are periods when mental, material [matters] are to be so altered in the affairs of men as to be even bringing turmoil to those that have not seen that the *Spirit* is moving in His ways to bring the knowledge of the Father in the hearts and lives of men" (3976-15).

In reading 826-8, given in 1936, Cayce replied to a question that he had prompted before: "What great change, or the beginning of what change, if any, is to take place in the earth in the year 2000 A.D.?" He replied: "When there is the shifting of the poles. Or a new cycle begins."

Cayce had said in 1933 that "a change was eminent in the earth," which "begins in '58 and ends when the changes wrought in the upheavals and the shifting of the poles, as begins then the reign in '98" (378-16). The consensus is that he meant *the reign of Christ.*

The year 1936 was a portentious one, according to Cayce. In that year he predicted not only pole shift but also the return of Christ as He became "manifested before men." This did not mean, as we might expect, that He would appear to all people physically, although many in the past and present have declared that He has appeared to them visibly. But He would appear in the manner he said John the Beloved would appear—that is, pointing the way "in the minds and hearts" of men and women. He spoke of earth changes to come in relation to this tremendous event, "when His light will be seen again in the clouds"(3976-15).

Those scientists who have studied this specific prediction as to major earth changes observe that such a pole shift has been linked to the rising and subsidence of the earth's crust and to earthquake activity in these times. See John White's *Pole Shift,* a thorough treatise on the subject.[8]

This reading (3976-15), given in 1934, was perhaps the most profound of the World Affairs collection, central to all the rest. It covered earth changes but ranged to the Second Coming of Christ. It referred to the time in which it was given, but it looked far ahead of that time to what seems to be the very social, political, and religious milieu of the 1990s. "So shall ye see those in lowly places raised to those of power in the political, in the machinery of nations." Is that not what we now see happening? Once oppressed people are catapulted to political power in the world arena, their oppressors thrown down.

In the context of this prophecy is considered also where America stands, what her role has become. America "has, does harbor within its bosom those things of other lands that are making, as it were, a leaven to the whole. And here, there, for as given, His messenger shall appear there. Hence, is finding those that make the paths straight."

As I understand this passage, as America has welcomed the refugees, those "yearning to breathe free," she has received in return a rich heritage of the world's cultures and has become a depository for the high ideals of many religions. This acts as a "leaven" that gives back again abundantly to the world.

We noted earlier that Freemasonry has its beginnings in Egypt. It was in Egypt that Jesus and John the Baptist were initiates in the Mysteries, according to the Cayce data. It is in Egypt that the Great Pyramid stands from the time of Atlantis and is termed by scholars "prophecy in stone." Though it would seem that Egypt and America have little in common, there is in fact an important relationship of which most Americans are unaware. High spiritual understanding, said Cayce, was reached in early Egypt and was preserved in Christian teachings to culminate in the founding of America. Freemasonry teaches that the picture on our dollar bill of the Great Pyramid with its missing capstone is a symbol of our spirituality as a nation. We have until this day been building the material foundations of our nation (the eagle side of the seal). In the capstone is placed the all-seeing eye. The capstone is not in place, signifying that it must await a future time for completion of America's destiny.

In his book *America's Destiny*, Theodore Heline states: "According to the prophetic promise of the Great Seal, it is the destiny of the United States to bring forth a New Order of the Ages. Such is the declaration in the Latin words on the reverse side of the Seal: *Novus Ordo Seclorum*. . . . The establishment of a new order of the ages will call for a new social system based on cooperation, good will, and right relationships; it will mean a new financial and economic order in which justice will prevail . . ."[9]

In a Cayce reading of 1934 he was asked, "Is America fulfilling her destiny?" Cayce replied that rather should the question be sought: "are individuals fulfilling their own destinies?"

"If there is not the acceptance in America of the closer brotherhood of man, the love of the neighbor as self, civilization must wend its way westward—and again must Mongolia, must a hated people, be raised" (3976-15). After describing the earth changes he said would take place, he stated: "As to those things that deal with the mental of the earth, these shall call upon the mountains to cover many. As ye have seen those in lowly places raised to those of power in the political, in the machinery of nations' activities, so shall ye see those in high places reduced and calling on the waters of darkness to cover them. And those that in the inmost recesses of their selves awaken to the spiritual truths that are to be given, and those places of those that have ministered in places will be brought to light, and turmoils and strifes shall enter. And, as there is the wavering of those that would enter as emissaries, as teachers, from the throne of life, the throne of immortality, and wage war in the air with those of darkness, then know ye the Armageddon is at hand" (3976-15).

What is the meaning of the words "the mental of the earth"? Says Heline: "The power of the present race is centered in mind, the power of the coming race will be centered in the heart."[10]

So the explanation evidently is that there will be—and now is—consternation among us as we shift from our education in mental pursuits alone to what William Harman has called "global mind change." That is, a new "search for wholeness" that includes education of the heart—a metaphysical viewpoint of ourselves and the universe.[11]

The "emissaries . . . teachers . . . from the throne of life" wage war on planes beyond our knowledge or understanding.

Opposing them are great numbers of "those that have hindered and would make for man and his weaknesses stumblingblocks." These dark forces "shall wage war with the spirits of light that come into the earth for this awakening. . . ."

Do we not see the effects of the hosts who hinder us: the tragedy of chaotic politics and religious rivalry in the world that tear whole nations apart, the hellish drug traffic, the climate of moral decadence that destroys families and lives?

There are those on earth—"the sons of men"—who have been calling the spirits of light "into the service of the Living God." These people are the ones who call by their prayers throughout the world on behalf of their weaker brothers. They include many churches and prayer groups everywhere. As I report in *Edgar Cayce on Prophecy*,[12] the readings contain a reference to Livingston, Montana, which was to "have much to do with many, many nations" (3651-1). At the time of publication, 1968, there was no clue as to what it meant. But in the 1980s the Church Universal and Triumphant purchased a large ranch just north of Livingston as its new headquarters. It had been centered in Malibu, California, and before that, in Washington, D.C. A major feature of that church's worship service is the use of the spoken word in which the entire congregation does indeed call with unusual consistency and persistency on emissaries and teachers of the light into the service of the living God! That church has established centers throughout the nation and the world, and its leader, Elizabeth Clare Prophet, by lecture and study programs, books and tapes, has brought her message—based on Christ in all major creeds—to people everywhere.

In reading 3976-15 also was given the prophecy that "John, the beloved of the earth" was to come as a messenger: "not as a forerunner, but as a messenger. . . !"

Who shall proclaim the acceptable year of the Lord in Him that has been born in the earth in America? Those from that land where there has been the regeneration, not only of the body, but the mind and spirit of men, they shall come and declare that John Peniel is giving the world the new order of things. Not that these that have

been proclaimed have been refused, but that they are
made *plain* in the minds of men, that they may know the
truth and the truth, the life, the light, will make them
free. . . .

When, where is to be this one? In the hearts and minds
of those that have set themselves in that position that they
become a channel through which spiritual, mental, and
material things become one in the purpose and desires of
that physical body! As to the material changes that are to
be as an omen, as a sign to those that this is shortly to
come to pass—as has been given of old, the sun will be
darkened and the earth shall be broken up in divers
places—and *then* shall be *proclaimed*—through the spiritual interceptions in the hearts and minds and souls of
those that have sought His way—that *his* star has appeared, and will point (pause) the way for those that enter
into the holy of holies in themselves . . .

In the spiritual realm it is not necessary for a physical manifestation of a soul to make itself of effect among us. Thus,
John becomes for us a messenger in spirit "in the hearts and
minds" of many. God is "first the God of the individual. As
He is manifested in the heart and in the actions of the individual, He becomes manifested before men," says this reading. As we become aware of the winds of change in our lives,
in the world about us, John appears in the work of those
serving as true channels of his message. Those who were with
Edgar Cayce when this reading was given that "in '36 he
will appear!"

Gladys Davis's note here is: "Beginning of new age of
spiritual awakening?"

This is directly related to Cayce's prophecy that there
would be those to "proclaim the day of freedom from the
bonds of those who would rule" (3976-4). He meant freedom
from political and economic bondage, from class distinctions,
for freedom is of the spirit, a gift of "the awakening." In a
notation here, we are referred to Genesis 32:30 for the origin
of the name "Peniel." It is the name Jacob gave to the place
where he said, "For I have seen God face to face, and my

life is preserved." Gladys Davis noted: "Could this mean that John the Beloved had been Jacob?"—in a previous incarnation.

Whom did Cayce mean by "Those from that land where there has been the regeneration, not only of the body, but the mind and the spirit of men"? This could only be America where the foundations of government were based on Christian belief and Aquarian understanding. Those who work in the study and use of the Cayce data have been a part of the regeneration of body, mind, and spirit of all who can accept it. They are indeed declaring "the new order of things" as they teach the holy concepts offered, as the work grows, reaching millions.

In the Book of Acts 1:11, Jesus Christ is reported by good witnesses, his apostles, to have been taken up to heaven by a cloud. Two men (angels?) appeared and declared Jesus would return just as He left. In the Book of Jude, verses 14 and 15, we're told ". . . the Lord cometh with ten thousand of his saints, To execute judgment upon all." The new order for the world will be under Christ's rule, according to John's Book of Revelation. What can we expect in that new dispensation?

In 1932 Cayce was asked, "Please explain what is meant by: 'He will walk and talk with men of every clime.' Does this mean He will appear to many at once or appear to various peoples during a long period?"

Cayce's answer was, "As given, (in the New Testament) for a thousand years He will walk and talk with men of every clime. Then in groups, in masses, and then they shall reign of the first resurrection for a thousand years; for this will be when the changes materially come."

The reign of Christ will be understood, then, to be visible to all people, but also even more important, in the minds and hearts of mankind.

In the manner as He sat at the peace conference in Paris in the heart and soul of a man (President Woodrow Wilson) not reckoned by many as an even unusually Godly man; yet raised for a purpose, and he chose rather to be

a channel of His thought for the world. So, as there has
been, so will it be until the time as set. As was given of
Him, not given to man to know the time or the period of
the end, nor to man—save by their constituting themselves a channel through which He may speak . . . Be
thou then a channel . . .

(364-7)

This last statement was typical of the way Cayce charged
us and the whole world. A reading might be given to one
person or perhaps a small group, but often it carried a challenge far beyond its original target. Not only were we sum-
moned to be a channel, we were also given insight as to how
to be a channel: to learn from Jesus as one who illustrated
the path toward Christhood by His own experience. That is,
as we grow in understanding and evolve throughout lifetimes,
we will one day ascend to mastery over all limitation, as did
Jesus. In the readings we are told that He had many incar-
nations on earth before His final one as the Christ. Here we
are reminded that He walked and talked with men, not only
in that period, but also before, as Joseph who rose from slavery to high authority in Egypt, as the Priest of Salem, and
other great men of the Old Testament (364-8). Thus He was
the pattern for our spiritual progress toward God.

In keeping with the compassion of Christ here affirmed, we
are given: "And God shall wipe away all tears from their
eyes; and there shall be no more death, neither sorrow, nor
crying, neither shall there be any more pain: for the former
things are passed away" (Revelation 21:4).

And Cayce assures us that, like an elder brother who sees
your sorrow or pain, "He will not leave thee desolate but will
come to thee—but not unless invited."

3

"Freedom! Freedom!"

What, then, of nations? In Russia there comes the hope of the world, not as that of sometimes termed the communistic, of the Bolchevistic, no. But freedom! Freedom! That each man will live for his fellowman . . . (3976-29, June 22, 1944)

These data of a twentieth-century seer relate to changes we see happening now to the dispensation prophecied since the time of Christ. According to the wisdom of the ages, it is a time of transition and cleansing. While this book was written, the world changed to the extent that what was happening in January 1990, in January 1997 seemed ancient history. So much change has taken place that one book cannot encompass all that could be said. Democracy and freedom have been won; world consciousness has been challenged. Attempting to make this an account of the Edgar Cayce readings as they relate to today's world-transforming events, I have necessarily limited the scope of it to highlights of what is fast becoming history.

Cayce foretold much that can relate to none other but these turbulent decades. Not only that, but he gave us wise suggestions about adjusting to a higher, more joyous environment of the Spirit. The wisdom of the ages he prompted is ancient but new still to many of us: the old understanding giving way to greater insight. The Age of Enlightenment is the age of the individual, and he constantly referred to the starting place of all world conditions: ourselves. By each one's thought, actions, day by day, he said, we create our lives, for better or worse. Thus, decisions based on principles are the stuff of which our personal lives and the life of the planet, of the cosmos itself, are made. Because, he said, we are cocreators with God.

As an example of the import of Cayce's message, we can see for the first time what he meant in a reading in 1944 that Russia would be guided by her friendship with America in learning the ways of freedom. Such did not seem to be possible in that faraway day of opposite ideologies that bred fear of nuclear destruction for all the world. But Cayce predicted that cooperation would be called for among nations to solve economic and military problems threatening the peace and well-being of millions. Cayce declared, "Mankind is his brother and thou art thy brother's keeper!" (3976-16)

Since the 1930s, the advice and wisdom of this man have been studied, taught, and practiced by increasing numbers in most of the world to improve life materially and spiritually. His more than 14,000 documented readings are known around the world because of the interest of scholars, physicians, physicists, and geologists who find in them the ring of truth. In particular, the principles of healing in the Cayce data have been found to bring dramatic results of healing, as physicians and their patients testify. Can we accept his readings as they deal, as well, with the healing of a very sick world? Can he have been so right in his diagnoses of ill people, and so wrong in diagnoses of social and political ills of the last decades of the century? We present this book as a report on what he had to say about the chances of world recovery from a rather long-term illness—that is, the chances for a democratic world order of peace, freedom, and prosperity for all people, at last.

With the sudden decline of communism brought about by Mikhail Gorbachev in the 1980s, the world has found welcome respite from tensions of past decades. President Gorbachev, who came to office in 1985, soon called for his country to restructure Soviet policies under perestroika. The new political and social environment was to be characterized by openness, freedom to speak out: glasnost.

It is certain the nations have never before experienced such a change as this. A new era has arrived in which cultural exchange and understanding have been met by Eastern bloc countries and Western democracies alike in joy and relief from fear and distrust of the past. One of the early happenings in 1989 that delighted us were seaport visits by American and Soviet sailors. American school students visited Russian cities, met with Russian youth. Educators and politicians traveled to talk to their counterparts or to speak to audiences.

Summit meetings took place between President Ronald Reagan and President Gorbachev. Such meetings continued between the Russian leader and President George Bush, and then between President Bill Clinton and President Boris Yeltsin.

The new structuring and good will permitted millions of people in Eastern Europe to congregate without being gunned down by police. In nonviolent demonstrations they demanded their freedom, calling for the end of communism and replacing it with democratic rule. It was a glorious time.

We saw for decades the oppressive use of power by leaders in Europe, Africa, South and Central America, and many other places. We witnessed in 1989 the tremendous changes taking place as oppression gave way to the demands of millions of people, most successful, those of communist Russia and her satellites.

The hated wall between East and West Germany was torn down with great passion and contempt for what it had stood for. Communism's seventy-year-old grip of entire nations within many borders was triumphantly challenged. It was due to the enlightened leadership of Gorbachev, who took office in 1985 as general secretary of the Communist party of the Soviet Union and added the office of president of the USSR, that is, chairman of the Presidium of the USSR Supreme Soviet, succeeding Andrei Gromyko. In 1989 he was elected to the newly created office of president with greater power, under a reformed political system that he himself designed. His turnabout leadership after years of the cold war now made it possible for an open relationship between his country and the United States.

Under President Reagan, the cold war was still continuing,

but the long years of détente in Washington-Moscow relations were coming to an end. Reagan and Gorbachev met in Geneva for a superpower summit that marked a major coup for Reagan: The Russians agreed to establish a new relationship essentially on Reagan's terms. Arms control, star wars, and human rights were top priorities to be worked out in later summits.[1]

History tells of the beginning of communist rule in Russia in 1917 by the Bolsheviks under the leadership of V. I. Lenin. The Czar had abdicated following the socialist revolution. After a week of fighting, the Bolsheviks were in charge.

Aided by the Western Allies, who supplied them with war materials, the "White" armies, under former officers of the Czar, challenged the Red Guards of the Bolsheviks and prevailed. British and American forces took Murmansk and Archangel. But the Red army won. Economic chaos and famine followed, and many people died.[2]

Dan Graf, professor of history at Virginia Wesleyan College, has spent a lifetime studying Russian history. He told me that he and Mrs. Graf have made many visits to that country. They have friends there, who, says Dr. Graf, "as your friend will give you the shirt off their back. We have been entertained lavishly with food and vodka, though these perhaps cost a month's wages."[3]

I attended a public lecture by Professor Graf in the fall of 1991 in which he spoke of the precarious Soviet position then. I later asked for his comments on the historical aspects of the Russian communist experiment. Concerning the 1917 revolution, he wrote: "As I see it, Lenin's hope was to seize power in Russia in an attempt to spark a world revolution of workers against the existing capitalist system. Meanwhile, a bitter civil war in Russia and the devastated condition of the country, thanks to World War I, left few options except to establish a 'temporary' dictatorship of the party based on the soviets (workers' councils) which had sprung up during the revolution. When the world revolution failed to materialize, the new Soviet regime was forced to improvise. Lenin died (1924) before a new direction was firmly established. Stalin destroyed his rivals and imposed a dictatorship (1927 +) the thoroughness and ruthlessness of which, I expect, exceeded anything Lenin ever considered."[4]

The long decades and the magnitude of such oppression seem an unlikely prelude to what in 1944 Cayce was to declare: "What then of nations? In Russia there comes the hope of the world, not as that of sometimes termed the Communistic, of the Bolshevistic, no. But freedom! Freedom! . . ." (3976-29)

And throughout the world today, the cry has been in the 1980s and 1990s: "*Freedom!*" From the millions of the Eastern bloc nations of Europe, from the minorities around the world, from blacks of Africa and throughout Europe, the Americas, the third world, it is insistent with centuries of slavery and is sounded through the earth like the toll of a great bell.

Cayce's concern was with "those who would rule," freedom denied those who lived under that rule. Neither under the czars nor their supplanters, the Marxists, would there be change for the Russian people.

States Graf, there were two factions to the "Russian Social Democratic Party" or Social Democrats: the Bolsheviks and the Mensheviks. Both were Marxist, but "most historians, I think, would argue that the Mensheviks were much closer to Marx's tradition than was Lenin. His was the more radical faction and it placed much emphasis on conspiratorial party organization and the role of the party as an elite 'vanguard' of the industrial working class—the proletariat. Lenin broke with the Social Democrats in 1903. I believe that Lenin's dogmatism and insistence on a tightly knit party led from the top fits the Cayce comment about 'those seeking to subjugate others to the will.' " Under the New Economic Policy, Lenin's relaxation of economic controls began in 1921 and continued, says Graf, "until 1927–28, when it was supplanted by Stalin's forced collectivization and the 5-year plans. During the 1940s the Stalin regime relaxed controls over culture, literature, religion, etc. in order to appeal for popular support for the war effort."[5]

*   *   *

Said Cayce in 1932, "Europe is as a house broken up. Some years ago there was the experience of a mighty peoples being overridden for the gratification and satisfaction of a few, irrespective of any other man's right. That peoples are going through the experience of being *born* again and is the thorn in the flesh to many a political and financial nation in Europe—in the world but out of same. With the prayers and supplications of those that may pray—even as Abram or Abraham, 'If there be fifty, will it not be spared?' Then the hope of Europe depends upon *you*, in your home today! In . . . the same manner as did the life of Lot, or of the other peoples of Sodom and Gomorrah."

"What is the name of that nation referred to?" was the next question.

"Russia!" was the reply (3976-8).

Certainly the devout, dedicated members of Cayce's group heeded that man's call to pray for Europe. "If there be fifty . . ." referred to Genesis 18:23–24.

Have not the Russian people now shown evidence of their being "born again"? Of triumphant and no doubt prayerful rebirth out of their long bondage to godless ideologies?

Communism was a real "thorn in the flesh" to the United States and the other nations because Russia's totalitarian rule posed a possible threat to the free world from nuclear attack. The entire Eastern bloc was "in the world but out of it" for those bleak decades—shut away from the progress and prosperity of the West because of their bureaucratic incompetence that stifled production and trade with other countries.

Moreover, capitalism was to the Soviets the great sin; religion, the "opiate of the people." Eastern bloc people had no independence and little control over their lives. The prophecy Cayce gave in 1944 continued thus: "Freedom! That each man will live for his fellow man! The principle has been born. It will take years for it to be crystallized, but out of Russia comes again the hope of the world. Guided by what? That friendship with the nation that hath even set on its present monetary unit, 'In God we trust' " (3976-29).

Still another reference to Russia as world leader of religious thought was given in August 1933: ". . . out of Russia, you see, there may come that which may be the basis of a more world-wide religious thought or trend, see?'' (3976-12)

Many times, Cayce emphasized that the fatherhood of God, the brotherhood of man would be "the only true, basic foundation of the world of the future."

In 1932 Cayce was asked: "What should be the attitude of so-called capitalist nations toward Russia?"

"On Russia's religious development will come the greater hope of the world. Then, that one, or group, that is the closer in its relationships, may fare the better in the gradual changes and final settlement of conditions as to the rule of the world."

We assume he meant the United States, for he advised that Russia would be "guided by her friendship" with the United States.

"Should the United States recognize the present (communist) government in Russia?" was then asked.

"Many conditions should be considered, were this to be answered correctly," replied Cayce. "You could say 'yes' and 'no' and both be right, with the present attitude of both peoples as a nation, and both be wrong; for there is to come, there *will* come, an entire change in the attitude of both nations as powers in the financial and the economical world. As for those of raw resources, Russia surpasses all other nations. As for abilities for development of same, those in the United States are the farthest ahead. Then these *united*, or upon an equitable basis, would become—or could become—powers; but there are many interferences for those already investments, those already under questions, will take years to settle" (3976-10).

We did see change in the attitude of the United States and the Soviet Union regarding finances and economics. Soviet bloc economy is in chaos, people there continued to suffer shortages. The United States and other nations, seeing their plight, organized political science and economic seminars in those countries to teach them the ways of the West. Affluent Western nations including the United States found ways to grant loans, bring business opportunities for new entrepreneurs.

Even before the prophecies given above, as early as 1927

a forecast was given by Cayce that is consistent with those given years later. It was at that time seemingly unrelated to the realities of world affairs, impossible for any future time. But today we can see clearly what he meant.

"The world awaits the coming of those who will proclaim the day of freedom from the bonds of those who would rule either through prestige or through political influence" (3976-4). At that time, this statement appeared just a utopian improbability. It was uttered a brief nine years after World War I at a time when peace was being sought in a relatively friendly world. In 1921 a peace treaty brought Poland a large part of Russian territory in reparation for taking over Poland. Germany, too, had to pay for having started the war. After the 1929 crash, however, worldwide depression led to the rise once more of totalitarian rule.

In hindsight, we see that Cayce foresaw the fifty-six years ahead in which Hitler and Mussolini imposed their rule from 1933 to the end of World War II, and Stalin created the communist brand of oppression on millions of Russians and their neighbors from 1945 onward. Much change took place after 1927. How could Cayce's followers then have understood, in the context of their own postwar world, what Cayce was telling them? Everyone at that time was innocently unaware of the oppression that would arise in just a few years.

Cayce added enigmatically, "Then, ones so chosen by their fitness as will come through holy communion with this high purpose will be the first to begin" (3976-4). The strange statement was given in a reading for creating a better world.

Policy would be found "only in Him in Whom there was found no guile." Only in His tenets might such an undertaking be realized by those who sought to build "an invisible empire within the hearts of men" (3976-4).

Mindful of the long history of despots, who were often self-deluded, Cayce then cautioned the group rule "not as an iron rule of the oppressor; not as one seeking to subjugate others to the will—but *making* the will one with that universal force as is necessary to bring everyone to that throne of grace, of faith, of hope, of love, of *all* those conditions necessary to build hospitals, churches . . . and help others to help themselves'' (3976-4).

Since that time, contrasts have abounded between those who have wielded power for self-aggrandizement and those who have taken power rather in the interests of the people. Consider Manuel Noriega who was divested of his role as suspected drug lord and dictator of Panama by the United States as 1990 began.

Also think of the Romanian hard-line communist President Nicolae Ceausescu and his wife Elena who for twenty-four years led an oppressive government and massacred thousands of people who protested their harsh totalitarian rule. They were executed by their own people in Bucharest on Christmas Day 1989, the last of their kind in the Warsaw Pact to be driven from power. The people who had suffered under their cruel regime cheered.[6]

Consider, too, the new President of Czechoslovakia, Vaclav Havel, whose New Year's message at the Berlin Wall then was: ''People, your government has returned to you!''[7]

The year 1927 was in the midst of a period of isolationism in America. The League of Nations, begun in 1920, with its humanitarian, peacekeeping goals, was the first attempt for all nations to maintain peace. Although the United States led in its formation and covenant that were the basis for the peace treaties after World War I, the United States refused to join, despite President Wilson's urging. Other nations then began dropping out, just at a time in the 1930s when such a powerful deterrent might have prevented World War II.

Against this background of failure by the nations to create what could have been an opportunity for tremendous good, Cayce's friends were attempting to work with the Creative Forces for the same goals. They were not dreamers, only, but practical, successful people. ''Remember,'' Cayce told them, ''large oaks from little acorns grow. . . . Remember it was the still, small voice, and not the wind nor the lightning, that was the voice of the Creative Energy that rules the world. Remember, then, that action—with the correct purpose—builds in the hearts and minds of individuals who are co-workers and ambassadors of that living force we call God'' (3976-5).

The name of their organization would be "the Association of International Investigators." It would be incorporated under the laws of the states. Capital might be, said Cayce, "in the billons" (3976-5). This would all be possible if the group held to the high discipline of Christian principles.

Over a period of several years, the readings show, the group received information and guidance. They were told that the first step was to choose "those who would give self in holy communion with this purpose" and that they choose to be of themselves "to be used as an instrument . . . for the saving of the good in human principles."

"*. . . for the world awaits the coming of those who will proclaim the day of freedom from the bonds of those who would rule*, either through prestige or through political influence. . . . Then, ones so chosen by their fitness—as will come through such communion—will be the first to begin. See? For as each are chosen, through these same forces, there may be given their perfect fitness. . . . As these seek, let's give to each their place, their niche, their abilities, their conditions, concerning such ideals" (3976-4, italics added).

From this brief insight into the hearts and minds of those drawn to Cayce's side, we gain insight into the hearts and minds of their counterparts today. These words just quoted could well describe today's new leaders who are proclaiming the day of freedom throughout the world.

Edgar Cayce himself was described by the Source as one "lowly in heart—ever seeking to do good, as good is understood by him, and willing ever to be used as an instrument . . ."

The others were given spiritual advice to follow "the dictates of the heart." If, in the intense seeking by that little group back in 1927, they did not carry out their magnificent ideal, they perhaps created the matrix for what was to follow in this day—the thought form granted us by the Creative Forces for proclaiming the day of freedom, by those prepared for the task.

What has determined "the fitness" of those who have this day declared the day of freedom? There have been throughout decades of dictatorship those who have courageously resisted tyranny. They have held differing degrees of power to do so and not only political; they have protested in whatever ways they had at hand, enabled surely by their own communion with the purpose of freedom, their individual "fitness."

When Cayce was giving guidance for creating a humanitarian organization, Stalin was carrying out his purges. States Graf: "In 1903, Marxian socialist Lenin, fired with revolutionist plans, had organized the Bolsheviks. His Marxian program was resisted to the point of death during years of civil war and bitter suffering by the Russian people. It is certain that Stalin and Lenin, as well as Hitler, were those Cayce referred to as "seeking to subjugate others to the will."[8]

That communism twisted the idea of service and brotherhood to serve tyrants was obvious. Reagan was right: The Soviet Union was an evil empire for seventy-two years.

The Association for Research and Enlightenment, Inc., together with the Edgar Cayce Foundation, today is a worldwide organization that has carried the high ideals of the Cayce readings to millions of people. Since Cayce seemed to see the whole picture, in the first of these readings in 1927, he must have been aware of the ominous fact of Stalin's success that year in overthrowing such enemies as Leon Trotsky, for the following year Stalin became supreme ruler of Russia. It is most significant that the American seer's reading on world affairs should volunteer, at that very moment of infamy, the message of the eventual downfall of Stalin's despotism. He did not name any of the leaders, "those who would rule," or those who would proclaim the day of freedom; it was early in the unrolling of the scroll of history, and only time would reveal the meaning of his words. That they were given in the first World Affairs reading for people wanting to know, not for themselves alone but for their fellowman, set the consciousness, perhaps the tone, for such forevision.

It is not for me to say definitely what Cayce meant at all about "those chosen by their fitness to proclaim freedom from the bonds of those who would rule." But if this is not the day the world has been waiting for, as he predicted, what day can we imagine it to be? The circumstances, the totally unexpected events taking place in our world, together with

the players in this cosmic drama of the ages, strangely match
the uncanny Cayce scenario for those with "eyes to see."

Cayce pointed out that bonds of rule could be either
through "prestige" or "political influence." He made the
distinction because the first is a subtle bondage by those with
wealth and power over those with less money or power. Political influence is by law and police force, as well. Both can
be damaging to human life and spirit.

In 1931, his friends asked for help with international economic problems of the day. He replied that fear on the part
of those who control or direct investing was the reason for
the imbalance. The answer was a return to trust in God, not
in the power of self.

They then asked: "Is there today in operation an outer organization representative of the anti-Christ forces which has
power to subvert governments as well as institutions? And
how counteract them?"

The answer was that every soul turn to the power within
and give God a chance in their lives. Power can destroy only
as man himself gives it power (3976-24).

He addressed the issue of freedom versus slavery and economic hardship. "Those who are hungry care not as to the
source of power." Thus, as long as rule has been practiced
through economic advantage, there has always been some
form of slavery.

In this reading was asked: "What should be our attitude
toward the Negro and how may we best work out the karma
created in relations with him?"

The answer was: "He is thy brother! They that produced,
they that brought servitude without thought or purpose have
created that which they must meet within their own principles,
their own selves." Blacks, said Cayce, should be taken on
the basis of "their own individual fitness" as in association
with every other people. God "hath made of one blood the
nations of the earth" (3976-24).

The Emancipation Proclamation by President Lincoln in
1862 was America's first step to free the slaves. The Thirteenth Amendment of 1865 ended slavery in the United
States, but laws still discriminated against blacks, Hispanics,

and other racial and ethnic groups, including the Indians. The Civil Rights Act of 1964 established a policy prohibiting discrimination in employment among minorities. But discrimination can be, and is too often, covert and hard to prove. Spurred by blatant poverty and inequality in America, in 1964 President Lyndon Johnson set up such agencies as the Office of Economic Opportunity. The vision put forth was "the Great Society." Programs were designed to provide housing, education, and job opportunities for both black and white people.

However, by 1968, money and confidence in the economy were scarce. Corruption, greed, and rivalry among those participating in the programs escalated. Riots took place in the streets. The Vietnam War was costing lives and money. By 1968 the Great Society was still only a dream of the future.

The struggle for freedom, whether in Africa, Asia, Europe, or America, is the same, it seems, although under different kinds of oppression. While communism or czarism imposes great burdens upon its own people, denying basic freedoms, even massacring them, democracy makes it possible to make changes for the better. The blacks in America have progressed far in recent decades in education and political and social status, though more than 130 years have elapsed since their emancipation.

In contrast, for communist nations just emerging from their bondage, total freedom is instant but precarious.

Cayce presented the same criteria of leadership for all nations, as valid as they were in the 1930s. Thus, whether we are talking about freedom of minorities in America, South Africa, Europe, Burma, Haiti, or Sri Lanka, he set forth a single platform:

> Then those who are in power must know that they *are* their brother's keeper, and give expression to that which has been indicated in "Thou shalt love the Lord with all thy heart and mind and body, and thy neighbor as thyself."
>
> For all stand as one before Him. For the Lord is not a

respecter of persons, and these things (oppression under totalitarian rule) cannot long exist.

(3976-19)

This was in 1938 and referred to Nazi Germany as well as to communist Russia.

The Nietzschean creed that God is dead had influenced Europe away from Christian belief. Since Nietzsche's death in 1900, communism has risen and fallen. The theories of Lenin and Marx have been declared dead, and God is still worshiped in churches everywhere. Cayce followers asked: "Upon what religious thought will fall the greatest responsibility in leading the world toward the light of understanding?"

The answer, central to all the rest, and repeated often, was: "That as is comprised in that as has been given, whether it be from the Greek or the barbarian, whether it be from the bond or from the free, 'Thou shalt love the Lord thy God with all thine heart, and thy neighbor as thyself!' " (3976-8).

Dr. Yuri Shmarov, a specialist on Middle East affairs with the Diplomatic Academy in Moscow, spoke in the fall of 1989 to American college groups on American-Soviet cooperation to resolve Middle East tensions. I attended one of his lectures at the Graduate Center of Old Dominion University and Norfolk State University in Virginia Beach. Although I listened with some feeling that this was perhaps part of a communist ploy, his sincerity was evident. He was, of course, a diplomat, and his audience was thoroughly disarmed by his candor. He said, "Perestroika brought me here" to speak on Soviet-American relations. He urged cooperation between the Soviets and Americans in joint action to prevent escalation of the arms race in the Middle East. We can only use our influence, he said, by pressure groups dealing with Israelis and Arabs, to minimize friction. Shmarov further suggested joint commissions on many other issues and an international conference on the Middle East. He pointed out the peacemaking potential of the United Nations and the appointment of a secretary general for the Middle East.[9]

The Russian professor said a "new international order" is seen now by the United States and the Soviet Union as theoretical rather than practical, unfortunately. There is no political infrastructure as yet. We seem to agree on the "promise of a new world," which must be given with sincerity. International agreement involves, he added, human rights, environment, Middle East oil, water resources, population growth, employment, peaceful reconstruction.[10]

Asked how he had reacted to the revelation that the history textbooks in the universities of Russia had to be revised, he said ruefully, "Yes, they were full of lies." He said that he had to explain the deception to his fifteen-year-old son, and this was difficult for him.[11]

As I sat listening to this man, I thought of the time of World War II that soon after brought on the cold war and its tensions. I was like many others not quite ready for what I was hearing: a Russian professor bringing the message of peaceful cooperation after so much estrangement the past forty years! But I recalled that Cayce had foretold cooperation among nations.

Some Western observers indicated that they were wary of continuing communistic ideology and practice that persisted at the heart of the Soviet government—that things were moving too fast for the hard-liners to catch up. Besides, the nations of Eastern Europe, including Russia, were involved in old ethnic and religious hostilities, dating back centuries.

David Selbourne, a British writer on that region, wrote: "A Soviet withdrawal could encourage long-suppressed nationalism that is already bubbling up in half a dozen places from Serbia to Transylvania and Silesia. There is no love lost between the peoples of Eastern Europe."[12] This was borne out later. Such was the civil war (or national conflict?) between Armenia and Azerbaijan in the southern Soviet Republic; the war in Yugoslavia among Christians, Muslims, Croats, Serbs. This ethnic hatred, cynically called "ethnic cleansing," was cause for relentless bombing of Sarajevo, rape of Muslim women by Serbs, as the Muslims stood helpless without weapons. Over years, it created tragedy for thousands of men, women, and children already living in grinding poverty and hardship due to inflation, housing shortages, and pollution. Distrust was evident in Romania when that country revealed it would boost defense spending to reinforce its border with Hungary. The saying was that although things have changed, things stay the same. East German writer Stefan Heym stated, "Communists across the bloc retain control of the instruments of coercion—the police, military, and security forces. . . . In the middle ranks, the same people are still there."[13]

Cayce's 1927 prophecy declared that the world awaits the coming of those who will proclaim the day of freedom. It was fulfilled many times. One of the great voices out of Russia was that of the late Andrei Sakharov, internally exiled exponent of freedom, brilliant physicist, recipient of the Nobel Peace Prize in 1975. He was without doubt one of those to whom Cayce referred: as Russia's leading dissident, a proclaimer of the day of freedom. During the last week of his life in December 1989, Sakharov opposed Gorbachev in the Congress of People's Deputies on the issue of "Gorbachev's refusal to allow debate on the Communist Party's constitutional monopoly on political power." Gorbachev was ignoring telegrams Sakharov showed him from Russians demanding multiparty democracy.[14]

Living and speaking for freedom as he confronted the staid, unmoving powers still in control, Sakharov spoke for all dissidents opposing the communists into the 1990s. According to David Satter, a longtime observer of the Soviet Union, in the official Soviet press there were still taboo subjects. "A heavy veil of secrecy envelops the soviet military. . . . While Gorbachev readily releases information that discredits his predecessors and rivals, he exercises strict control over media coverage whenever he chooses."[15]

Satter goes on to state that other Soviets have spoken out, such as "Sergei Kuznetsov who was sentenced to three years in a labor camp for slander and resisting the police. His real crime was writing articles critical of the KGB in Sverdlovsk." Another is Edward Kritsky, "arrested in the West Ukraine in 1980 for carrying a sign calling for genuinely free labor unions. He is imprisoned at Goris, a city in Armenia."[16]

Yuri Nikulin, the well-known director of the Moscow Circus, "was nominated as an independent candidate for the Soviet Union's new Parliament. . . . Party leaders blocked a vote with a series of delaying tactics that lasted far into the night. . . . At election time, party loyalists had a solid majority. . . ."[17]

At the first session of the Congress of People's Deputies, Yuri Vlasov, a former Olympic weight-lifting champion, began a speech that set a new standard for public discourse in the Soviet Union. The KGB constituted 'a threat to democracy,' he said. The KGB is not a service but a real underground empire that has not divulged its secrets yet—except for some excavated graves. And despite such a history, this service retains its special, exceptional position. States Satter: "Three years ago anyone criticizing the KGB in public would have been put in a mental hospital, but Vlasov's address was broadcast nationwide."[18]

"Prominent economist Nicolai Shmelyev said that 'the exploitation of workers in the Soviet Union was the highest of any industrial country.' "[19]

We have come to the last decade of the twentieth century on a note of victory for millions of oppressed people. The strong current of communism has receded in the 1990s, as freedom has won out.

In the United States for the first time, to receive his Medal of Freedom from President George Bush, Lech Walesa was interviewed in November 1989 by Robert MacNeil for the *Nightly News Report.* He is recognized as the man who, with Solidarity, took the lead in 1989 to encourage all of Eastern Europe to break away from communism. He said, regarding union of Europe, that "the situation has to be brought back to normalcy. It was not normal that Europe disintegrated. . . . Let's remember that one nation (Poland) disappeared. It calls for payment. It should not happen again. Reunite Europe, but not like Hitler did."[20]

(Poland did disappear. In 1939 Russia and Germany signed an agreement dividing Poland between them. After World War II, Poland was given back most of her territory). MacNeil asked, "What would be Poland's kinship with the Germans?"

"I was thinking of a single Europe," Walesa replied. "I'm an incorrigible romanticist." Much earlier, he said, the idea got started. "I talked with people responsible. Many are now prepared: a united nation can be powerful." He spoke of one Europe integrated economically, however. In explaining how it happened that the process was opened, he explained, "I have to say I'm a practicing Catholic believer. . . . There is no force capable of reversing the reforms. The only possibility is the future victory. . . ."[21]

Walesa admired George Bush. "I believe Bush sees to the interests of this beautiful country. I'm a Pole and have to give him credit. . . . He can facilitate but says, 'Help yourself and the world will help you. I have to take care of the United States.' I think that's wise. Nobody else (but Bush) was willing to support Solidarity. He's a wise and brave man."[22]

There are, he added, great opportunities for business in Eastern Europe. "The problem is infrastructure." At that time, he was not interested in high office, although he was offered that of prime minister of Poland. "I'm a free man. I felt freest when I was an electrician. . . . I want to be the serving one."[23]

It was by such self-effacing leadership that Solidarity has successfully led the Polish government.

Looking back, we can see that Walesa's role in Solidarity's success in 1989 was part of the start of the new order of freedom. Like dominoes, at the same time, Panama was set free from Noriega's dictatorship, under the U.S. Operation Just Cause; Havel took over Czechoslovakia; the Berlin Wall came down.

As for Walesa, he continued to work behind the scenes. In the fall of 1990 he announced he was running as a candidate for the presidency of Poland. He did, and he won. In his leadership that has proved so effective, he appears to be one of those Cayce meant "proclaiming the day of freedom, rising from low to high estate." Changes they bring cause great turmoil among those who fail to understand that "the Spirit is moving in His ways to bring the knowledge of the Father in the hearts and lives of men."

In 1932 Cayce described Europe as "a house broken up." From political, economic, and religious freedom as Eastern

Europe recovers from her long bondage, a united Europe is possible.

WRITERS OF RUSSIA

Pressure to conform in the arts to what the Soviets called "socialist realism" had begun in the 1920s under Stalin and created a stultifying torpor in all the arts. "In the years since Stalin's death in 1953, Soviet literature has benefitted from a gradual abatement of the paralyzing terror which had been the chief instrument of rule since the early 1930s," wrote Max Hayward, known for his many outstanding essays on twentieth-century Russian writers.[24]

One great Russian writer is Alexander Solzhenitsyn, whose *One Day in the Life of Ivan Denisovich* and *The Gulag Archipelago* were novels about Stalin's concentration camps. He was evidently another one of those of whom Cayce spoke who protested by means of their writings against the tyranny of their own time, "proclaiming the day of freedom." In addition, he wrote open letters to the Writers' Congress and the Board of the Writers' Union denouncing the censorship of Soviet literature and failure of the Writers' Union to protect the interests of its members. He was not allowed to publish in Russia after that, but *The Cancer Ward* and *The First Circle* were published abroad. He wrote the latter based on his experience of four years' imprisonment in an institution "in which scientists and technologists were confined in comparatively mild conditions as long as they agreed to work on special projects, such as new spying gadgets." He was sent there "on the strength of his knowledge of physics and mathematics." Because of disobedience, Solzhenitsyn spent four years in a labor camp. *The Cancer Ward* followed his hospitalization for cancer.[25]

Many other writers in the Stalin period found themselves in trouble with Soviet officials who tried to force them to hew to the communist ideology. Boris Pasternak wrote the epic *Doctor Zhivago* in which he puts the 1917 Bolshevik revolution "in the broad context of eternity and nature." He sided with a fellow writer, Osip Mandelstam, who had written a poem describing Stalin as "a murderer surrounded by braying and whinnying half-men." Such criticism was of course censored. Pasternak, with another writer and literary editor, Olga Ivinskaya, pleaded for Mandelstam's life. Stalin, who fortunately respected writers who said what they thought, did not execute the errant dissident but sent him into exile. He later died on the way to a concentration camp in a subsequent time of terror.[26]

Stalin continued to hassle Pasternak. To punish him, he had Olga Ivinskaya, Pasternak's companion and the inspiration for the heroine Lara in *Doctor Zhivago,* arrested and sentenced to five years in a forced labor camp. "As one can judge from several of the poems (such as 'Parting') in the *Zhivago* cycle devoted to her, Pasternak was infinitely distressed by this cruel blow. But it did not have the desired result. He made no concessions and went on writing the book which, as no one had ever done before, he was to settle accounts with the epoch through which he had lived."[27]

As if fulfilling their roles, these very ones "so chosen" have indeed appeared on the world scene: not proud political aspirants but heroes of the people such as Pasternak, Solzhenitsyn, Walesa, Havel. It is people like them, I think, whom Cayce meant: chosen by their fitness made possible by their "communion" with Higher Purpose. Walesa as a religious man spoke in religious terms, telling his questioners in America that the fate of his people in Poland was in God's hands.

Where did these dissidents acquire their courage?

Preceding the great freedom movement in Eastern Europe has been a religious movement that has never abandoned the church, both Roman Catholic and Protestant. There are countless souls in that part of the world who can be considered among those "chosen" of whom Cayce spoke so long ago: They spoke by their very audacity to defy Soviet authority against atheism. They are akin to those suffering religious persecution in China.

As oppressed nations rise around the world, there comes Cayce's promise that future governments will be based on "the ideals of the Ages"; governments that "make the will of leaders one with the Universal Force,'' and not self-seeking.

Can people who have never enjoyed self-rule suddenly be able to run a government? The trend appears to be surprisingly well-founded as people are caught up in an unprecedented new consciousness of hope and faith.

4

"OUT OF RUSSIA"

. . . comes again the hope of the world . . . (3976-29, June 22, 1944)

. . . here a new understanding has and will come to a troubled people. Here, because of the yoke of oppression, because of the self-indulgences, has arisen another extreme. Only when freedom of speech, the right to worship according to the dictates of the conscience—until these come about, still turmoils will be within. (3976-19, June 24, 1938)

A NEW UNDERSTANDING

THE FIRST MENTION OF Russia in the Edgar Cayce readings was in 1932 in response to a question: "What can be the trend of events in the political and economic conditions in Europe?"

There followed the answer: There, "peoples are going through the experience of being *born* again." That nation, he said, was "Russia!" (3976-8)

In the same year, "What should be the attitude of so-called capitalist nations toward Russia?"

Cayce's reply was: "On Russia's religious development will come the greater hope of the world!" (3976-10)

The next time was in 1933 when he was asked, "Give the outstanding events in Russia through 1938."

"These should be presented rather after there have been

those changes in that to be presented . . . that out of Russia, you see, there may come that which may be the basis of a more world-wide religious thought or trend—see?'' (3976-12)

In the final World Affairs reading, Cayce gave a kind of ''farewell address'' that summed up all the major nations and their characters and problems to be overcome. ''What then of nations? In Russia there comes the hope of the world, not as that sometimes termed of the communistic, the Bolchevistic, no. But freedom! Freedom! that each man will live for his fellow man! The principle has been born. It will take years for it to be crystallized, but out of Russia comes *again* the hope of the world . . .'' (3976-29).

It is difficult to know without doubt what Cayce meant by the word ''again.'' Only if we take the sentence in the context of the account of RaTa as a young priest of 10,600 B.C. does it make sense. RaTa (Edgar Cayce) was born, said his own readings, of a daughter of Zu in the area south of the Caucasus Mountains of southeastern Russia. He joined a tribe of Caucasians called ''the people of Ararat.'' Today, it is site of the smallest former Soviet republic of Armenia. But the area seems to have significance from antiquity. Mount Ararat, 16,946 feet high, is in Eastern Turkey near the border of Iran, thought by some people to be the location of Noah's Ark.

People of the RaTa period were interested in ''seeking for the understanding as to the evolution of the souls of men,'' states Cayce. ''Thus, RaTa saw a great need to help the less advanced people of his time, those who were still primitive in their development.'' He was accompanied by the son of Ararat's king and a large entourage of nine hundred people as they migrated from the Caucasus into Egypt. There they conquered benevolently and began the work of regenerating souls. RaTa himself was highly advanced (not a god, as Cayce declared, but with clairvoyant and certainly godlike spiritual powers). After a strenuous sojourn in which age had taken its toll, he was able to regenerate himself. For his work of regenerating whole nations by the laws of right use of creative energy, he chose Egypt. There he was able to build, over time, a high culture that worshiped the One God. There are ''many peoples, even nations, that were influenced by the material activities of the entity in that experience" (294-147). Eventually he instigated the temples there and with the great initiate, Hermes, built the pyramid. In these temples were nurtured the ideals of beauty of mind and spirit, of the body whole and perfect. For this purpose was built the Temple of Sacrifice (a holistic hospital utilizing spiritual healing) and the Temple Beautiful (where was continued healing of mind and spirit with the help of all the arts).

It was this life experience that was seen by friends of Cayce to be replayed in his life in the twentieth century. He was serving once again as "one to be used as that medium of transferring those ideas, ideals as are ready to be given to those who would put same into effect" (3976-5). To those millions who recognize him, he is a humble spiritual teacher returning at a time of need for spiritual awakening in *this* day.

What did he mean when he prophesied that *out of Russia would come the hope of the world*? Let us remember that RaTa journeyed from the southernmost regions of *Russia*, between the Caucasus Mountains and the Caspian Sea. The advent of the priest into Egypt, say the readings, "was one of the most momentous occasions or periods in the world's history" (900-275). Why? Because RaTa's mission as a high priest in Egypt of prehistory was to influence civilization down to the present.

This is certainly a tremendous statement. RaTa, the priest, was in that time and to that extent the hope of the world. Has the hope of the world of the twenty-first century *again* come out of Russia? And how?

Why did Cayce say that "out of Russia" would come the hope of the world? Why should he have not said, out of America, or England, or perhaps Italy, or India? They have not, as Russia, had a history during the past seventy years of atheism.

In Russia, the churches were used as museums or storage buildings; church leaders were persecuted and parishioners punished by loss of their rights to education and first-class citizenship. How is it possible that a nation so deprived of its spiritual autonomy, its very right to think and to speak from heart and mind, could be the source of the hope of the world?

We in the free world cannot imagine being so shackled in spirit. We take for granted our right to worship or be atheistic. It is private business, this, or we can make it public business as to what we feel and think, fear or dream. We are free to grow, learning as a nation as well as individuals how to make wise choices in social and domestic issues, foreign policy, economics. Our free press is the envy of journalists and poets of nondemocratic countries.

During the worst of their sufferings, from the 1920s and 1930s to the 1970s, Russians and their satellite neighbors may have been truly atheist, or only pretended to be. But in their adversity, as Cayce told us, they were being *born* again. Living in a free country, we could only read about their condition. From books and plays that escaped Soviet censors, through the eyes of those who lived the ordeal, we can know something of what it was like. And television has at last shown us their new faces, let us hear them speak for themselves.

In my attempt to know what Cayce really was seeing for this time, I realize that these apolitical, non-office-seeking leaders I point out may not be what he saw, nor those dissident writers before them, but they surely bear an amazing resemblance! As they appear, we begin to see a set of traits found in them that are the antithesis of power-hungry sycophants and tyrants of the past. Those traits that it is obvious they possess in common are humility, dedication to human rights, selflessness, courage, and a certain nobility of soul, a brand of spirituality that marks true democratic leadership. They are invariably people who have earned their place in life by their own efforts and not by political favoritism. In their comments about themselves, about God and "fate," they revealed consciousness of a higher Purpose guiding them.

It would seem, taking all we have said about the manner in which there would be produced out of Russia the hope for the world, that Mikhail Gorbachev must be one of the most important of those "chosen" to bring it all about. Was he a dissident? No, he came up through the regular Party channels and is, from all accounts, an atheist. From the book *Behind the High Kremlin Walls* by Vladimir Solovyov and Elena Klepikova, we have a rare glimpse of the intrigue, secrecy, and deception of Soviet power figures, past and present; thus, the world of Mikhail and Raisa Gorbachev. It is written by a husband-and-wife team of Russian journalists who today live in the United States.

Gorbachev was born in Privolnoye, Stavropol, in southern Russia near the Caucasus range. He was there in 1942 and 1943 when Hitler's armies occupied the area and were headquartered in that village. He graduated with a degree in law from the University of Moscow. In his sophomore year he joined the Party and became politically active. While his comrades drank when they got together, he imbibed little, proving him to be the exemplary Party worker.[1] As a young lawyer, he competed for position against other young apparatchiks, winning out because of his intelligence, zeal, and very likable personality. He was not aggressive but obliging; he worked well with his peers; his superiors were pleased with his efficient and correct manner.[2]

Gorbachev was a true Party man. He was assigned to his home province early in his career but finally moved up the ladder to greater posts after being there twenty-three years.[3]

In 1960, "The modest and businesslike Gorbachev, who is not given to gross flattery, did not at first glance attract the notice of many of the influential men who later became his patrons, nor of Kulakov, Suslov, Andropov, nor Gromyko."[4]

Gorbachev was by 1970 promoted to be first secretary of the agricultural system of "the Stavropol Territory, sole master of a huge domain about the size of Austria or of Denmark and Switzerland taken together."[5]

In his book *Perestroika: New Thinking for Our Country and the World*, which Gorbachev published two years after becoming president, he makes a powerful statement that reflects the profound break from past Soviet thinking. Yet in it he holds fast to the socialist way of life, and to Lenin and Marx as his historic mentors. So a Western reader peruses the pages with ambiguous feelings, for the utter failure of communism that had proved so final was not yet seen by loyal Soviets to be reason to throw it over.

He freely admits to the many problems. "At some stage," he writes, "this became particularly clear in the latter half of the seventies—something happened that was at first sight inexplicable. The country began to lose momentum. Economic failures became more frequent. Difficulties began to accumulate and deteriorate, and unresolved problems to multiply. . . ." A "gap in the efficiency of production, quality of products, scientific and technological development, the production of advanced technology . . . A country that was once quickly closing on the world's advanced nations began to lose one position after another. . . ."[6]

For these and other related social and economic reasons, he wrote, perestroika became "an urgent necessity." He described his socialist society as "ripe for change." His stand regarding America is that it is "a power with whom we shall have to live and build relations." He pondered America's "enemy image" and deplored "inflammatory" American broadcasts about the Soviets.[7]

Neither science nor politics seems adequate to save us entirely from the ravages of disease and drugs, from the imbalance of economies. We have the power, however, to change the way we think, the attitudes we hold, and can thereby change our destiny. According to Cayce, "Mind is the builder." And the first lesson in the *Search for God* studies he gave the first Study Group was cooperation. It is that lesson which was recognized by Gorbachev as he strove to lead a divided world toward working together rather than in the attitude of confrontation.

Nothing so well illustrates the power of cooperation and the group mind as the spectacle of thousands of Eastern bloc protesters seeking freedom in the streets. And now the tasks of designing new governments challenged the leaders who have taken over in the wake of the communist collapse.

Those countries have gone through much tribulation during the past decades, but it has made them stronger in their faith than we had guessed. Alexander Solzhenitsyn in 1979 said that he could not recommend Western society in its present state as an ideal for the transformation of Russian society. "Through intense suffering, our country has now achieved a spiritual development of such intensity that the Western system in its present state does not look attractive." He added that he thought the Western world was in a state of spiritual exhaustion.[8]

It has been the writers of Russia who have, over the years of communist despotism, provided articulate protest against the obliteration of freedom and human rights. The very prolific Solzhenitsyn, in *One Day in the Life of Ivan Denisovich*, tells his own experience in a forced labor camp. The brutal cold of Russian winters was matched by the brutal inhumanity to which prisoners were subjected. In an interview with Nikita Struve in 1976 he said that the publication of *One Day* brought hundreds of personal recollections from people who had lived in the camps. It was out of the "vast torrent of material" that he then wrote *The Gulag Archipelago*.[9]

Another essayist, John Dunlop, states in *"The Gulag Archipelago": Alternative to Ideology* that "what Solzhenitsyn appears to be maintaining is that only Christianity offers an effective antidote to Marxism-Leninism, only it can exorcize the demons which have been rending Russia since 1917." Further, Solzhenitsyn used a superior ethical stance—rooted in a "point of view"—that characterized many of the believers he observed or heard tales of from his fellow zeks (prisoners).[10]

"Solzhenitsyn believes that his own arrest and the dramatic reversal of his personal fortunes had a salutary effect on his life. As Dr. Kornfeld, a Jewish convert to Christianity, tells the future writer shortly before being murdered in the camps: '... I have become convinced that there is no punishment that comes to us on earth which is undeserved.' "[11]

One of the major concepts in the Cayce readings is that we are all responsible for our fate: Results are never without cause. As Cayce so aptly stated for one person, "every tub must sit on its own bottom."

Whereas the good Jewish Christian referred to causes and results confined to this life only, Cayce of course suggested the long-term view that in ancient philosophies and religions include the system of reincarnation and karma. Says Dunlop, it was this encounter with Dr. Kornfeld that seems to have been the spark for Solzhenitsyn's conversion to religious belief. He arrived at the conclusion that "the meaning of earthly existence lies not, as we have grown used to thinking, in prospering, but . . . in the development of the soul."[12] He had arrived at the most profound reason for understanding the Christian doctrine.

The purpose of life had long before been explained by Edgar Cayce thus: "Then what is the purpose of each soul entering a material manifestation? That it may be a witness-bearer for and unto the glory of the Father which has been manifested through the Son, even Jesus; in making then those activities through, and in which, such may be the purpose, the desire of the individual entity" (1722-1).

People who came to Cayce were led to seek counsel about their soul growth. One person asked, "What is holding back my spiritual development?"

Cayce replied, "Nothing holds it back but SELF" (987-4, MS 1). Whether one believes or not in reincarnation, this has proved a valid axiom for Christians everywhere. We are expected to be in charge of our souls, minds, and bodies. We can't blame others, or circumstances, for our lack of spiritual development. We, only, are responsible.

This is not to say, however, that Solzhenitsyn believed in reincarnation, only to point out the Christian view as is taught throughout the world being a large factor in his life and works.

The excellent collection of essays by Max Hayward, *Writers in Russia, 1917–1978,* is a source of broad and deep insight into the soul of Russia and its seventy-two-year bondage under communism, 1918 to 1990. He is the outstanding scholar of Russian literature, famed translator, and brilliant critic of twentieth-century Russian letters, according to the book jacket. He was a graduate of Oxford and served in the British Embassy in Moscow from 1947 to 1949 "during Stalin's fearful purge of intellectuals—an experience that left him irreversibly committed to the culture the dictator was determined to destroy." His essays deal with the dissidents in Soviet literature at the time of Stalin, Nikita Khrushchev and Leonid Brezhnev and include firsthand encounters with communist domination and its effects on Russian writers.

He speaks of Christianity in Russia as formerly including the intelligentsia, which was not officially recognized as a class separate from the church.[13] ". . . both, in their different ways, contended for the soul of the nation, and that some outstanding members of the intelligentsia were actually sons of priests." He says that the Russian church was totally subordinated to temporal power only in the eighteenth century under Peter the Great, "not for nothing widely regarded as Antichrist incarnate. . . . The church nonetheless remained the chief visible repository and guardian of the country's millennial traditions and, for most people, the only source of mystery and ritual in an existence which would otherwise have been intolerably cheerless. . . ."[14]

An impressive corpus of speculative religious thought that arose in part outside the church in the late nineteenth and early twentieth centuries showed that Russian orthodoxy was "capable of an intellectual vigor certainly no less than that of the secular systems of belief which competed with it. . . ." There was "a restlessness which often drove people of all social classes to set off in search of the ever-elusive combination of truth and justice summed up in the untranslatable word *pravda*." The intelligentsia were constantly searching for "all-embracing formulas or systems of ideas which might seem to provide not only a complete view of the world but also a total solution to all its problems." It is the reason "for the almost incredible ferment produced in Russia by German philosophy" such as Hegel, Fichte, and Marx.[15]

Hayward states that the October Revolution was for some Russians religious, transcendental. "Symbolists Blok and Bely interpreted the Revolution as a millennial event, equaled only by the coming of Christ. Sergei Yesenin mistook the grand designs of the Bolsheviks for a plan to build a rural utopia" of universal reconciliation and brotherly love.[16]

Another clue to the Russian spirit is their traditional way of referring to each other as "brothers." In addition, a standard form of address between officers and men in the communist Soviet army was, "How are you serving?" The answer was, "I serve the working people."[17] These terms relate comfortably with Christian principles. In the spiritual life, the idea of serving rather than being served is to make of the custom a noble one.

Walesa as a free man told his TV audience in America, "I want to be the serving one." He reflected the old religious tradition, expressing humility and love of others, echoing Cayce's "Freedom! that each man will live for his fellow man!" Cayce declared that the ones to proclaim the day of freedom would be chosen because of their "fitness." It is the fitness of the spirit he meant, as well as whatever talents and abilities they had. For many of us have the same abilities, but only those with moral stamina and fortitude founded in God are able to stand against the powers of darkness.

Czechoslovakian playwright Vaclav Havel, president following the "Velvet Revolution," is one more of those who fit the description of this unique breed of leader. In his youth he was denied a university education, so he drove a taxi by day and attended night school. When at nineteen he made an appeal to a conference of young writers to remember the forgotten poets of their country, he was severely criticized. He began writing plays that poked fun at communism's decadence. After the Prague spring of 1968 his books were removed from libraries, his plays were banned. Then he started selling his plays abroad and thereafter rode every day to the brewery, where he was forced to work, in a Mercedes-Benz![18]

He was jailed for a total of five years because of his "subversive" activities, which included founding the Charter 77 human rights organization. Like Solzhenitsyn, he wrote in prison. "What is now considered a masterpiece of dissident literature, *Letters to Olga*, is a collection of his prison letters to his wife."[19]

In his visit to the United States in February 1990, Havel expressed his admiration for our American founding fathers. But he is not looking to capitalism to solve the problems of his country. He is reported to have said of his own sudden rise to the presidency of Czechoslovakia that, "This was not my choice. It was fate. But I accept it and try to do something for my country because I live here . . . I have a responsibility to something higher than family or country."[20]

"Higher than family or country?"

Havel's statement reveals him as a "true Aquarian." For astrologers say we are moving fast into the millennium when we will be influenced by the Aquarian ideal of brotherhood, of being aware of ourselves and mankind rather than only family and tribal (national) allegiance. I believe, based on the Cayce concept and what we know of the Aquarian, that Christianity will be practiced as the true source of enlightenment in the Aquarian Age. Looking back 2000 years, reminded of the history of mankind during those centuries, we can see that the Piscean Age was a growing experience toward realizing the Christian ideal.

What will be the emphasis? Although we will be even more aware of our own worth as individuals, we will be influenced to reach out to each other and all mankind in friendship and good will. Nationality and race will mean little; rather, oneness of all races and faiths. But "Raise not democracy above the Fatherhood of God, the Brotherhood of Man," said Cayce.

This Aquarian concept has been with us in the teachings of Christ for 2000 years. It is expressed in His concern with the individual, yet His outreach to all people on earth. For 2000 years we have been given His teachings and His Presence to protect and encourage us through the centuries when nations were built too often on despotism. Aquarius will bring to us inspiration and vision and knowledge that will be, said Cayce, "of the heart."

Reading between the lines of Cayce's references to Russia, in particular, one senses loving compassion for her people, as if he were seeing them as those who know Russia and her neighbors best. As one studies the Russian culture, especially through the novels of Solzhenitsyn and Pasternak and the short stories of Chekhov and Dostoyevsky, there is a sensitivity and warmth in the protagonists, an abiding belief in a spiritual universe, because of the religious heritage of the authors. In stories of everyday people of the nineteenth and early twentieth centuries, there is frequent allusion to religious practice. It seems not an acquired faith so much as an innate indwelling of idealism.

This high consciousness is just as evident in the conversations of several visitors from Russia and the former republics of the Soviet Union who have visited this country. They have come forth on television with unselfconscious acknowledgment of God's relationship to their experience. It is as if they feel free to speak in America where belief in God is cherished. In that freedom, Walesa stated unabashedly to Robert MacNeil that the fate of his country rested with God. A Russian journalist on the same program prefaced a statement with: "If you believe in God and read your Bible . . ."[21]

We in America take our religious freedom for granted. They don't.

For Americans of the 1990s, it is no less a time for change than it is for the rest of the world, because we share the reckoning. Embroiled in domestic wars against drugs and moral conflicts in which values of the past are questioned, we are not quite so ready to attempt to fix the rest of the world.

However, it is America, Cayce reminds us, that has led the world "in its freedom of speech—in its activities towards freedom of service toward that God, as according to the dictates of the conscience; showing that *natural* advancement or evolution of men's minds toward that of a *one* God, *one* purpose, *one* ideal—with many *ideas* of expressing same, but *one* ideal!" (3976-9)

States this reading, within the major consecutive cultures of our history, man has evolved in his perception of what is the ideal. At the time of Cain, self rather than service was the norm. In the Egyptian period were the Israelites, "with their advancement to which the ones chosen were sent for instruction and servitude for their rebelliousness in that land of promise. And with their raising to that . . . ability, through the raising up of the leader to lead them out—(Moses)—came the lawgivers . . . to become that channel through which mercy, grace, should come to a tired, weary, war-ridden world, in peace to all mankind—through the Prince of Peace, of the house of David, of the stock of Judah, of the sons of Jacob, of the seed of Abraham—the father of the faithful!"

Cayce then recalls for us the Greek civilization in which the arts, including philosophy, expressed what was the highest in man's consciousness and is for us still treasured. For the Romans, leading the world by military and political power, the criterion was the law (3976-9).

Gorbachev, being a lawyer, has declared that his country will recognize not a rule of men, as in the past, but a rule of law. It must be clear to us, though, that even the law is not enough, that man's laws did not save Rome from eventual destruction. The highest rule will be, according to Cayce, not man's laws alone but the law of "*One* God, *one* purpose, *one* ideal!"

When Dr. Shmarov told his audiences that the United States and the Soviet Union should cooperate in trying to solve the Middle East conflict, he was reiterating Gorbachev's call for "cooperation, not conflict among all countries." "It's my conviction," wrote Gorbachev, "that the human race has entered a stage where we are all dependent upon each other. No country or nation should be regarded in total separation from another, let alone pitted against each other. . . . A great deal depends on the position of the United States and the West as a whole. . . ."[22] This is recognition that the world cannot be saved from nuclear destruction unless concern for our fellowman is shared by all. Perestroika, it seems, is a return to religious values, intended as such or not.

Various historians see Peter the Great and Ivan the Terrible differently. They are seen by some as precursors to Joseph Stalin. Others see them as positive figures: They were despots, but they were *enlightened* despots. Garrard describes the great reforms of Peter as "the origins of Russia's super-power status today."[23]

According to Nicholas v. Riasanovsky, the Mongolian occupation of Russia lasted from 1240 to 1480, when Ivan III (the Great) threw off Mongol control. During those 240 years, Russia was denied contact with the rest of Europe and therefore was without benefit of cultural and scientific ideas of the Renaissance. By the time of Peter (1682–1725), the Tatars and other Mongols were declining in their political power, being pushed back by such as the Christian nomads called Cossacks.[24]

Peter broke away from the Tatars, a branch of the Mongols who had controlled the great land by Oriental court rule. This was the type of rule practiced by Ivan the Great. He was first to use the title of "czar," borrowed from the Roman word "Caesar," retained along with the attendant autocratic rule that included the medieval feudal system of serfdom.[25]

Finally, Peter was able to send "a mission to Mongolia," beginning diplomatic relations with China.[26]

While in the sixteenth and seventeenth centuries, the rest of Europe and America were waking up to scientific understanding that brought the Industrial Revolution, Russia knew no such progress. States Garrard, missing were the treasures of the mind of classical antiquity: the literature, art, philosophy of the ancient world. "If the eighteenth century marks the beginning of the modern age, it does so for Russia no less than any other nation. The rise of modern Russia may be considered one of the most significant long term developments of the century."[27]

When we compare the consciousness of Russia's leaders of the past with that of recent leaders when Gorbachev and Yeltsin brought their reforms, we can conclude that the eighteenth century brought great growth in the consciousness of the Russian people, though it would be two centuries before they would throw off both czar and communist despot. As Cayce stated, few men can handle great political power and keep their perspective. Another example is Ivan the Terrible in the sixteenth century, grandson of Ivan the Great who finally took back Russia from the Mongols. Some historians, says Nove, see them as positive figures because of their humanitarian reforms.[28] The Russians finally saw Stalin with no redeeming qualities.[29]

Ivan the Terrible began his reign as a reformer, evidently a "good" czar happily married to Anastasia, whose loving influence on him and his kingdom has been recorded by historians. During his early reign, in 1551, a great church council took place in which Ivan (then not so terrible), in harmony with Higher Powers, presented his new legal code enabling participation in government by local churches in order to cut down former corruption and oppression of centrally appointed officials. But when Anastasia suddenly died and he suspected that she had been poisoned, his personality changed. He conducted a reign of terror, personally participating in horrible tortures and executions. His emotional unbalance led him to rages and more violence, in one instance, killing his own son and heir.[30]

His severe acts were taken particularly against a group called the boyars, the ruling class with large estates, who had usurped rule of Russia through the Chosen Council. It was this class that he tried to suppress. His paranoia led him to get rid of many former trusted allies. He set up what now would be called political police, dressed in black, riding black horses. Their purpose was to destroy those considered to be his enemies. This brought death and confiscation of property for many whom in his madness he thought were plotters against him. They might well have been treasonous.[31]

It was a different world by the time Peter took power, for Europe was enjoying new learning, philosophy, letters, music, and the production of material goods not before possible.

In his youth, Peter traveled in Europe, comparing the backwardness of Russia to the progress of the West. His zeal for reform was one of the great turning points in world history. His objective was to bring into Russia the benefits of Western learning and art lost during two hundred years of isolation because of the Mongolian invasions. He introduced Western dress and many reforms for Russia by encouraging scholars and teachers from Germany, France, England, and Holland to bring Russia into the Enlightenment.[32]

Peter did not attract the arts of the high Renaissance culture until late. He first brought in industrialists and merchants, technicians and craftsmen in various fields such as metallurgy, textiles, glass, and mining, to teach these skills to his people. However, he sought educators who would give Russia Western ideas as opposed to Oriental despotism. He found these among various philosophers such as Rousseau, who brought concern for human rights and means for freer development of man's potential. He favored the Protestant countries that brought also their rationalist, scholarly, and scientific philosophers.[33]

The Roman Catholic church had dominated Russians in the absence of the Renaissance. The Roman and Eastern churches had formally broken in the eleventh century. Peter the Great mistrusted the Roman Catholic church, opting for the influence of a Protestant bishop to redesign Russia's religious life.[34]

In the mid-eighteenth century the ideas of John Locke were adopted, with his emphasis on the total education of the young child. Education developed, too, from the ideas of Rousseau and his belief in the "natural man." It was "knowledge with a concern for the spiritual and moral development of the child, to create a new type of Russian, 'the true son of the fatherland, dedicated to the good in the moral, spiritual, political, and social sense.' "[35]

Peter also recognized the superiority of Jesuits in classical studies. Therefore, the Petrine schools "were founded on the European-wide Jesuit notion of education," which included both secular and religious subjects, and Jesuit schools were the most famous and successful. Scores were founded from 1580 to 1650. One of these was the Jesuit-run Kiev Academy which accepted Russian children from all ranks, and other countries who were 'defenders of the holy Greco-Russian faith.' "[36]

Peter's anti–Roman Catholic bishop, Feofan Prokopovich, had reverted to Orthodoxy. The bishop and Peter were of one mind, for Prokopovich was in essence a Protestant who wanted to reform the church. He declared in his *Ecclesiastical Regulations* that seminarists and the church fathers should study "the ancient and modern philosophers, astronomers, rhetoricians, historians, etc." By his authority, he made Peter supreme under God over the ecclesiastical, military, and civil authorities. All power was concentrated in the hands of the monarch and his government, including the leaders of the church.[37]

States Cracraft: "It would be difficult to exaggerate the importance of the [bishop's] *Ecclesiastical Regulations* and related documents in the creation and maintenance of the characteristically absolute Russian state of modern times and in the consequent secularization of Russian society. They embodied the fundamental principles according to which the Church governed until 1918.''[38]

There were many different views regarding what Russia was to imitate among the various Western models, but as thoughtful Russians compared their own character with the West, some came to appreciate their own national culture. As one writer, Fonvizin, said, "the Western Europeans may have more material wealth, but the Russians are somehow spiritually superior."[39]

Hayward states that Peter the Great is thought of as the "Anti-Christ" by many. Consistent with this view, Nove says that others see him and Ivan the Terrible "as enslavers of the people," with Peter as "the creator of manufacturing establishments staffed by slave labor, producing to order by the state." After his rule, he left the dark legacy of serfdom that was still present in the time of Catherine II, who ruled from 1762 to 1796. When challenged by Diderot about Russian serfdom, she replied smoothly: "I know of no country where the worker loves his land and his home more than in Russia."[40]

In the eighteenth century, however, there were others, such as the Freemasons, who were disturbed by the condition of the serfs as opposed to humanitarian ideas fostered by the Enlightenment. Catherine, whose role model was Peter, regarded the Masons as "seditious."[41] Like Peter, she brought further reforms in education, especially in medicine so that Russia could provide health care for her people. She fostered Voltairianism, which for most Russians "became synonymous with mockery of the Church."[42] She and Peter were lauded for civilizing Russia but criticized for misuse of power.

Cayce spoke of the use and misuse of power in the hands of mortals. In 1927, he addressed the group wanting to know how to create a better world based on the "ideals of the ages." "Same was the idea of Alexander when he sought to conquer the world," he replied, "yet the tenets of the ideal were forgotten in the desires of the flesh, and while the principles as set forth in the mind and heart of the man as the student under Plato and Archimedes, and Aurelius and others, the *man* became gored by the greed of power as to become the loathsome body. . . .

"Again we find the dream of such power in the mind and the hands of one" still living at the time of the reading and identified as Kaiser Wilhelm of Germany who ruled from 1888 to 1918 (3976-4). He believed as the kaiser before him in the divine right of kings. When Germany lost the war, Kaiser Wilhelm resigned. Regarding Hitler six years later, Cayce stated that "few does power not destroy, as men" (3976-13).

Another Alexander—Alexander II, emperor of Russia—was an enlightened ruler who saw the inefficiency of the government he had inherited. He was determined to free the serfs who made up a large part of the population. In 1861, among other major reforms, he emancipated them from their oppressive landlords. However, their freedom spurred them to revolution, which the czars of the past would have put down by force. The revolutionary actions by peasants and students were opposed by the educated, thinking people, who nevertheless criticized the government's weakness and ineptitude.[43]

Although now free, the peasants were worse off than before. They were kept under special laws and separate courts and penalties such as capital punishment, all of which added up to apartheid. And Alexander was repaid for his enlightened reforms by being assassinated.[44]

The last czar was Nicholas II, who presided over the first International Peace Conference at The Hague, attended by representatives from twenty-six states. The International Court of Justice was set up, which was to lead to subsequent peace efforts culminating in those of present decades. Such issues as disarmament, however, would have to wait until the 1990s. The Russo-Japanese War of 1904–05 ended in defeat for Russia and was followed by the Revolution of 1905. Many social and economic changes led to the assassination of Czar Nicholas in 1917.[45]

At the time of Kievan Russia (eleventh century), peasants

were free, but later, bondage became more common. Dependence on their landlords began when they made contracts for loans of money, grain, or farm tools. They paid back the loans with dues—quitrent—and performed work. The arrangement usually lasted for the serf's lifetime, as he could never quite catch up.[46]

By the seventeenth century, the system under the czars was based on the importance of the landlord gentry, the military service that protected the state.[47]

In the eighteenth century, large state lands were given to the gentry by Empresses Anna and Elizabeth. The peasants who were living on those estates thus became serfs. When the gentry was freed from compulsory service in 1762, the serfs demanded their own freedom. Anna had forbidden their right to buy land or establish factories. Before that, they had been forbidden to join the military to escape their condition. Under such controls the serfs sometimes ran to Siberia where no such laws existed. As in American slaveholding, landlords could transfer their serfs (legally termed property after 1754) to other estates. Peasant uprisings had been frequent in the past. After an especially dangerous one, Catherine made reforms that included recognition of the gentry on a permanent basis rather than on twenty-year terms. More than a million peasants were under a stronger legal form of serfdom, with greatly restricted freedoms.[48]

Cayce's concern was, as we have seen, with "those who would rule"; "freedom denied" those who lived under that rule. Neither under the czars nor their supplanters, the Marxists, would there be change for the Russian people.

States Graf, there were two factions to the "Russian Social Democratic Party" or Social Democrats: the Bolsheviks and the Mensheviks. Both were Marxist, but "most historians, I think, would argue that the Mensheviks were much closer to Marx's tradition than was Lenin. His was the more radical faction and it placed much emphasis on conspiratorial party organization and the role of the party as an elite 'vanguard' of the industrial working class—the proletariat. Lenin broke with the Social Democrats in 1903. I believe that Lenin's dogmatism and insistence on a tightly knit party led from the top fits the Cayce comment about 'those seeking to subjugate others to the will.'

"Under the New Economic Policy, Lenin's relaxation of economic controls began in 1921 and continued," says Graf, "until 1927–28, when it was supplanted by Stalin's forced collectivization and the 5-year plans. During the 1940s the Stalin regime relaxed controls over culture, literature, religion, etc. in order to appeal for popular support for the war effort."[49]

Historical accounts about Stalin continue to baffle our comprehension. He was in his youth raised in a church school and was enrolled later in the Orthodox Russian seminary to be trained as a priest. He became instead a revolutionist under communism, paid to incite the people against the tsar. He was exiled to Siberia many times, but always managed to escape. He changed his name to "Stalin" which means "steel." He wanted to be known, evidently, as "a man of steel." He joined the Bolshevists in 1903 and his ability to organize people and events brought him to the aid of Lenin, whose violence was matched later by Stalin's despotism.

Stalin, Nove declares, saw in Ivan the Terrible and Peter the Great his most relevant predecessors. As in most autocratic rule, fear was an essential part of both these systems and that of Stalin. Nove says that a Stalin critic, M. Gefter, thought Stalin was successful because he made himself needed in the Bolshevic agenda and deliberately strengthened his position by strategies assuring he would be needed by his heavy use of class warfare.

Why didn't the other Russian leaders at the time protest what they saw happening under Stalin? Nove says that when they met in 1934 for the 17th Party Congress, the potential opponents seemed unable to protest the millions of victims. Their uncertainties and confusion, and even their party unity, kept them from acting until it was too late to stop him.

Russia herself was invaded by the dictator from the West: Hitler. In 1932, Edgar Cayce foresaw changes that "would make different *maps* of the world." He was seeing what he called "the great catastrophe" that was coming in 1936 "in the form of the breaking up of many powers . . . The first notable change will be the acceptance or rejection of the world's interference, or court of last resort (The World Court of the League of Nations) as presented by France, and as rejected by America" in 1919 (3976-10).

France had formed the Little Entente—Czechoslovakia, Romania, and Yugoslavia—all of which wished to honor the Paris peace settlement after World War I. As Poland, they all feared Germany.

As Cayce forecast, 1936 was the beginning of the "breaking up" of Europe into two opposing factions. Fascist dictators Adolph Hitler and Benito Mussolini formed the Rome-Berlin Axis to retain power against the democratic victors of the war but also to fight communism. Hitler withdrew from the League of Nations and began his conquests of Austria and Czechoslovakia. At Munich in 1938, he threatened England and France with war. On September 1, 1939, he invaded Poland. In 1940 he invaded Denmark, Norway, Belgium, the Netherlands, and Luxembourg. He fought and occupied France. The Axis helped Spanish rebels to win the civil war against the loyalists. Thus, Europe was divided between the Axis nations and the democracies. World War II broke out, and Russia joined the Allies.

All this is to give some insight into historical culture trends that brewed fascism, revolution, Marxist influence toward communism, and the tragic results for millions of people. These pages are intended to present some major highlights that are necessary, however inadequate, to give some background for Cayce's views about what happened yesterday and today. Having had no democratic rule in the past, under the czars or since, the Russians and their satellite neighbors are having to adjust to the new political freedom. We saw for ourselves on television a Russian woman at the polls for the first time in her life, complaining that she didn't know whom to vote for! It was difficult for her to be given suddenly the responsibility of helping choose who will lead. This, we happily admit, is one of the downsides of democracy, but one that is highly favored over the alternatives. There was, says Nove, a lack of law and legality in Stalin's time. Gorbachev's decision to make the Soviet Union a nation of law rather than men, or the "personality cult" of the past, is understandable in the light of past misrule. He sent a group of young Russian lawyers, men and women, to the United States to learn from us how to make democracy work.

With freedom now for many, there is evidence of an epic shift in a few moments of "that natural evolution" we are privileged to witness within our own time.

5

"BORN AGAIN!"

That peoples (Russia) are going through the experience of being born *again . . ." (3976-8, January 15, 1932)*

RUSSIA'S RELIGIOUS HERITAGE

FOR CHRISTIANS AND JEWS, Buddhists, Hindus and Muslims, there is the higher law that guides and encourages us toward the light of freedom and God-consciousness. Conversely, that which has dominated Russian life for centuries has been the archetype of despotism from one leader to the next.

Repressed as it has been, Christianity was accepted by Kievan Russia from the Byzantines and has been the saving influence since that time. In a chapter by the chairman of the European Conference of Churches, Metropolitan Alexy, manager of Tallin and Estonian dioceses, states:

Of late we seem to be witnessing several discoveries of considerable significance for our life. A substantial part of our society has discovered that the idea of the Church being a harmful, doomed remnant in the backward consciousness of some of our citizens, an attitude predominant in the official ideology for many years, was an ignoble attempt to deprive the people of their historic legacy. Besides, it became clear that atheism at any price was not necessary, and moreover, it was harmful, because applying the principle was inevitably connected with violation of both the historic past of our country and the freedom of conscience of millions of our compatriots. I believe that our society has realized that all of us, both believers and materialists, are heirs to our great spiritual tradition; and it was that very tradition which introduced the truth of goodness, charity, and love into our life—the truth, which, if buried in oblivion, makes people pay dearly.[1]

He states that in 1988, the Russian Orthodox church celebrated the millennium of the "Baptism of Rus." It is recalled as a treasured religious event that changed the country from paganism to Christianity a thousand years ago. In 988 or 989, Prince Vladimir of pagan Russia wished the hand of the Byzantine emperor's sister, Anna, in return for having saved their country from Arabian invasion. Since Vladimir was a barbarian, the emperor insisted that he be baptized. He was, and was married to Anna. It was the fact of his baptism that is celebrated for its significance as a symbol of the baptism, not only of Vladimir of Kievans, but "the day Kievan Rus turned into Christian Rus."[2]

Kiev is known by historians to have been the first Russian state that flourished, until about the twelfth century when it, too, was overrun by Mongols. The Rus were a group or tribe of disputed origins who had settled Kiev, a large area of western Russia. There had been Christian influences before Vladimir's conversion, and though paganism persisted even after that, Vladimir's own conversion brought Christianity back to provide important advantages such as that of the highly advanced Byzantine culture. Vladimir was remembered not only as a mighty and successful ruler but was canonized by the church as the baptizer of the Russians, "equal to the apostles."[3]

The church has everywhere and always been centered in man's service to his fellowman. A striking contrast is apparent in the ways of God's people and the ways of a godless society. The tradition of those who worship the One God relates enlightened mankind to eternal laws of which Cayce spoke. They have been around, tested, and found workable for millennia. They cannot be bettered by the temporal, man-flawed systems that experiment with millions of lives over long years only to be found worthless because they do not take into consideration the spiritual reality which, if buried, "makes people pay dearly." In the time of Vladimir, those peasants connected with the church were engaged in operating hospitals, dispensing charity, educating the parishioners. But since those centuries, the peasants have been enserfed, thralls to the feudal system of powerful landlords long before the time of Peter the Great and Catherine II, and after their emancipation under Alexander II. Even after 1917, they were not really free. But in the time of Vladimir and the time of the early church, they were free men.[4]

According to Nove, under communism, charitable works were banned as presumably a form of "religious propaganda." Due to restrictive laws during the 1930s, thousands of priests were arrested; churches were closed and destroyed. It was the time of the Terror under Stalin. But even Khrushchev held a negative view of religion, and under Brezhnev, priests who tried to evade the restrictions by more intense service to their parishioners were jailed.[5]

In 1988, when the "thousand years of Christianity" was observed, came the opportunity for the church to seek amendments to highly restrictive laws and to create a better relationship between the state and the Orthodox church. Because of glasnost, Orthodoxy has begun to revive its influence. A "roundtable on 1000 years of Christianity in Russia" was held in which seven priests and seven lay academics discussed rehabilitation of victims of the 1920s and 1930s and the role of religion in establishing morals in society.[6]

For many years, Baptists and others from the West have been welcomed by Russian Christians. American churches have long supported the Society for the Study of Religion in Communist Lands. Leaders of Anglican churches in England have fostered religious freedom throughout the world. An American Presbyterian told me that he traveled with a group of Baptists in the mid-1980s to Bulgaria and Romania, which then were still under the old regime. He visited churches there, which he said were either Baptist or Orthodox. Some of them, he said, were packed.

In 1988 the "all union Council of Evangelical Christian-Baptists became aware, says Nove, of the charitable work of Baptists abroad. The Russian group was told that Baptists came into a Moscow hospital and helped "look after the patients, to carry out any difficult work. They refused any reward."[7]

Ada B. Bozeman points out that there are two differing religious cultures in Russia: those Christianized by Rome and those Christianized by Constantinople. The latter group were untouched by the great movement of the Renaissance, while among the countries greatly influenced by Western thought and Roman Christianity were the Baltics, Poland, parts of Germany, Czechoslovakia, Hungary, and Yugoslavia, which wound up behind the Iron Curtain. They had participated in the Western legal, political, moral system for centuries and had learned "what civil liberties are." Thus they have been continuously revolting since 1948.[8]

"The Byzantine-[Constantinople]oriented were not aware of such notions promulgated by the United Nations as human rights, being patterned after the imperial Byzantine tradition." Our failure to progress smoothly toward the new world order in 1975 is due, states this author, to our lack of understanding the great differences in Soviet bloc cultures. States Bozeman, former President Gerald Ford told the Eastern delegation that "the principles on which the Conference [on Security and Cooperation in Europe] in 1975 had agreed are part of the great heritage of European civilization which we all hold in trust for all mankind." Bozeman says, though, that other cultures do not necessarily conform to the Western mold.[9]

Just the same, from the Cayce vantage, all religions do recognize the One God.

The Russian Orthodox church has proved to keep the light of freedom of conscience burning, although theologians and Orthodox leaders have been reduced in the past to finding favor by developing "communist Christianity." They made pronouncements "to show that they associate the Soviet system with the kingdom of God on earth."[10] This is surely a travesty of true Christian belief!

John Adams's statement that America was "designed by Providence for the theatre on which man was to make his true figure" is consistent with Cayce's declaration that America has led the world in freedom of speech, of service to God being the natural evolution of man's growth toward one Ideal. The founding fathers held a vision that has inspired the world toward the same goal of freedom and democracy.

As we see Russia evolving toward that Ideal, from a very recent bloody past, there seems to be some secret movement of providence going on in her people and those she has held captive, as providence guided America. Like the Israelites who for forty years lived in the wilderness of Sinai until they came into Canaan, Eastern Europeans have been led through their own wilderness for a significant forty years. They appear to be entering their own Canaan, although not without turmoil.

With the progress of days, we are seeing strong evidence of the validity of Cayce's prediction that "out of Russia would come the hope of the world." But we are too close to events that are unresolved to fully acknowledge that this is so.

GORBACHEV AND THE CHURCH

In his book *Perestroika*, Gorbachev spoke admiringly of Lenin: "The works of Lenin and his ideals of socialism remained after the Revolution for us an inexhaustible source of dialectical creative thought, theoretical wealth and political sagacity. His very image is an undying example of lofty moral strength, all around spiritual culture and selfless devotion to the cause of the people and to socialism. Lenin lives on in the minds and hearts of millions of people. . . ." He termed Lenin "an ideological source of perestroika." He added, "Perestroika is a revolutionary process for it is a jump forward in the development of socialism."[11]

However, not only has the image of Lenin died in the minds and hearts of millions of people, but in Moscow and

Bucharest his statues were ignominiously pulled down and hauled away. The same fate has happened to statues of Joseph Stalin, as in Mongolia, where for years his likeness stood in Ulan Bator, the capital. The communists failed to persuade the Mongolians to accept socialism in place of their nomadic life and their traditional belief in Lamaism, a form of Buddhism.

The word "spiritual", which Gorbachev used to describe socialist thinking, presents Westerners with interesting insight into the way an atheist society looks at itself. For such a society to speak of itself as spiritual is out of context with its profession that man does not need God.

Despite his pragmatism, Gorbachev was a product of his Christian heritage of a thousand years. As Max Hayward indicates, Russian Christianity was formerly a meld of the Church and the intelligentsia. "Both contended for the Russian soul." Speculative religious thought outside the Church in the late 19th and early 20th centuries led the Russians to seek "the ever elusive formula" of truth and justice as a total solution to all their problems.

The natural assumption is that the foment produced by the philosophy of Hegel, Fichte, and Marx led to what the Russians of the 20th century decided was the answer: communism.

As we have seen, from the historians' view Peter the Great and the czars before him were predecessors to Stalin. They were a part of the Russian psyche, as much as the philosophers; after all, Peter was the one who brought the philosophers into Russian classrooms in the first place! With his emphasis on Protestantism and introduction of the philosophers of Europe to Russia, he altered the direction religion would take after him, despite the ambiguous slant left by himself and Ivan the Terrible as "enslavers of the people." All that surely had its impact on 20th century Russians and how they sought answers.

State Dusko Doder and Louise Branson:

"For the Gorbachev family and for everyone else in the region, 1931 was a turbulent year ...

"Stalin's cruel retribution was staggering in its scope and

it affected the Gorbachevs directly. Millions of farmers who actively resisted being herded into the collective farms were shipped off to Stalin's notorious gulag of prison camps flung across Siberia. Among them was Mikhail's grandfather, Andrei . . .

"[Gorbachev] was secretly baptized."[12]

One would think that, having lived under such repression as a boy and under later despots who used the KGB to put down any protest, Gorbachev would have himself become radical. But if he had, he would probably not have lived to achieve power that would ultimately free Russia and the Church.

In 1988, state the authors:

". . . Gorbachev was looking for a new way to approach the question of political reforms. Searching for allies, he found the Russian Orthodox Church. From his experience in Privolnoe, he knew that Christianity remained remarkably tenacious, despite seven decades under the heel of an invariably hostile state. His own grandparents were religious; he said in a visit to Britain in 1984 that his grandparents had kept icons in their house, hidden behind portraits of Lenin and Stalin. . . . [13]

"In the spring of 1988, he seized the opportunity for a dramatic gesture of reconciliation with the church. He sent the signal with unexpected live national television coverage of midnight Easter services at the Yelokhovsky Cathedral in Moscow. The gesture could hardly have been more spectacular; Easter is the most important holiday for Russian Orthodoxy."[14]

Under perestroika and glasnost, ideas were sought to create a better world. The *ideals* of American people, rooted in a variety of ethnic cultures but predominantly Christian and Jewish Biblical tenets, did not fit Gorbachev's. But his restructuring pointed to a more enlightened leadership than the atheism he avowed.

In 1946, Stalin had ordered the Ukrainian Catholic Church absorbed into the Russian Orthodox Church. History was made when Gorbachev visited the Pope on December 1, 1989.

Fred Coleman observes: "The Polish Pope and the Catholic Church had been instrumental in fomenting the independence movement now tearing the Soviet Union apart." Religious repression was outlawed by the Soviet legislature on September 26, 1990, with the passage of a law forbidding the government from interfering with religious activities. At the same time, Gorbachev ordered withdrawal from Afghanistan, and he normalized his relations with China and the Vatican. These laudable achievements led to his agreement with President Bush at the Malta meeting to work toward East-West amity. Gorbachev had met in 1987 with the head of the Russian Orthodox Church. "Freedom of choice is a universal principle to which there should be no exception," Gorbachev had declared before the UN in 1988. "It provided the key."[15]

At the back of his book, Coleman presents his ideas on the question posed by Lenin in his best known political tract: "What Is To Be Done?" He offers this:

Keep the Faith

The American motto 'In God we Trust' can help manage a future Russian threat. On this issue it is wrong to separate church and state. America's interest is to combine them. Religion was a major force behind the nationalist rebellions—from Catholics in the Baltics to Muslims in Central Asia—that helped break up the Soviet Union. Should dictatorship return to Russia, religious faith will again be a major source of opposition among Russian Orthodox, Catholic, Jewish, and Muslim believers alike. Western commitment to freedom of religion is a beacon of inspiration to them. . . . [16]

That faith is evident and strong. In Soviet Central Asia, where Muslims predominate, attendance at mosques has risen; copies of the Koran are in heavy demand. Atheism remains the doctrine of the Communist Party, but the law prohibits government funding for either religious activities or atheistic propaganda. It allows religious groups to set up societies and send people abroad for spiritual study. This victory for religious freedom, as well as for democracy, was recognized in October, 1990, as Gorbachev was awarded the Nobel Peace Prize.

The moral values Gorbachev has acknowledged as necessary in his restructuring of political, economic, and social conditions in Russia which he calls "democratic centralism" come closer to the ideal than has been hoped for. Judging by his reforms—free speech, free religion, peaceful congregation—it was the beginning of the possibility that all nations might meet on common ground that the free world had long shared.

Cayce's wise advice might have been given just yesterday: We are, after many years, still undergoing a reckoning that forces us, in fear of global annihilation, to begin to agree, to meet each other as brothers whom we must consider as we do ourselves. With the end of the cold war, the world did grow closer to acknowledging that we all are "our brother's keeper." But it's apparent to many that there is much change yet needed before that ideal is realized by both nations and individuals.

Fred Coleman, author of *The Decline and Fall of the Soviet Empire*, states that "1989 was a year of remarkable diplomatic triumphs" for Gorbachev, for he "settled his Afghan, Chinese, and German problems and established a good working relationship with the new president of the United States." All those accomplishments won him the Nobel Peace Prize for 1990.[17] His New Thinking was leading the world away from the nuclear trap it had built, toward the next step: a climate in which peace could be possible. The Biblical prophecy of a time when swords would be replaced with plowshares seemed to be coming about. Like Roosevelt and Wilson, Gorbachev to all appearances was "raised for a purpose" to work with others toward peace and a stable and secure world. As Cayce predicted, "out of Russia comes the hope of the world." Gorbachev appeared, too, the very embodiment of that hope, despite the fact he would not yield to the growing demand for independence by the Soviet Empire's fifteen captive republics.

The test came on March 11, 1990, when Lithuania declared its independence. To Gorbachev's dismay, the Lithuanian Communist Party in December, 1989, was the first to break with Moscow and declare itself an occupied independent state.[18]

In April, the Kremlin began its crackdown on Lithuania, imposing an economic embargo. The Lithuanians could no longer purchase such commodities as oil, coal, gasoline, and timber.

In the United States, Washington was taking a second look at its heretofore support of Gorbachev.

Serious deprivation to Lithuania of the necessary supplies was taking its toll. President Bush threatened to place sanctions against Moscow to show United States disapproval. However, he decided against it because such action could undermine President Gorbachev and worsen the Baltic crisis.[19]

Pope John Paul II sent Lithuania a message of hope. President Bush expressed his dismay. Until his crackdown began, Gorbachev's popularity in the United States had been growing. Douglas Hurd, Britain's foreign secretary, visited the Kremlin to talk about a solution. Lithuania was a small nation whose freedom was at stake. The stake included friendship between the two great superpowers and all it meant to the rest of the republics. But the West was not able to do much but cheer the Lithuanians on.

Fortunately, states Fred Coleman, Lithuania had the ability to withstand the economic blockade and could afford to be more independent than the other republics. "It was one of the few Soviet republics with surplus meat and dairy products. Not only could the republic feed itself, but the Lithuanians survived the blockade by bartering excess food for essential supplies from other areas of the U.S.S.R. that were desperately short of food."[20]

Gorbachev backed down, agreeing not to have Lithuania's declaration of independence repealed. The larger problem was the breakdown of the economy and rising demands for independence among the fourteen other republics. In May, food prices doubled. He tried to calm their fears. However, the economy was weakened drastically not only by inflation but also by corruption involving theft, speculation, and the black market.

By June, Lithuania's economic embargo was eased. Latvia and Estonia joined in grassroots opposition. The laws of the Ukraine soon would be recognized over those of Russia.

Due to the many problems, Gorbachev was bitterly chastised from all directions. Critics charged that perestroika was to blame, that his reforms were the cause for the Soviet Union's chaos. But he denied that. He pointed out his many democratic reforms. He met in compromise with Lithuania in which the Kremlin would end its economic blockade. By October, the Kremlin allowed shipments of fuel, raw materials, and consumer goods and promised to open talks on independence. Russia announced that Estonia's laws would henceforth be recognized over national ones.[21]

In early winter 1990, the Soviet economy was collapsing, with 80 percent inflation. Compounding ethnic unrest was chaos stemming from moves by the various republics to issue separate currencies. Wrote Marshall I. Goldman,

> It not only seems like a step backward, but that such a step means the Soviet Union as an economic entity has begun to disintegrate. . . . Not that the Soviet economy ever functioned perfectly, but in the process [of Gorbachev's program to change the economy], economic conditions have become much worse than they were. . . . Factories find it hard to obtain raw materials, which affects production. Lack of goods helps to promote strikes, which lead to demands for wage increases, which cause inflation as well as further disruption of production and shipments.
>   All this helps to explain why so many shops have been emptied of almost everything that will not spoil.[22]

Shevardnadze had warned that hard-line lawmakers were driving Gorbachev to dictatorship. On December 20, 1990, to make his point, he resigned. But Gorbachev said he would not so misuse his presidential powers of emergency. How-

ever, by 1991, growing economic pressures and demand for
autonomy by many republics, except for Romania, led to
harsh measures. He was driven to impose order by using the
KGB and military forces.

(A few months later I met a woman who had traveled to
Poland and Hungary in September 1990. She showed me a
Polish 50-zloty note bearing the likeness of a communist official, the eyes of which had been neatly punctured out. The
very worn little document, faded and tattered, seemed to sym-
bolize at once the fragility of most Eastern Europe economies—bitter defiance against the old regime and against new
dictatorship.)

Meanwhile, noncommunists kept winning elections. Ethnic
unrest continued.

According to Soviet authorities, it was at the request of the
pro-Kremlin National Salvation Committee that the Soviets
attacked the Lithuanian broadcast station January 13, 1991,
killing fourteen people. The Soviet government told the Lithuanian president that, due to the Lithuanian government's
failure to guarantee order, the Kremlin troops were growing
out of control.[23]

When Soviet tanks and troops moved in to close the news
media in Vilnius, the shock we felt suddenly broke the spell
of perestroika. It was a chilling turn to the past: Gorbachev,
staunch friend and partner in the new world order, ostensibly
based on nothing but good for us all, allowing the old world
order mentality to take over in the form of military force and
the KGB. He was sorely tried, it is true, by the impending
chaos he feared for the Soviet Union, which was threatened
with anarchy and ethnic bloodbaths if the republics fell apart.
He was fighting to hold the country of 285 million people
together to save central authority.

By January 1990, East Germany, Czechoslovakia, Bulgaria,
and Romania had all turned against communism.[24]

Fred Coleman was in the Soviet Union as a correspondent for
American news magazines for thirty years beginning in the
Stalin era. He witnessed the decline and fall of the empire
firsthand. He states: ''Though Lithuania proved to be the

spark, the Ukraine would play the crucial role in the eventual breakup of the USSR. The Ukraine was the largest Soviet Republic except for Russia, a territory the size of France with a population of 50 million people. It was also the Soviet Union's most important agricultural and industrial producer after Russia, accounting for a quarter of the USSR's food supply and nearly a third of its industrial output. As such, the Ukraine was absolutely indispensible to the Soviet economy.''[25]

Among the Baltic states, as well as Georgia and Armenia, men in the military were deserting, and civilians were dodging the draft. Soviet soldiers cracked down in such trouble spots to counteract growing defiance.

To save the federation, Gorbachev was given more power by the Soviet Parliament. Discontent had grown due to his failure to move forward the economy fast enough. Reflecting the concern of many nations, as the winter of 1990 deepened, Germany, Israel, Italy, and Sweden poured great offerings of food into Russia and the republics, while the United States sent medical supplies. An aid package was drafted by the European Community providing $2 billion in food and transportation over two years. At the same time, Gorbachev made deals involving loans and export credits to buy basic food and consumer products to fill empty store shelves.[26] But throughout the 1990s, there continued bread lines, hoarding, black market economy, and misdirection of gifts of food from abroad meant for the general population.[35]

In February, the National Salvation Committee advocated a return to dictatorship, to suspend Parliament, the presidency, political parties, and the press to ensure absolute power for its program to preserve the Soviet Union. What could we make of Gorbachev's crackdown on the Baltic states? Could he have called off the tanks and riflemen from attacking the freedom seekers of Vilnius and Riga? Had he changed to become a dictator with his newly gained powers? There were those hard-liners urging the Kremlin to use force. Observers suggested that perhaps he was no longer in control even before those outrages. Calls for his resignation came from the people of the Soviet Union, with opinion from other quarters that his Nobel Peace Prize be rescinded. Masses of people in Moscow, Riga, and Vilnius again thronged the streets demanding independence.

Even as Gorbachev denied he wanted to be a dictator, amid growing reports of widespread demand for independence by separation, he found it difficult to hold the Soviet Union together. Since the 1980s there had been uprisings among the various nations, large and small, including Georgia, Yugoslavia, and even the Muslim population of central Asia. Gorbachev tried to tell everybody that the Soviet Union was happy and friendly, when in reality many of those captive nations not only rankled against the Russian regime but also fought among themselves. Even as he tried to reform the old ideology, he was forced by events to make concessions. However, at this point, his new support of a hard-line attitude toward breakaway republics caused his critics to think he was returning to the old autocratic mind-set of past Russian leaders. It is true that he continued to admire Lenin as the inspiration of perestroika and glasnost. A product of communism, he looked at his previous achievements as a new *phase* of the communist experiment, not so much as a break from it.

Responding to Gorbachev's change to a harder line, Boris Yeltsin, Russia's first elected president, went on television on February 19, 1991, to ask Gorbachev to resign. The Kremlin then attacked Yeltsin in return with fury.

In February came still another test: This time, the military forces were supporting the government in trying to get the people behind a huge rally intended to save the Soviet Union. Was the Russian military about to stage a coup? Army cadets were ordered to help the demonstration by keeping the crowds in line, which would mean shooting their own countrymen if necessary. They refused to report for duty.

Meanwhile, from Albania came reports of arrests and deaths in clashes between anticommunist demonstrators and supporters of Stalinist Albania. In Yugoslavia, there was turmoil between those who desired secession and those who opposed it. Separatists in Georgia brought out troops against the nationalists. War broke out between the Yugoslav army tanks and helicopters clashing with Russian forces. Armenia and Azerbaijan, long at odds over territorial disputes, fought in the streets.

All the republics desired independence. To those dissenting, Gorbachev presented a treaty offering self-governing autonomy in how they managed their territories and their power system. The new name would be "the Union of Sovereign Soviet Republics." It was a liberal, and on the surface a reasonable break from the former system. It guaranteed self-determination for all of them except in defense. But of the fifteen republics, at least six refused to sign: Armenia, Georgia, Moldavia, Estonia, Latvia, and Lithuania.[27]

In April 1991, Soviet soldiers continued their harassment of the Baltic countries. They occupied buildings such as the Communist party headquarters in Lithuania. They forced their way into the printing plant in Vilnius and beat some of the several dozen armed civilians who had been on guard.[28]

HALTING STEPS TOWARD A FREE ECONOMY

Gorbachev announced his radical restructuring plan of the economy in October 1990. He had renounced Marxism and Leninism and now espoused democratic practice patterned after that of free nations.

But he was at the same time indecisive as to putting it into practice. States Marshall I. Goldman, throughout the centuries of serfdom, and later communist rule, the Russian people had little experience with private ownership, either of property or business. "Gorbachev's move toward a free market and private ownership was hedged about with vagueness: uncertainty over its slow timing, opportunities for bureacratic meddling, options for acceptance or rejection at the regional level."[29]

In addition, "Much of this indecision stems from Gorbachev's reluctance to abandon the way of life associated with communism. . . . In particular, he has frequently expressed his determination to spare the Soviet people inflation and income inequality. To the extent he sees such undesirable prospects as features of capitalism, he will have to decide whether they are outweiged by the advantages capitalism brings.''[30]

President Bush showed support for Gorbachev's intention to reform the economy, but he refused to recognize his accountability while he aided third world countries such as Cuba. While the rest of the world admired and respected Gorbachev, massive unrest by hundreds of thousands once more in the streets at home signified his loss of all popular support from his own people. Calls were made for his resignation.

BORIS YELTSIN TAKES CHARGE

In September 1990, Boris Yeltsin, president of the Russian Republic, long supporting democratic reform, had led the Russian legislature's Presidium in blocking Gorbachev's request for more power. Concerned by the failing economy and its effect on political stability of the empire, they wanted new tactics. The people were in favor of a free-market economy.

In March 1991, hundreds of thousands in the streets protested Gorbachev's apparent turn toward dictatorship, demanding his resignation. Between Yeltsin and Gorbachev there had been animosity they seldom could contain. Yeltsin added his call for Gorbachev to resign, to be replaced by the Federation Council, made up of presidents of the fifteen republics. Under Yeltsin's plan the republics would still be a union but with power to override Moscow.[31]

More rallies were held throughout Russia. A national referendum was to be held March 17 to vote whether or not to preserve the Soviet Union. But six republics refused to hold it. Meanwhile, anticommunist Serbians in Yugoslavia wanted new elections to replace communism with freedom and democracy. Serbia wouldn't back its hard-line communist president to demand a nationwide state of emergency, which could bring a military crackdown.

Soon after that, Boris Yeltsin demanded an end to the Kremlin's use of the army for political purposes. His call for harmony, that the republics agree despite their differences, was perhaps the reason he had received high approval from voters. He had been denied, however, more authority.

Yeltsin introduced an economic plan for his Russian Federation that included luring foreign money with more rubles to the dollar. He also offered land and factories to be sold to private concerns. It was what Gorbachev's "500 day" plan had tried to do to begin a market economy, but it was obstructed by those who opposed capitalist methods. Yeltsin proposed a coalition government for the country.[32]

To keep the union, Gorbachev changed the name of the empire to the Union of Soviet Sovereign Republics, dropping the word "socialist" but retaining its essential intent. On June 6 he asked for financial aid from Western democracies as he made his speech of acceptance for the Nobel Peace Prize in Oslo. But Secretary of State James Baker made it clear he thought the Soviets must try harder to be more self-sufficient.

Reformer Russian President Boris N. Yeltsin won the election against Gorbachev on June 12, 1991, as the first president of the newly formed Russian republic's Congress by only four votes. His democratic changes were thought to be radical, but he asked cooperation in forming a new political party based on the "Democratic Russia" movement.[33]

A Moscow summit in August 1991 took place to deal with START agreements and economic issues. In the treaty, both the United States and the Soviets cut long-range nuclear missiles—about 15 percent of the American arsenal and 25 percent of the Soviet. They limited the modernization of intercontinental missiles and kept verification procedures.[34]

In the past year, President Bush had approved for the Russians a $1.5 billion farm export credit and had not imposed trade restrictions on them. Although Gorbachev hoped for still more aid, one of Bush's chief aides noted that the Soviets were "in a period of instability. We're prepared to assist dramatic change but without being foolish in the process."[35] Since 1983, it had been Gorbachev's main goal to reform the economy. But for him, and for most people of the empire, since capitalism had been anathema, economics still remained obscure and enigmatic.

Gorbachev's critics said he was more interested in preserving his own power than saving the empire. But because Bush admired him, in spite of the critics, by July 1991 he wanted to teach him capitalism.[36] He made another proposal that portended great benefit to both countries: establishment of joint ventures between the two countries, such as developing Russia's energy resources. Bush asked the Russian president to recommend test projects for oil and gas development with American companies. The Russians would receive US-backed loan guarantees.[37]

Sure enough, six years later, that proposal of George Bush became reality. The first filling station to sell gasoline from Russian oil opened for business July 28, 1997, in Altavista, Virginia, where AO Lukoil Holding, Russia's oldest oil company, said ninety-nine more stations were planned for the United States this year, with two thousand planned for the future. Lukoil is contracted to build and operate gas stations through Nexus Fuels, a Texas-based gasoline retailer. The stations will be built and operated at Food Lion stores, Shaw's Supermarkets, Richfood Holdings, Inc., and Supervalu, Inc.[38]

Cayce previewed that very scenario: ". . . there will come an entire change in the attitude of both nations as powers in the financial and the economic world. As for those of raw resources, Russia surpasses all other nations. As for abilities for development of same, those in the United States are the farthest ahead. Then these *united,* or upon an equitable basis, would become—or could become—powers . . ." (3976-10). This reading added that "it will take years to settle." (See Chapter Three: "Freedom! Freedom!")

We note he did not say "the Soviet Union." He said "Russia." Does this happy new capitalist venture of a nation of retired communists fit the ominous "world order" of the invisible government? It's doubtful, based on what the Russian people's experience with communism has been. We're told they look at their seventy years under it with loathing. All people in the empire have had relatives, or known of neighbors, who were taken away by the KGB and never seen again. It was typical of dictators since Stalin who killed millions of bright, good people who happened to stand in his way. It was an ordeal the Russians and their former captive nations are not likely to repeat or recommend to the rest of us. Reports reach us that the young are quite cynical as they contemplate entry into the millennium. Their only "security" was a sparse living wage in return for blind compliance with the most despotic rule in history. Now, many are finding their spiritual roots, which are considerable. Hopefully, democratic politicians of the new commonwealth, and those independent states once captive, will encourage their participation.

THE COUP

Suddenly, on August 18, 1991, the Soviet hard-liners who were angry about Gorbachev's failure to improve the economy, his arms control concessions, and the unruly republics, brought about the coup that ousted their president. Gorbachev and his family, vacationing in the Crimea, were held under house arrest. Heading the coup was Vice President Gennady Yanayev, whom Gorbachev had trusted along with the other coup members.

But the coup was short-lived. It had no constitutional legitimacy, having been carried out without the knowledge even of the Communist party. A state of emergency was declared; there was dissension among the coup committee. Resistance among the republics grew. The Estonian republic declared its full independence, and great demonstrations took place in Petersburg and Kishinev, capital of Moldavia.[39] It was clear that the plotters had underestimated the will of the people for their liberation.

Now Boris Yeltsin appealed to the Russians to defend the Parliament building and prevent the junta "from reintroducing a concentration camp regime."

"They understand," he told the people, "that things have reached the point that if they lose, they will lose not only their armchairs, but they will be seated on court benches." He warned the junta would stop at nothing to keep power.[40]

Armored vehicles that had been ordered by the coup leaders were surrounded by demonstrators, as violence brought three deaths among the volunteers. Yeltsin himself was seen standing on top of a tank outside his headquarters, denouncing the overthrow in the harshest terms. He then demanded of the plotters that he meet Gorbachev. He called for work stoppages throughout the nation, but there was little response.

Yeltsin's popularity among the Russians was evident, however, as they rallied to his side as he made his stand.[41]

*   *   *

"Soviet people power put President Mikhail S. Gorbachev back in charge of the Soviet Union on Wednesday, ending a coup that made the world tremble for three days."[42]

That people power was strengthened by the very Russian army troops that defected to the side of Boris Yeltsin, the thousands of troops that would probably disobey orders to fire on their own countrymen.[43] It was a historic moment that attests to the sovereignty of the human spirit despite centuries of oppressive rule. It was perhaps a very crucial moment in the winning of freedom for all of Russia and Eastern Europe, not to mention other communist nations. Triggered by the coup, bringing about opportunity for the masses to confront tanks and tyranny successfully, came the moment of truth. And the leadership to give it voice was in place: Gorbachev, greatly shaken, being forced to admit communism's failure; Yeltsin, the courageous defier ready to take the helm. The day it was over, August 22, was heralded in triumph. It marked the end of long decades in which the United States must consider nuclear threat from communist Soviet Union, its thrust around the world a constant "thorn in the side" as Cayce termed it, to all nations.

President Bush announced the same day that United States would again send food shipments at least the following winter. More such humanitarian aid would depend on Russia's economic reforms.

All needed reform would prove to take both men to provide Gorbachev's statesmanship, Yeltsin's popularity, and economists who offered their advice. Soviet President Gorbachev let it be known he was willing to work with the new Russian leader. It was a time of unity between them, although they had become enemies by misunderstandings and mistakes on the part of both. Just after Gorbachev returned to the public eye after his harrowing experience under house arrest, as television viewers watched, Yeltsin behaved toward him with something like malice.

But following Gorbachev's personally painful disavowal of

communism, there were ovations in the streets from great crowds shouting, "Gorby! Gorby!"

Fears were expressed by some that another coup by hard-liners could occur in the future. But other experts thought that again much depended on Gorbachev and Yeltsin as to their positions in relation to the democratic process and to each other. Though Gorbachev had not faced the test of running for elective office, he remained strong. How they handled the economic crisis in the 1991–1992 year would determine whether or not there would be chaos and a return to dictatorship.

Edgar Cayce used the words "Freedom! Freedom!" in foretelling the movement in Russia to defeat communism. In August 1991, another great demonstration of thousands outside the Russian Parliament chanted the Russian word for "freedom" again and again. Strange coincidence or psychic perception?

Some people thought the revolution was not over but just beginning. There was much left ahead that had only been thought about in overhauling the complex Kremlin machine—in reform, in dealing with breakaway republics, in the economy abandoning collectivization.

Besides, many see decay of moral values, corruption, and ignorance of business ethics. Some said that large business concerns rule the government. President Havel has been outspoken about the decline in principles. In Czechoslovakia, as well as in the Soviet Union, there is reported much the same thing. He has shown before that he is well aware of the tremendous importance of maintaining and living the moral values that brought the former Russian empire to freedom. But they have had to deal with the communist holdouts against economic reform. As in Russia, there is high inflation and crime, even after reforms of the economy under communist rule. But by 1992 Czechoslovaks were enjoying material prosperity, although inflation continued. Christ stated: "And ye shall know the truth, and the truth shall make you free" (John 8:32). The values Havel holds include the very notion of freedom itself but not that it be used to fleece one's fellowman!

In line with Cayce's view, on May 3, 1991, Pope John Paul II took to task financial powers that exploit the poor for higher profits. He "hailed Marxism's demise in Europe but warned about unbridled capitalism." It was "an essential part of the Christian message." He said "vast multitudes are still living in conditions of great material and moral poverty."[44]

In that regard, the law is, as Cayce states, that conditions are created first in the heart and mind. We anticipate his prediction fulfilled: that Russia and all Eastern Europe, for that matter, will overcome their past through rebirth under God. It will be possible by distribution of Bibles we hear has been made in the former empire. In such countries as Lithuania, because of religious repression, because there were not many Bibles, the young people have never heard of the Hebrew prophets and kings, the rich religious history of the Old Testament four thousand years ago in the lands to the south of Russia. They would be able to relate to the Exodus under Moses as the Hebrews left Egyptian bondage, having been in bondage themselves to past "pharaohs" under nearly a century of repression when God was exiled, along with the best of the Russians.

As the Hebrews under Moses, the Russians and their satellite nations are hopefully undergoing spiritual rebirth, retrieving their own great heritage of Christianity. The Spirit appears to be moving among them. As Cayce foretold, through their suffering, the Russians and the people they once held in bondage are being *born* again, reborn as nations, however traumatic the process. To bring them a message of hope during their trials, many evangelists have gone to Russia to offer the Catholic and Protestant religions, as well as those of Eastern origin. However, President Yeltsin banned any but the Russian Orthodox church. It has, after all, a history of more than a millennium.

The new revolution meant Gorbachev could no longer hope that the empire might prevail; but there were signs that the phoenix would rise from the ashes, on wings of democracy. It did, in the form of a proclamation of the death of the Soviet Union and the birth of a commonwealth—President Boris Yeltsin's new Commonwealth of Independent States.

The agreement of December 21, 1991, recognizing each republic's present borders, was signed by eleven former Soviet republics and Russia. Russia, the Ukraine, and Byelorussia sought to unite all twelve republics with a stable military, economic, and political relationship.[45]

Coleman points out that Gorbachev "managed to accomplish the seemingly impossible task of dismantling the unworkable Soviet system, not the way he intended, but effectively nonetheless." He declares that the problems Gorbachev faced and the responsibilities he shouldered were "colossal."[46]

"Mikhail Sergeyevich resigned on Christmas Day, December 25, 1991. Thirty-three minutes later, the red Soviet flag with the Communist hammer and sickle came down from the Kremlin walls. In its place flew the red-white-and-blue flag of reborn Russia. All that remained from the Communist era that had shaken the world for most of the century was the Lenin Mausoleum on Moscow's Red Square. Fittingly, the most enduring symbol of Soviet communism was a tomb."[47]

Boris Yeltsin, as the new elected head of state in Russia, now found his role an uneasy one. By mid-January 1991, there were street protests over food shortages, absenteeism in the factories, old ethnic animosities—all dangerous symptoms of massive anger among the people. Morale in the military was low due to poor housing conditions. Many deserted or sold off weapons and equipment.[48]

Yeltsin thought freeing prices would result in a better economy eventually. Inflation was 450 percent due to price hikes. He set up a privatization program for small businesses. And Western aid had begun to arrive. Opponents of Yeltsin warned, however, his economic reforms could produce hyperinflation and a return to totalitarianism.[49]

He tried to assure the people that economic hardship would be over by the end of the year. But of course hardship would continue in the former empire throughout the following years, as transition to an economy based on free-market reform was slow.

President Bush had warned that the danger of nuclear proliferation remains. At the same time, the Pentagon told a Senate panel that though threats to American security were remote, the cuts in military spending cannot safely exceed those Bush had proposed.[50]

In its annual *Military Forces in Transition,* published in September 1991, the Pentagon was reported to play down Soviet military power as a menace; that the August coup accelerated reform of the Soviet military because it rendered it, along with the Communist party, the security services, and the military-industrial complex, no longer in a position of influence. Gorbachev's 1987 policy was to reorient the armed forces to a purely defensive posture. But military leaders choose to keep it flexible as well.[51]

Observers in the United States thought that we should not be lulled into thinking the threat from military aggression no longer existed. In fact, General Colin Powell stated in March 1992 that U.S. military power should be kept strong in the presence of world instability in many countries.[52] Arms-control agreements were volunteered by both the United States and Russia's new commonwealth for slashing arsenals but keeping those needed for defense. During the last decades of the twentieth century, many world leaders were appearing to help bring about peace, those highly visible and those behind the scenes, in place by the grace of God. It seems God knew how to pick the right men and women for the job. So, in particular, it was the strong peacemakers Reagan, Bush, Gorbachev, and Yeltsin who were on hand at the right time to lead the world into a new order of peace on earth and good will to all people.

6

IN PURSUIT OF PEACE

> ... the conditions throughout the nations of the
> world ... are a challenge to every thinking person:
> that ye are not alone to pray for peace but are to
> PURSUE peace—by living the second phase of the
> divine injunction, "thy neighbor as thyself." (3976-
> 22)

WHERE PEACE BEGINS

MEMBERS OF THE EIGHTH ANNUAL Congress sat quietly
in the living room of the A.R.E headquarters on Fourteenth
Street in Virginia Beach. It was ten-fifteen the morning of
June 13. Outside, the lake sparkled in the summer sunshine.
As they prayed, peace fell about them. Edgar Cayce prepared
to give his reading (3976-22) for the 1939 Congress. Present
with him were Gertrude Cayce, his wife, and Gladys Davis,
his stenographer.

They were mindful of reports of the rise of Hitler, his
marching into Prague three months before, and in May, Germany and Italy signing their pact pledging mutual support.
Cayce and the group around him wished to have a discourse
on the ominous world situation.

As usual, they received more than they had bargained for!
The reading did not dwell on details of what was transpiring
in Europe. Instead, it gave them a very unique and spiritual
basis for understanding the relation between how nationalism
develops and our individual purpose. We find it of equal value

today, although our circumstances include a world that has overcome tyranny and even wars to a great extent. He spoke not of war, but of peace:

> In giving a dissertation upon World Affairs today, it may be well to look, for a moment, upon that which has come to pass in the affairs of the nations of the earth since the records have been kept of man's doings. Also it may be well to look at those promises, as well as the warnings that have been a record of those peoples in their attempts to present a manner of moral, religious, and secular life of the various peoples.
>
> These, to become illustrative in the minds of individuals, must be referred, then, to individual attainment or individual application of those things which have been and are still ruling factors.
>
> Man finds himself endowed with body, mind, and soul; and each phase of his consciousness is seeking for the satisfying or gratifying of the longings of those phases of his nature.
>
> Hence we find there are in the experience of man three desired purposes, or three natural laws pertaining to his material existence: survival of his species, or the preservation of life; to give expression of his own concept of life; and (third) to be heard, to be noticed in his activity.
>
> Out of this individual purpose grows that position or condition known in various groups or countries as nationalism, patriotism, and the ability to rule—or force his concept upon others.
>
> These are conditions which exist in man's experience today.
>
> Then look, for the moment, upon those standards that have been proclaimed in the varied lands. To us here, as individuals, we have accepted, we do accept those tenets of the Nazarene, Jesus of Nazareth, whose whole gospel was combined in that message, "Ye shall love the Lord thy God with all thy heart and mind, and thy neighbor as thyself." And then, as to make this become a more practical experience in the lives of individuals, He gave: "A

new commandment I give unto you, that ye love one another.''

That we as individuals may make compatible, then, those relationships of Creative Forces or God upon the one hand, and the nature of man in materiality upon the other hand, is the need of THIS day, this age. For He WILL indeed come again,—and woe be unto him who is found wanting!

In the experiences of the earth, of the nations, since those periods of the war to outlaw war (WWI) there has grown more and more the desire and the purposes for PEACE. Not as a peace at any cost, or any price, but a peace that is compatible with man's nature, man's purposes, when that purpose, that aim, that desire is made compatible with the spiritual law as given by that Teacher.

When this is compared with all the varied experiences of groups, of nations that have had, that DO have a following of some other teacher, we have found, we will find that the BASIC principles ''Ye shall love the Lord'' are at the core, the heart of every one. The manner of its application to the fellow man has been and is that variation, that has made for the application of man's desire in the relations to the other two phases of man's consciousness.

But since those periods when man has been made to THINK, not only of the sources of man's spiritual, but his mental and material desires,—more and more has gone up the prayer from individuals, groups—yea, whole nations have joined almost as one; and more and more of the secular things are being put aside.

Hence we find at this present time, NOW, the conditions or the circumstances throughout the nations of the world, or in the earth, are a challenge to every thinking person; that ye are not alone to pray for peace but are to PURSUE peace—by LIVING the second phase of the divine injunction, ''thy neighbor as thyself.''

Then, today, we are to answer within our individual consciousness, ''Am I my brother's keeper?'' Not ''What does the world owe me?" but "What contribution can I, as an individual soul seeking God, seeking to know His face, make that may hasten the day of the Lord?"

For we as individuals, as we look about us, realize more and more that indeed we live and move and have our being in Him—and we are becoming mindful also OF "from whence we came." And we realize that as He has given, "If ye will be my people, I will be thy God" applies to me, to you, to each soul that has been blessed with the consciousness, the awareness, of life.

For Life itself in all its forms and phases is indeed a manifestation of that we worship as God.

We realize that selfishness, jealousies, those things that make people afraid must gradually be put away.

First, then, as an individual, self must be conquered. Rather than raising thy voice, then, that YE may be heard, raise thy voice that HE thy God, may be heard!

WHO, then, is thy God? Is it thyself, thy body, thy ego? Rather look, then, to Him who is able to keep you from falling, but is able to keep you in strength of His might by thy desire, thy purpose, thy aims being "Others, Lord! Others!"

(3976-22)

As Cayce spoke these words, again world war was at hand. The world was not wise enough to avoid the great wars of that time. But today, it seems, many leaders have learned from the past and seek peace, "not at any cost, but that which is compatible with man's nature and spiritual law."

Leaders in 1939 were attempting to gain peace through appeasement. As Cayce has implied here, such peace would be a form of slavery for those yet free. Yet it must be compatible with spiritual law as given by Jesus of Nazareth. Thus his words reach long into events of the 1990s.

Reaching long into the past, as well, was Cayce's reference in reading 3976-26, given two years later, in response to a request for astrological aspects of the world at war and the great changes that were taking place among nations: Europe's national boundaries, and the destruction of much of our culture. America had given England the Lend-Lease agreement to supply arms to that country in March but was not yet at war.

In this reading, given April 28, 1941, Cayce said that as many understand, history repeats itself.

As to those experiences paralleling the cycle of astrological activity now—beginning on the morrow—there will be the Sun, the Moon, Jupiter, Uranus, and Venus all in the one sign.

When last this occurred, as indicated, the earth throughout was in turmoil, in strife.

There are still influences indicated in the lives of groups banded as nations, banded as peoples, still influenced by these happenings.

What then, ye ask, is the influence that makes for this great change that may be expected?

The powers of light and darkness, as then, as sixteen hundred (1600) years before. As in those periods, so to-day—we find nation against nation; the powers of death, destruction, the wrecking of that which has been and is held near and dear to the hearts of those who have through one form or another set ideals . . . to each it will become a personal thing, a personal condition. Thus it will require—yea demand—that there be an expression on the part of each as to that given 3200 years ago when the injunction was given: "Declare ye today WHOM ye will serve! As for me and my house, we will serve the living God."

(Joshua 24:15)

To what world change was he referring sixteen hundred years ago? It was the era of the decline of the Roman Empire due to internal moral decay, to revolution and barbarian invasions in the early centuries A.D. to 476 when one of the leaders deposed the last Roman ruler. In great numbers, Goths, Huns, Lombards, and Vandals swept through Europe. The invasions, lasting several hundred years, brought down the great Roman Empire that had protected the high culture of the civilized Roman world, with its treasures of literature, philosophy, and art garnered from the classical Greek civilization and, before that, the Egyptians and the Arabians. For centuries, the empire had been weakened by moral and spiritual decay. Under Byzantine despotism brought by Diocletian, democratic government disappeared. Science and letters, which had been treasured for six hundred years, were supplanted by ignorance and superstition. The empire was ruled by barbarian kings who brought anarchy and total dissolution of the once beautiful and cultured cities of Europe. Thus, civilization was overrun by the powers of darkness, forces we don't always recognize until too late. Nor do we always realize that there are those who would confuse us. One Bible reference sounds a warning: "Woe," said Isaiah, the prophet, "unto them that call evil good and good evil; that put darkness for light, and light for darkness; that put bitter for sweet, and sweet for bitter!" (Isaiah 5:20)

If Cayce's answer to achieving peace begins with ourselves, conquering self, where is the discipline to be found to begin? And why should any sane person think he or she alone can make the world safe from destructive forces, those forces of darkness? After all, the other guy doesn't seem to be doing anything about conquering *his* orneriness, *her* jealousy and sneaky doings!

That is admittedly part of the problem and the very reason some good people who befriended Cayce asked for the solution. Many of Cayce's followers were Bible students, Sunday school teachers. They wanted the in-depth guidance Cayce afforded, both as an outstanding Bible teacher and as a clairvoyant. So the small groups drawn to his work in Virginia Beach began a project they called "A Search For God."

Over time, lessons were dictated through the sleeping Cayce. The twenty-four lessons given in Books I and II have found their way to study groups around the world. The first lesson in the series is "Cooperation." It teaches cooperation with God and our fellowman and applies to nations and groups as well as individuals. With the other twenty-three lessons it provides a foundation for practical soul growth.

At the beginning of that first lesson is this Bible quotation:

"Finally, be ye all of one mind, having compassion one of another, love as brethren" (I Peter 3:8).

An affirmation follows: "Not my will but Thine, O Lord, be done in me and through me. Let me ever be a channel of blessings today, now, to those that I contact in every way. Let my going in, my coming out be in accord with that Thou would have me do, and as the call comes, 'Here am I, send me, use me.' "

The first chapter, based on Edgar Cayce readings 262-1 through 262-5, begins:

> Cooperation in the physical is defined as acting or operating jointly with others, concurring with others in action or effort. In the spiritual it is more. It is losing sight of self and becoming a channel through which blessings may flow to others. The blessing is cooperation in action. Whether in the spiritual or physical, action is necessary to put cooperation into operation—thus those who would come together for a common cause must have united action in the pursuit and realization of a common end.
>
> The best of life is ours, not at the expense of others, but in harmonious cooperation. In every successful organization the law is in effect. The heavens declare the Hand which formed them was the Hand of unity, order, and harmony. All nature follows the same law. Each part of the human body performs its duty without a thought of the other, yet fully depending each upon the other.
>
> When self is lost in the Ideal, cooperation is the natural result. It is the natural consequence of self-service, self-sacrifice, self-bewilderment in Him.

In June 1942, Cayce was asked to give before the Eleventh Annual Congress a discourse on "a spiritual and practical concept for World Peace, giving suggestions for individuals and group operations to make it effective." Cayce complied.

> In the study of the history of various groups, in their varied activities through the earth, these in the most part have sought that which would satisfy or gratify the ideas and

ideals of the few—or those that were set in power from various sources, or by circumstances as had arisen in the affairs of men in varied portions of the earth.

Today we find a world at war. . . .

Then, through whom, from whence may man gather an idea, an ideal to which he—as an individual or as a group, or as a nation—may adhere with impunity; to which purpose, to which ideal, to which surety he may put his faith, his confidence?

As has been indicated, it is not in individuals or in personalities. For these have failed. . . . Then, there must be the looking to HIM who has overcome the world; who hath known death, who hath known wars, who hath known trials, who hath known tribulations; who hath met man on his OWN consciousness of physical, mental, and spiritual emotions. . . .

Then, we find, peace in the world must begin first within the heart and purpose and mind of the individual, prompted by that something which answers within— even as has been given, "My spirit beareth witnesss with thy spirit, as to whether ye be the children of God or not." . . .

(3976-27)

WITHER THE UNITED NATIONS

"In whatever state we find society let us meet it upon its own level: as we look up, we lift it. That is cooperation."[1] Since 1945 the years have brought change, not by the whim of fate but by a change in our collective consciousness. There are still laggards left such as Saddam Hussein, Quaddafi, Castro, we hope the last of their kind. By what means have we been able to deal with "those who would rule" in our midst?

As many see the Western world, we are morally bankrupt, possibly heading toward a dark age and not a renaissance. But there have been attempts, through institutions political, religious, and humanitarian, to help protect us from further wars, to solve third world poverty. One of the most potentially powerful institutions has been the United Nations.

The United Nations was formed in 1945 in order to deal with war, poverty, and human rights. But by 1980, the UN seemed to be of no effect in that agenda.[2] Governments around the world, frustrated by failure of the UN to create a peaceful, kinder world, opted to deal directly with each other rather than depend on an organization failing its mission. Yet the work went on with little interest by the public. During those years, we saw the Korean and Vietnam wars; Middle East tensions, racial strife, and international terrorism.

The ideal upon which the United Nations was founded was in line with Cayce concepts: unanimity, cooperation among the five permanent members of the Security Council—the United States, the Soviet Union, Britain, France, and China. The UN embarked by 1973 on first studies of environmental concerns, international exploitation of the sea's resources, the population explosion.[4]

Novelist Alexander Solzhenitsyn in his undelivered Nobel award lecture viewed the UN harshly, criticizing it on the grounds of its moral destitution: "... in a world without morality, the U.N. was "born without morality." It "has rejected consideration of private complaints—the groans, the cries, the prayers of isolated little people who are merely people."[5]

Lately, mankind has discovered the moral, the spiritual law of cooperation that benefits everybody. We see evidence of it in many ways, in joint efforts to solve social, political, and economic problems, or to improve our environment, which was not the case in years past on the level of mass participation. We have seen unaccustomed unanimity among nations: thousands freed from oppression, economic and political cooperation of many countries in a domino reaction. Those such as North Korea have met with economic collapse due to a kind of paranoia against the rest of the world.

It was in the same years, 1990 and 1991, that in the United States and Africa progress in race relations was dramatic.

From the 1980s there seem to have been steps toward a point in time we are again talking about: the shaping of the new world order under what amounts to spiritual principles. It began with Gorbachev, but it would not have been possible without the timely metamorphosis of humanity everywhere longing for a better world, implemented hopefully by the United Nations.

At the UN General Assembly meeting on October 1, 1990, as the world watched Operation Desert Shield in the Persian Gulf, President Bush again defined the UN and its place in the new world order. "The UN is finally becoming what it was intended to be: a center for international collective security that can help bring about a new world order and a long era of peace. . . . We should strive for greater effectiveness and efficiency of the UN. . . . We have a vision of a new partnership of nations that transcends the cold war; a partnership based on consultation, cooperation, and collective action . . . united by principle and the rule of law and supported by both cost and commitment, a partnership whose goals are to increase democracy, increase prosperity, increase the peace and reduce arms. . . ."[6] He set before the world the ideal. Would it become the reality?

When Desert Shield turned into Desert Storm in January 1991, we had realized it was by then a time of testing once more. Would the world coalition live up to its commitment?

Cooperation is the first lesson in the A.R.E. book *A Search for God.* Logically, world changes taking place presage our readiness for subsequent lessons in the future—all of them leading to a kinder, gentler society. They continue with (2) "Know Thyself" (3) "What is My Ideal?" (4) "Faith" and continue.[7]

Cayce spoke of "man's consciousness," referring specifically to the three phases: spiritual, mental, material. In this he recognized man's nature as threefold and thus recognized the relationship we have not only to mental and material things, as important as they are to our well-being, but also our relationship to spirit: "For we as individuals, as we look about us, realize more and more that indeed we live and move and have our being in Him. . . ."

As he pointed out, since World War I, the world was seeking, praying for permanent peace, and although it did not happen in their time, their prayers and longing, added to those today, had perhaps paved the way for a new world of brotherhood.

Among his reported crimes against his own people, Saddam Hussein had violated the trade sanctions agreement and invaded Kuwait August 2, 1990. The UN Security Council had given the right to stop violation of trade sanctions by force.

When January 15, the deadline for Iraq to withdraw passed, Bush's reason to go to war was not the official one: to drive Hussein out of Kuwait and restore the government. Rather, it was to reduce his military potential and eliminate his political capability. Hussein had the power to destabilize the Middle East with "his million man army, his megalomaniac vision and his weapons of mass destruction." Congress voted overwhelmingly to give Bush the authority, after long and anguished debate.[8]

Moreover, the vote represented a major diplomatic victory for the United States. U.S. officials had had a difficult time persuading the Soviet Union, China, and third world countries that Hussein would comply with the UN, that the trade embargo against Iraq needed enforcement. Thirteen of the council's fifteen member states, including all five permanent members, voted for the resolution. Cuba and Yemen abstained.[9]

Rather than all naval operations under UN control, the resolution allowed the United States and other governments to retain complete authority over the forces they committed to enforcing the blockade. Iraqi ships were under surveillance by American or allied warships in the Persian Gulf and Red Sea.[10]

The United Nations Security Council has the power to determine the existence of any threat to peace or act of aggression and to settle the dispute "by negotiation, arbitration, recourse to the International Court, or by other peaceful means."[11] Diplomatic efforts by both U.S. and foreign representatives were led by United Nations Secretary General Javier Pérez de Cuéllar to convince Saddam Hussein to withdraw from Kuwait.

When diplomatic negotiations failed to liberate Kuwait, the

United States mobilized American, British, and French troops in the Persian Gulf under General H. Norman Schwarzkopf. On February 23, 1991, "one of the most violent battles in the history of modern warfare" began.[12]

By February 27, Bush declared victory: "Kuwait is liberated!"

Ideas as to what means nations take to achieve peace have varied, and some have been successful. Over the years, we have witnessed diplomatic persuasion, economic sanctions, embargoes, blockades, military action covert and overt, all in the interests of bringing about peace. Usually, it has been force that was needed against the troublemakers, the "strong men." Countering them, the efforts of Reagan, Bush, and Carter with their peace missions, and Arias Sánchez of Costa Rica, surely led us by their service closer to what Secretary of State James A. Baker called "a whole new international order."[13]

According to Carla Anne Robbins, the Gulf War turned out to put a new face on solving national conflicts. "Bush and Baker's success in forging an international alliance to oppose Iraq—and especially their ability to bring Moscow and the Arab states on board—left them dizzy with possibilities. . . . The new consensus could solve most any problem . . . even the seemingly insoluble Arab-Israeli conflict."[14]

Most outstanding of all was the tremendous leap forward in August 1991, when the United Nations exhibited historic success in its concerted determination, at the urging of President Bush, to condemn unanimously the invasion of Kuwait by President Saddam Hussein of Iraq. It is one more example of the necessity and the effectiveness of cooperation. The American adage is still, "United we stand, divided we fall."

Moreover, after the Arab countries held a summit to decide what stand they should take, it was followed by the unprecedented Arab nations' pledge to stand with the West in opposing Hussein, despite the fact his was a "brother" nation. The Arab countries have traditionally respected their own brand of cooperation and solidarity among themselves, to the exclusion of the same with the West.

Collaboration of almost all the world was of course based not on brotherhood alone but on the economics of oil. As in the past, expansionism, and wars that are fought in its wake, is rooted in some opportunity seen in exploiting neighboring countries. The action taken in August related directly to the world's stake in energy from the oil-rich fields of Kuwait and Saudi Arabia.

These developments in what President Bush calls "the new era" reflect the new consciousness shared by people everywhere working together, and not only for selfish reasons but because they seek to answer, as Cayce advised, "Am I my brother's keeper?" If we understand cooperation as a divine attribute, we can interpret the historic changes as signs of world soul growth!

Human rights was the issue in an interview with UN Secretary General Javier Pérez de Cuéllar following the Gulf War. He told Charlayne Hunter-Gault regarding atrocities by Iraqi soldiers against Kuwaiti people, "The security of the whole region is the issue for members of the Security Council. Stability is needed in the whole area [the Middle East]. I am fully involved in maintaining peace . . . it is my dream." He added, "but not peace at any price."[15]

In Iraq a popular uprising was reported against Hussein's loyalists in many towns in the south by Iraqi opposition leaders. The Republican Guard was firing on civilians. The opposition leader called the uprising "a spontaneous movement . . . Hussein can't maintain control long."[16] But despite sanctions against Iraq, which Hussein ignored while his people suffered, he remained in power.

The Atlantic Charter was issued in August 1941 by President Franklin D. Roosevelt and Prime Minister Winston Churchill. It declared their hope for making war obsolete and world security permanent. The UN, then with only twenty-six countries, pledged to carry out the charter goals, based on UN principles which, says Leland Goodrich, are "not legal rules . . . but general principles for the guidance of member states and organs."[17]

Those principles can be thought of as reflections of the ideals of the brotherhood of man, the fatherhood of God, as they establish a standard in world peace, human rights, sovereign authority of each nation, large or small.

The new world order has evolved, as Cayce suggested it would, from the time of the League of Nations to the United Nations today. Change is evident in the differences between the Covenant and the Charter. One important revolutionary difference, states Goodrich, is that the UN Charter states something not given in the Covenant: "the Organization shall ensure that states which are not members of the United Nations act in accordance with these Principles so far as may be necessary for the maintenance of international peace and security." That is, formerly, only the major powers were members of the League, and other nations did not have to abide by its principles. Further, membership has evolved to include *all* nations. In 1946, its last year, the League had forty-four member nations. The UN in 1990 had 160 member nations.[18]

This noted authority on international relations states further that the Covenant of the League of Nations and the Charter of the United Nations have the same objective: maintenance of peace and security, with the difference being that the UN today serves a much broader objective. In its earlier years, "As a peace organization, the United Nations had as its principal purpose the maintenance of international peace and security on the basis of the new order resulting from the victory of the Allied powers. Consequently, members were expected to be willing to accept—and join in guaranteeing against any change by force—the new postwar order, an important part of which would consist of the arrangements to be decided upon by the principal victor nations."[19]

With its present policy expanded to include third world countries, responsibility is expected of them as well as of the major powers, as much as they are able to provide in leadership, decision making, and even financial support. Further, the Charter of the UN goes beyond peace and security to provide for humanitarian aid to all nations.[20]

According to history sources, such aid was introduced in the Covenant of the League of Nations, in efforts to prohibit slavery, to aid war victims, and more. But the United Nations of today implements a wide range of economic and social objectives not attempted by the League. Included are the Charter's provisions for human rights, justice, social progress, and international peace and security, with membership open to all who want to join.[21]

On April 23, 1990, the UN General Assembly met for the eighteenth special session on international economic cooperation. As Secretary General Javier Pérez de Cuéllar said in his opening speech, the time has come "to be bold." He asked for "an agreed upon global agenda for the 1990s. . . . Success requires that we be more forward and outward looking than our cautious human and political nature normally allows."[22]

THE UN AND WORLD ECONOMY

According to the *United Nations Chronicle*, September 1990, "The meeting on May 1, 1990 brought about a landmark international consensus on the future world economy: a 38 point Declaration on International Economic Cooperation. It set forth the most important challenge for the 1990s—"the revitalization of economic growth and social development in the developing countries." It called for "sustained growth of the world economy and favourable external conditions. Also: "this major challenge has to be addressed in the context of increasing interdependence and integration in the world economy."[23]

Among the 136 speakers addressing the special session were the president of Cypress, the prime minister of Peru, three deputy prime ministers, and 39 foreign ministers. All countries are involved, states the Declaration, and share responsibility for the state of the world economy and humanitarian development. All are urged to mobilize human, financial, and physical resource through effective national policies. All countries are expected to reduce military expenditures "and integrate environmental concerns" into their national policies. The Declaration points out that the developed countries create the major pollution and are to take the most responsibility to eliminate it."[24]

The Declaration consensus found that "the 1980s marked the beginning of fundamental rethinking towards the achievement of economic development. A gradual convergence of views on economic policy is emerging." It must have flexibility, creativity, innovation and openness. "Until the 1990s, Eastern European countries have not been involved in the world economic system. Now the international community is asked to support the efforts of Eastern Europe countries to integrate themselves into the world economy, without detracting from the high priority placed on international aid to developing countries," said Assembly President Joseph N. Garba of Nigeria. He pointed out that it had taken ten years to achieve.[25]

The UN thus provides for "all Governments—developed and developing alike—in the areas of debt, development aid, environment, open trading system, stable commodity markets and a large role for the UN in helping revitalize development." Its goals include the interests of non-self-governing territories for which the UN has an obligation to promote to the utmost . . . the well being of the inhabitants of those territories, "and to ensure their political, economic, social, and educational advancement."[26]

It would seem that the Masonic and Cayce prophecies regarding future world economic conditions based on shared ideals of brotherhood are coming close to being fulfilled. Especially emphasized was the urgent task of solving regional conflicts, under the Security Council's aegis. Various leaders expressed general agreement that "improved relations between the two superpowers—the U.S. and the USSR—with further progress in disarmament would surely lead to progress in solving regional problems."[27]

Yasuhiro Nakasone, prime minister of Japan, saw the world becoming a "global village" leading to increasing interdependence among countries. One of the most urgent world concerns is the two million Central American refugees described in "Bullets and Diplomacy." The sum of $121 million is on the way as international aid to the refugees and displaced persons in that region, after a meeting of the Follow-Up Committee on the International Conference on

Central American Refugees in June 1990. The countries with the most refugees are Belize, Costa Rica, Honduras, and Mexico. "Largest contributors are Sweden, the European Community, Italy, and the United States, in that order. About 20 countries pledged contributions."[28]

"The Meeting asked affected countries to agree that projects in favour of refugees should promote the participation of women, development of children, conservation of ethnic and cultural values, and protection of the environment. "In 1988 a \$4.3 billion Special Plan was adopted by the General Assembly to help reconstruct the region as peace is attained." Stated Constantine Zepos of Greece, the Declaration was "a balance of concepts." He said that Assembly members showed "good will, cooperation, and common sense" in arriving at a solution that, "if not ideal for everyone, met the interests of all, up to a certain acceptable degree."[29]

Important precedents have been made by the UN, a major one being the resolution adopted on the formal cease-fire in Iraq. So states Jeffrey Laurenti, executive director of Multilateral Studies, the United Nations Association of the United States of America. Author of several books, including *One Earth, Many Nations,* Laurenti says that the step was a major one because it is intended to avoid "victor's peace" like that made at Versailles. It will avoid also excesses of enforcement action. He spoke to a group at Virginia Wesleyan College in April 1991. The first precedent was set when the UN allowed the action to liberate Kuwait from Saddam Hussein's Iraq. "The Persian Gulf crisis was a clear-cut case of flagrant aggression. The last such case was the invasion of Ethiopia by Italy in 1935, which helped lead to World War Two. With British help, the country won back her freedom in 1941, and joined the UN."[30]

As a result of this precedent, no nation can now take action without the UN. For the first time, Laurenti points out, the UN invoked sanctions. But economic sanctions are okay for individual nations. Further, the military forces will be able to give the Security Council power. But with the great powers, it is a problem to get interests in sync. With all this, the UN force envisioned in the Charter now engages the possibility of keeping peace that was not thought possible before now.[31]

With the swift and decisive ending of Desert Storm on February 27, 1991, President Bush triumphantly declared victory. Then began his battle for peace. His resounding success in that victory was greeted with applause around the world. Americans once more were confident in our strength both military and moral, as we witnessed the high-spirited professionalism and good will of our troops.

Cayce's insistence that it is the individual who is important was underscored by the action of one man and his spontaneous response to the suffering of the conquered Iraqi soldiers. The image of our television screens of an American soldier comforting "enemy" prisoners said much of ourselves as a nation. Said the American, "It's all right! It's all right!" as he realized that the Iraqi expected to be killed.

It *was* all right. As that brief, revealing moment unfolded, we realized what made us great. We are a nation founded on the ideals of the brotherhood of man. They carry over into our compassion, the mark of nobility.

"Then, today we are to answer within our individual consciousness," said Cayce, the question "Am I my brother's keeper?"

Clearly, neither diplomacy, nor bullets, nor even good intentions will be enough in the new world order. There is a secular norm of right thinking such as "good will, cooperation, and common sense" as Constantine Zepos of Greece characterized it.

"PERESTROIKA OF THE MIND"

Many countries have won their freedom since 1989, but it has not always brought peace. As Gorbachev's brave beginnings brought freedom to the Eastern bloc, peace has receded in demands for independence met with Soviet military violence.

Happily, a map of freedom presented in the February 1991 issue of the *World Monitor* portrays more nations free than not free. An article by former Arizona Governor Bruce Babbitt in the same issue points to "the New and Improved South America." The map shows that most of South America is now free, or partly free, and Central America and Haiti are partly free.[32]

However, it is the process of democratization that has begun and is not yet complete. Leonard R. Sussman, senior scholar in international communications of Freedom House, New York, says that what is needed is perestroika of the mind—"the restructuring of the entire citizenry's understanding of what a civil society should be. Civil education for the purpose of creating a democratic society is not an easy or rapid process, but it must begin even as the institutions and process of democracy are set in place."[33] He quotes Gorbachev's musings that, "We were among the last to understand that in the age of information sciences the most valuable asset is knowledge, springing from human imagination and creativity." He added, "We will be paying for our mistake for many years to come."[34]

In February of 1990 Gorbachev approved a unified Germany, and East German Premier Hans Modrow called for a single, neutral German state. Dr. Ralf Brinkmann, a West German native and assistant physics professor at Old Dominion University, had spoken to an Old Dominion University group in January about the problems in East Germany. "If there is no quick, peaceful action to reunify Germany within a year, no solution is possible to present problems there," he said.[35]

The thirty-year-old electrical engineer had been in the United States for two and a half years as a visiting scholar on a scholarship at Chicago University. From Braunschweig, near the East German border, he told the O.D.U. audience that the problems of East Germany are legion. "Although the communist party in East Germany lost 1.1 of its 2.4 million members in the last three months, the communist apparatus is still working with tens of thousands of full-time employees. They still have access to East Germany's vast resources, with full control of the media. The opposition is divided into 35 different groups which have to work with practically no resources and without any access to the mass media. The economic picture is even worse. Industry is completely out-dated, with production less than half that of West Germany. . . . The public communication system is insufficient, out of date. The environment is devastated with severe air, water, and soil pollution."[36]

The problem is encountered not only by Eastern Europe but also by great sections of the world just learning the art of democratization. In the vanguard of those helping such countries is Professor A. E. Dick Howard, executive director of the commission that wrote Virginia's new constitution. He is professor of law and public affairs at the University of Virginia and chairman of Virginia's Commission on the Bicentennial of the United States Constitution. For several years he has been a consultant for constitutional draftsmen in other states and abroad, traveling to various places where he helps leaders to write new constitutions. He has consulted in such places as Brazil, Hong Kong, the Philippines, and, more recently, Hungary, Czechoslovakia, and Poland.

I attended a lecture he gave January 13, 1991, as Virginia Beach began a series of open forums on "The Bill of Rights and Beyond." His topic was "Mr. Madison, Meet Mr. Havel: The Global Legacy of the Bill of Rights."[37]

"History has never seen a country unravel as fast as Russia," he said. The Europeans correlate their past experience with the American example, as it is not practical to copy the American constitution wholesale. The building blocks of the Bill of Rights, he said, are principles. For fledgling democracies, after drafting a constitution, the next task is "making it work." He cited important challenges in the tough times ahead as the right leadership and building institutions, universities, and political parties.[38]

"I took Hungarian people to the polls, voting places, to show them how they work," Howard said. The most important part, he tells new constitution makers, are the civic virtues, the duties as well as the rights. "Civic virtue is the living heart of the Bill of Rights."[39]

In Europe, "They know Thomas Jefferson's name . . . the American example is in the minds of the Europeans. . . . A Pole told me that 'every Pole is a little Thomas Jefferson.' "[40]

Just as Cayce said, it is the American example that would lead the world toward the new world order. Such people as this expert bring reports that bear it out. Howard thinks evolving governments will succeed in making their own rights documents but will need a lot of help from the United States. "The New World Order is helping countries like them, not just winning the [Gulf] war," he stated.[41]

Countries struggling to join the free world find much conflict in the freedom process. In December 1990, Baptist Haiti Mission directors Wallace and Eleanor Turnbull wrote me during the dangerous and uncertain preelection time in Haiti. "At present, we are stocking everything from cement to salt and pepper, as no one knows what the next day will bring. Candidates are from the whole spectrum of Haitian society, desiring to be president, senator, or village mayor. Their reputations vary equally. Assassinations and a deadly bombing of a candidate's supporters have the whole nation jittery. Yet the majority of Haiti's people of voting age have registered, determined to escape the nonentity of the voiceless through their ballot."[42]

They were referring to the election in which Jean-Bertrand Aristide replaced Lieutenant General Prosper Avril on December 16.

At the Baptist Missions, Haitian children are given an education and Christian teachings. "Our days are filled with the joy of sharing and often hours of paperwork to satisfy various government offices, knowing that satisfying them will mean hope and opportunity to many in need—need of medical care, need of schooling that will provide tools of knowledge for life, and need of the Light that came with Christmas."[43]

The Turnbulls explained that the ongoing school and church construction was interrupted because of preelection violence. "Fearing blocked roads and worry over their families, the men bolted for home."[44]

The March 1991 issue of the *United Nations Chronicle* reported that there was violence in Port-au-Prince, the capital, on December 5 when at the end of a pro-Aristide rally, hand grenades were thrown, killing seven people and injuring fifty others, including women and children. Ugly violence, free electoral process, and voting were closely monitored by the United Nations Observer Group for the verification of the elections in Haiti. Success was due to "the determination and discipline of the Haitian people, the professional behaviour of the Haitian army."[45]

Life is difficult enough for the children without having to suffer such trauma. Many areas do not have proper school buildings. The children eagerly meet in primitive arbors with log benches to hear their lessons. In February 1991 there were no other reports of violence against the children, but school was canceled for much of the election period. It was Haiti's first free and democratic election.

Haitians still look forward to an uncertain future. After the elections, there were many reminders of the violence that had taken place. Friends of the Mission were asked to pray for President Aristide and the new Parliament. He was known in Haiti as a radical Roman Catholic with Marxist views. He was reported to express anti-American and anti-Protestant views. There is a desire among some of the radical leadership to return to voodoo as the cultural religion. Among the population, it was hoped that the new president would be moderate and work with all segments of Haitian society and not suppress Protestants, who were known to pray that he open his eyes to the complexity of the problems of Haiti.

The ideal for achieving the new order, if all countries could accept it, can be found in Edgar Cayce's insistent claim that "We are our brother's keeper." He said that "if the ideas and the ideals are rather that each should be, each will be, each purposing to be, a channel for presenting brotherly love, kindness, patience, longsuffering, just being kind—and if these are rather the propaganda, if these are rather the promptings . . . in every phase of every association . . . we will find more and more that there will be drawn the greater dawn of every form of helpfulness, hopefulness, in the experience of an individual, a family, a state, a city, a nation" (3976-17). Would not we see the dawn for a better world?

Cayce referred in 1936 to America's own beginnings in creating a democracy. "What read ye, how interpret ye that which prompted this land in its separating itself or binding itself (as a nation) for a functioning in the affairs, the experiences of man? These become the basic forces in the economic relations of a peoples of any nation. . . ." He was referring to colonial America's economic situation with England: taxation without representation in Parliament. In addition, the colonies sent England raw resources, and England turned them into products and sold these back to the colonists and other world markets. The result was a trade imbalance intolerable to the colonies.

There has been seen a general parallel between the democratization of Eastern Europe today and that of the American colonies of the eighteenth century, with economic relations the "basic forces" common to both.

Contrarily, freedom of expression granted those under Soviet rule has brought forth old ethnic and nationalist grudges to stir brother *against* brother. Thousands of Jews are seeking to leave the Soviet Union because of renewed acts of hatred against them. And for all their great progress that has continued worldwide changes, democratic Russian leaders must cope with a hard core of communists who would return to the oppressive regime rather than deal with new, unaccustomed freedom.

Racial and nationalist conflicts continue to rage in the world—in South Africa, where, however, much progress has been made through the leadership of Mandela and de Klerk; in Nicaragua; in Mexico. America, too, is not wholly free as blacks, Asians, and Indians suffer discrimination and sometimes violent confrontation. Crime, including murder, rape, and robbery, has seemed to escalate, with need for more law officers and cooperation from law-abiding citizens.

Nevertheless, there is everywhere the belief expressed that the world will never be the same. In spite of imperfect conditions, optimism is high. How has the great change been carried through, triggered by Gorbachev's vision, if not through the change of consciousness everywhere taking place?

"How shall this (one Ideal) be brought about?" asked

Cayce. "As they each in their own respective sphere put into action that they know to be the fulfilling of that as has been from the beginning, so does the little leaven leaven the whole lump." The leaven appears to be working.

7

BULLETS AND DIPLOMACY

In the experiences of the earth, of the nations, since those periods of the war to outlaw war, there has grown more and more the desire and the purposes for PEACE. Not as a peace at any cost, or any price . . . (3976-22, June 13, 1939)

SUPERPOWER AGREEMENTS

THE LITTLE LEAVEN—the prayers and longing for peace on the part of people everywhere—is evident. For both the Soviets and the United States, under both Reagan and Bush, arms have been viewed in the light of mutual concern for the dangers of a world bristling with nuclear weapons. Reagan and Gorbachev held their first summit meeting in Geneva, November 19–21, 1985. It was the result of both men finding common ground: the universal desire for lasting peace.

Arms control was the principal concern. Stated Caspar Weinberger, secretary of defense, arms agreements on SALT II and the ABM Treaty were not about reduction in arms but about limiting what growth the Soviets would make. . . . It's a license for expansion. . . . The President wants verifiable and very real reductions down to parity on both sides.'' He said the Soviet Union had violated the ABM Treaty.[1]

Ronald Reagan and Mikhail Gorbachev actually talked about doing away with thousands of nuclear warheads. This was in response to demands of the people: Just months before, Pacific Islanders drew up a treaty to be signed by eight nations to make the South Pacific nuclear free. Other such zones have included Latin America and Antarctica. Still others were to protect the Nordic and Balkan regions. The Antarctic Treaty in 1959 led the trend. In the 1968 Nuclear Non-Proliferation Treaty, one hundred nations agreed not to acquire atomic arms, while other treaties ban placement of atomic weapons on the seabed and in orbit around the earth.[2]

Such bans have been made in major cities of the world by "no nuke" resolutions: in London, Sydney, Vancouver. Nations of the South Pacific—Australia, New Zealand, Fiji, Western Samoa—sought banning. The object was to prevent destruction by the superpowers.[3]

Major issues were arms control, human rights, the Mideast, and Russia's presence in Angola and Afghanistan. During the Geneva talks, both leaders were trying to deal with their mistrust. Reagan declared that it must be overcome. He said to Gorbachev: "I've explained to you that when we had a monopoly on nuclear weapons, we didn't use it. Why don't you trust me?"

Gorbachev replied: "Do you believe that I wouldn't attack you?" They were both anxious to explain their side. They found respect for each other that would help in their subsequent talks.[4]

How NATO allies saw the summit in November 1985 was indicative of "rising expectations," particularly on arms control. From a West German paper: ". . . a confrontation between the two [superpowers] is no longer a serious danger." French President Mitterrand said, "the simple fact dialogue has started again "is a sign of hope." But Britain's *Financial Times* said that "*little or nothing has been achieved.*"[5]

By August 1986, talks in Geneva continued as Reagan and Gorbachev agreed on arms control. Reagan said he would delay missile defenses yet not upset his SDI ("Star Wars") deployment schedule. But the United States was slow to guarantee Gorbachev's radical proposal to eliminate the intermediate-range nuclear forces from Europe.[6] In April 1987, Gorbachev's proposal to eliminate nuclear weapons by the year 2000 went for months while U.S. leaders could not decide to agree: Shultz thought careful compromise was best, while the Pentagon conservatives urged Reagan to renounce Salt II.[7]

The second summit continued their talks in Reykjavik on October 11 and 12, 1986. An economic summit in Venice in June 1987 turned out to be another one on arms control. Reagan's wisdom in recognizing Gorbachev's ordeal of change—and his own willingness to change America's stance—was greeted with relief by the world. He was a primary force in the entire freedom movement, another one of "those chosen" to bring it about. The two men were beginning to think alike, though no one thought the Geneva summit had accomplished much.

In Washington, December 7–10, 1987, heads of state signed a treaty to eliminate intermediate-range and shorter-range nuclear missiles. It was the result of six years of work to ban all ground-launched medium-range missiles. Two days of intensive talks had taken place in Geneva between Soviet Foreign Minister Eduard A. Shevardnadze and Secretary of State George Shultz.[8] Shevardnadze called the agreement "historic."[9]

Under the terms of the treaty, the Soviets eliminated four times as many missiles as the United States and roughly six times as many warheads. The weapons were to be eliminated within three years, and inspectors for both sides would monitor compliance for another ten years after that.[10]

The fourth meeting was held in Moscow, May 29–June 2, 1988. Its principal subject was the control of INF (intermediate-range nuclear forces), following work done by Shultz and Shevardnadze in Geneva and after debate on the Senate floor. But although the meeting did not resolve differences on arms control, particularly mobile, land-based strategic nuclear missiles, it was termed positive.[11]

In the area of human rights, Reagan was reported to have met with prominent Soviet dissidents and pledged to them in an emotional meeting that the United States will remain "unshakable" in its commitment to human rights. According to Columnist Donald Kaul, President Reagan's performance in the Soviet Union was "truly remarkable" . . . it "knocked their socks off. He spoke to an audience of Soviet intellectuals and drew this response from a leading Russian novelist: " 'One thing pleased me especially—his religiousness. This feeling of responsibility before God, as we say here in Russia, this created a feeling of sincerity. Hearing this religious vocabulary from a politician, I'm not used to.' They loved everything he said over there. . . ."[12]

Cayce said, "Not peace at any price."

Although Cayce taught in the readings that peace should be pursued by application of spiritual law—that out of the heart and mind, all conditions are created—he did not advise caving in to aggression. He said that America could be saved from invasion by the *prayers*—"and the living of same"—of the sixty-four people present at his dissertation June 23, 1940, if they so desired.

Prayer is a powerful force. Negotiation between right-thinking people, if it is not appeasement, is also powerful. If they are combined, think what such a formula for peace might bring! It would amount to the alternative to aggression from any source: passive resistance, which, as practiced by Mahatma Gandhi against British rule, won for India her freedom.

In the 1980s, with much of the world communist, the Reagan Doctrine could not be one of passive resistance. It took the dedication of many good people and massive military force. In an article based on an interview with Reagan in August 1990, Michael Ryan stated:

. . . Ronald Reagan has not been given much credit for the profound changes that have occurred in the Communist world in the last few years. I wondered, did he believe that the massive military build-up that he undertook during his eight years in office helped to explain why Mikhail Gorbachev finally called a halt to the Cold War?

"Yes," he said without hesitation. "Because the Russians had it all their way before. . . . If it's a case of rebuilding the military or reducing the deficit . . . I have to stand on the rebuilding of our national security. . . . Yes, I want to eliminate the deficit—it's necessary that we do so. But the first and prime purpose of the federal government is the national security of the American people."[13]

The Reagan Doctrine holds no less persuasion for third world areas such as Central America, Cambodia, Korea, the Philippines, Pakistan, and Burma, where these countries have been contending not only with communism but also such ideologies as Islam.

In July 1990, Muslim extremists put Prime Minister Arthur N. R. Robinson and forty other hostages under a four-day seige in Port-of-Spain, Trinidad. Nine people died, with looting of food stores and even appliances by hundreds of hungry poor.[14]

A group of black Muslims claimed that the government is corrupt and the coup was intended to stop poverty and the destruction of Trinidad and Tobago, two islands composing a Caribbean nation with high unemployment and skyrocketing food prices. Agreement was reached with Robinson to resign immediately and elections to take place within ninety days.[15]

The Korean peninsula was divided in 1945. In the Korean War, June 25, 1950 to July 27, 1953, capitalist South Koreans fought the communist North and communist China's troops. Fifty-four thousand Americans died.[16]

Its importance to the post–cold war era of the 1990s is made evident in that it "encouraged seven American presidents to draw lines against Communist subversion from Vietnam to El Salvador, drew an Atlantic America irreversibly into Asia, and helped catapult what had been a declining military establishment to the forefront of American foreign policy. If the Berlin Wall was the symbol of the division of Europe, the border between the two Koreas is its Asian counterpart."[17]

When Mikhail Gorbachev and South Korean President Roh met earlier in June 1990, "they may have started a thaw that could someday eliminate the most visible remaining vestige of the cold war: the division of Korea. Moreover, in this spring of reconciliation in Asia, both Beijing and Moscow are taking new steps toward diplomatic rapprochement with Seoul, a government that Communism's twin giants had tried to destroy in 1950 and in the 40 years since have ignored, denounced, and sought to subvert. Even the relentless enmity between the U.S. and Kim Il Sung's Stalinist regime has begun to soften. ..."[18]

In the 1990s in Seoul, South Korea, the issue has long been reunification of communist North Korea and democratic South Korea to become one nation again. Students have rioted and been subjected to clashes with police, arrests, and beatings. The violence has sparked increasing public anger from older residents.[19]

In 1988, on the forty-third anniversary of Korea's liberation from Japanese colonial rule, President Roh Tae-woo proposed a meeting with North Korean ruler Kim Il-sung. But resentment was brewing protests against American military presence in South Korea. Students, led by radical leaders, said the government of South Korea was using the Olympics of September 17–October 2, 1988, to impose authoritarian rule, demanding that communist North Korea be host for the Games along with South Korea. Fighting broke out, with riot police as targets for rocks and firebombs. The protesters hurled firebombs into U.S. Army headquarters in Seoul, in anti-American protests during the Games, contending that the forty-two thousand U.S. troops stationed there under a mutual defense pact enforce the division of the Korean peninsula. They demanded withdrawal of the troops.[20]

On July 20, 1990, South Korean President Roh called for an end to their cold war and proposed unrestricted travel between them. "The time has come to end total division," he told the nation in a radio and television broadcast. He said that South Korea would open its border at Panmunjom in the demilitarized zone for five days as of August 13 and "accept brethren from the North without restrictions." He noted that President Kim Il-sung had proposed conditional free travel on January 1 and added, "I am convinced there will be no obstacle."[21]

Nevertheless, in a report on July 27, 1990, when the prime ministers agreed to meet, renewed dissention broke out over arrangements to conduct a crossing by North Koreans into South Korea. There was to have been a joint reunification rally, but the crossing was canceled in a setting of name-calling, protest, and rhetoric.[22]

* * *

In the Philippines, President Corazon Aquino ruled perilously since her husband, Benigno Aquino, was assassinated by communist guerrilla rebels. Six U.S. military bases, of strategic importance, provided stability in the democratic island nation. She took over after the ouster of Ferdinand Marcos. She was forceful in contending against former Defense Minister Juan Ponce Enrile, an ambitious rival who, in December 1989, attempted a coup against her and failed. He was jailed but, according to reports, denied his association with disgruntled military factions that made a series of coups.[23]

On June 3, 1990, neighborhood vigilante groups were formed to help fight the rebels. Restrictions were announced on the American troops, Defense Department civilians and military dependents at Clark Air Base. Both Clark and Subic Bay bases are the largest U.S. military installations abroad, and U.S. officials said in the 1980s that they were essential for protecting eastern Asia from Soviet military expansion.

Since 1969 the United States has been the Philippines' main supplier of arms in their ongoing conflict with communist rebels. There have been about forty thousand U.S. military personnel, dependents, and Defense Department civilians stationed there.[24]

Recent decades of turmoil were created by oppressive governments in not only the Philippines but also other Southeast Asian countries such as Burma. There, the same struggle between brutal government and pro-democracy advocates proceeded contemporaneously with those of Trinidad and Haiti, half a world away.

Another Southeastern nation in turmoil in 1988 was Thailand, where on July 24, Muslim separatists reportedly attempted to disrupt the general elections by violent means. They are a minority in Thailand and a majority in the province bordering Malaysia. They torched seven rural schools and a health clinic where voting booths had been set up. Four of the schools burned to the ground and the other buildings were damaged.[25]

Due to communist aggression in Vietnam and Cambodia, many thousands of innocent men, women, and children have lost their lives or suffered economic hardship, homelessness, hunger, and disease. They have become refugees, fleeing from their homelands as war engulfed their provinces.

Nicaraguans have fled over their borders to Honduras and Costa Rica. Cubans have found sanctuary in America. Southeast Asians have fled Cambodia and Laos into Thailand or America.[27]

These dispossessed, frightened victims of communist insurgency looked inevitably to America, although some do manage to enter Europe, not without some immigration problems. In America, there is strong resistance to refugees, regardless of the pitifulness of their plight. But Senator Rudy Boschwitz, who has worked for the East Asians, thinks that although refugees are not a popular subject, and there is great resentment of them, they forget that their own grandparents or great-grandparents were refugees. He states that 600,000 refugees, including Cambodians, enter the United States every year. They are consumers, create new jobs, are energetic and strong.[28] They have had to be: The boat people who made it to our shores are an example.

The United States ended military involvement in Southeast Asia in 1975, but the suffering there continued. Thailand was an unwilling reception center for Vietnamese who worked their way through the war zones of Cambodia to seek safety in Thai camps. Under their leader, Pol Pot, the communist insurgents Khmer Rouge killed hundreds of thousands of Cambodians from 1975 to 1978, when they were invaded by the Vietnamese. In the 1980s, the Khmer Rouge conquered Cambodia. Near the Thai-Laotian border there was misery and death. In Thailand illegally, Vietnamese and Cambodians hoped for new life in the West. In Site Two—the largest of the Thai camps—lived 160,000 people. Thousands of Cambodians were interviewed for resettlement in the United States. Placards read: ''We Need Education; America Can Help Us.''[29]

For Cambodia, the peace treaty that the UN had proposed months before became a reality, leading to free elections in the future. The UN had conducted a transitional government for eighteen months. It was described as ''the most ambitious peacekeeping task ever taken on by the world body." The move was accompanied by a scathing condemnation of the Khmer Rouge for their killing and torturing of more than a million Cambodians. "The world has not forgotten," said Baker.[30]

The guerrilla group was to keep a share of power because their cooperation was needed to keep peace. Along with the Hun Sen government and two noncommunist guerrilla groups, signing the treaty were representatives of eighteen other nations. Seventy percent of the country's fighting forces were to be demobilized; thirty-five thousand refugees from Thailand camps would be repatriated.[31]

The Cambodian peace accord paved the way for reconciliation between the United States and Vietnam and Laos; it also improved ties with China. Initial talks on full diplomatic and economic relations with Hanoi could begin immediately, said Baker. They would be governed by the degree with which Vietnam continues to cooperate with the US on the very, very important issue of our prisoners of war and our missing in action. It would require a halt to its military intervention in Cambodia and a full accounting of the two thousand, three hundred U.S. servicemen still missing from the Vietnam War. Diplomatic, travel, and trade relations were to follow.[32]

FIGHT OR FLIGHT IN CUBA

In Miami, Cuban exiles planned for the day they could help overthrow communist dictator Fidel Castro. For more than ten years, veterans of the 1961 Bay of Pigs invasion, when the United States sent Cuban exiles to their homeland to overthrow Castro, conducted regular drills, along with younger Cubans anxious to be a part of the action. "We have not stopped since 1961," said brigade leader Pedro Rojas, sixty-eight.

The Sunday drills began with the raising of the American flag, to a recording of "The Star-Spangled Banner" and the Cuban national anthem. After roll call, they performed maneuvers. "This is our message to Cuba," said Rafael Cabe-

zas, another Bay of Pigs veteran. "We have only a few dozen
men, but behind us is 30 years of history. We want Castro to
know that at the last moment, we are ready to sacrifice our
lives."[33]

Meanwhile, Cubans were swamping European embassies
in Havana for permission to receive asylum in Belgium,
Spain, Italy, Switzerland, and Czechoslovakia.

As the Cubans poured into the embassies, European diplomats asked the Cuban government for more police protection to prevent further forced entries there by Cubans seeking
to leave. The Cuban Foreign Ministry blamed the United
States for "inciting" the run on the embassies.[34]

PANAMA LOOKING FORWARD

Since 1979 the United States has reduced its presence in
Panama and will return Panama back to her people December
31, 1999. But civil unrest marked Panama City March 2, 1988
when a strike erupted by opposition groups confronting government military with bomb threats at the Panama Canal. The
United States had intensified economic pressure on General
Manuel Antonio Noriega to limit Panamanian access to funds.
The strike was called by the opposition National Civic Cru-
sade to protest Noriega's rule. Most businesses closed down
for the third day. A government truck was burned. Civic Cru-
saders marched in the streets in an effort to stir the largely
passive resistance to Panama's military-backed government.[38]

An abortive coup against Noriega brought about a state of
emergency on March 8. Further confrontations occurred between the military-backed government and opposition groups
that organized street protests and made bomb threats. More
strikes were threatened by the opposition National Civic Cru-
sade to protest Noriega's rule. On March 8 in Panama City,
Noriega's military forces used truncheons and tear gas to disperse demonstrators protesting his leadership. Banks closed
because of cash shortages and fear of a run on banks. In New
York, Miami, and Boston, U.S. District judges froze Panamanian assets after suits were filed to prevent Noriega's government from withdrawing funds.

Panama's United States ambassador, Juan B. Sosa, recognized President Eric Arturo Delvalle rather than Noriega.[39] Manuel Noriega had entered into business with the Medellin drug cartel of Colombia and used the Bank of Credit and Commerce International to launder the cartel money in Panamanian banks. Then he made a deal with Fidel Castro to move the drugs into the United States. In 1988 he was indicted for drug smuggling.[40]

In July 1989, covert activity was instigated by President Bush to oust Noriega. American economic moves to topple Noriega brought public life to a standstill, but he was defiant. Banks remained closed for nearly three weeks. The armed forces of Panama went without pay. Businesses were paralyzed, as stores closed and people went hungry.[41] Economic sanctions were imposed until the United States invaded Panama in December 1991 and overthrew the Panamanian dictator.

Like President "Teddy" Roosevelt, both Reagan and Bush believed in "shaking the big stick" in Marxist countries, which are invariably run by dictators. However, the United Nations opposes all invasions whether to conquer and control, or to set the people free.

During the Gulf War, Bush welcomed the United Nations' collective approval and security. Under Bush in the 1990s the United States was foremost in the United Nations security and humanitarian campaigns. Reagan and the United States in the years of the cold war were not as supportive of the United Nations as were Bush and Clinton later.

In all the cases in which the United States during the Reagan administration sent troops to other countries, that action was greatly appreciated. When Reagan sent in troops to free Grenada, the people cheered in gratitude. When President Bush sent in forces to oust General Manuel Noriega from his dictatorship of Panama in 1989, the people cheered in gratitude. American troops that he sent to Saudi Arabia were heartily welcome for their presence in the crisis there. American involvement has been criticized, as well, for its absence: Bush received much criticism for not sending troops to help the Iraqi rebels overthrow Hussein!

HAITI

Many dictators have held Haiti hostage to their rule over decades. The election on December 16, 1990, of Jean-Bertrand Aristide brought hopes for a better future as Haiti's first elected president. In 1988, men armed with guns and machetes burst into a Roman Catholic church and killed at least three parishioners, wounded sixty, and burned down the building. Police, under the military rule of Lieutenant Colonel Namphy, stood by but did not try to stop the crimes that were compared to the terror characterizing the twenty-nine-year-old Duvalier dynasty.

Namphy was then toppled by Lieutenant General Prosper Avril. Hope for democratic reforms dimmed.[41] In March 1990, Avril was overthrown after violent demonstrations. Aristide was elected in Haiti's first election in thirty-one years, but he was ousted in a coup that resulted in 150 deaths and more than 300 wounded. Soldiers attacked at random. Security forces in a slum area went house to house shooting indiscriminately, acccording to a radio broadcast.[42]

Only four days before, Aristide had addressed the United Nations General Assembly. He was quoted in an interview that, "Democracy has won out for good, the roots are growing stronger and stronger." The coup began with mutinies at an army training camp and at a police station in Port-au-Prince.[43]

President Bush called the coup "outrageous" and cut off all aid to the island. An international embargo was placed on Haiti by the Organization of American States, which arranged a meeting between Aristide and his opponents on November 23 in Cartagena, Colombia. Exiled in Venezuela, he offered concessions to the Haitian parliamentarians, apparently to no avail. They had criticized him for his handling of the presidency.[44]

A great exodus of Haitians left the country for Florida or Guantánamo Bay Naval Base, Cuba, during the months that

followed; many drowned, while others were rescued from
capsized boats by the U.S. Coast Guard. They claimed they
were frightened to stay in Haiti because they had supported
Aristide.

Haitians were thought by some U.S. officials to be leaving
the country due to economic problems. Officials at a U.S.
refugee camp said that more Haitians were received into the
United States than were returned.

In 1994 the United States sent troops to Haiti to restore
order which was not happening under Aristide. In fact, in
1995 many of his opponents were murdered.[46] When Rene
Preval was elected president, he was faced with severe economic problems and subsequent discontent among the population. When political violence escalated, the United Nations
sent in peacekeepers. They were to leave by August 1, 1997.[47]

INDIA

India, striving to remain democratic, was torn by riots after
the assassination of Rajiv Gandhi, on May 21, 1991, as he
campaigned for reelection as prime minister. He had been
elected immediately after the assassination of his mother,
Prime Minister Indira Gandhi, in 1984. Voted out of office
in 1989, he led the opposition while the coalition governments of V. P. Singh, and then that of Chandra Shekhar, both
fell.[47a]

Gandhi was called India's leading politician and a symbol
of national unity. He had worked to bring the many religious,
political, and ethnic factions of India together which were due
to the Hindu nationalist Bharatiya Janata party and others.[47b]

In Pakistan in 1990, war was feared with India following
the sudden dismissal of Pakistan's democratic Prime Minister
Benazir Bhutto, who had criticized New Delhi's harsh crackdown on a Muslim separatist uprising in Indian-held Kashmir.
She also "restrained militants, however, from openly aiding
Kashmiri Moslems, which would almost automatically trigger
war No. 4." The United States brought heavy pressure for
talks, but exchange of gunfire occurred in mid-August 1990,
after banishment of Bhutto's civilian government and ad-

ournment of talks. She was ousted in a bloodless coup by militant Gulam Ishaq Khan.[48]

In May 1998, India set off nuclear testing underground, twice in several days' time, alarming the rest of the world that Pakistan would now activate nuclear defense. A chain reaction among the other nations was feared as well. Clinton declared economic sanctions against India, and India agreed she would halt further testing.

In April 1990, Nepal, a small nation between India and China, democracy won out over the long-term repressive monarchy. Protests by hundreds of thousands of people in the capital, Katmandu, took place in unprecedented pro-democracy demonstrations. They were fired on by police and scores were reported killed or wounded. At midnight King Birendra announced he would lift the ban on political parties.[51]

"We are liberated!" acting president of the Nepali Congress Party declared, as crowds marched through the streets.[52]

The cold war is over, but there are still social "earthquakes" affecting millions of people. Many are not safe from attacks or free from abject poverty and ignorance. We have witnessed "ethnic cleansing" among Muslims and Bosnians in Yugoslavia. Corruption between leaders in Mexico and drug traffickers brings cocaine, heroin, and marijuana to the rest of the world to kill the youth and make billions for traffickers in Colombia, Mexico, and Ecuador. In most of Latin America, the people have poor housing, no jobs, and few schools. Only the wealthy few have a good life.

Elsewhere, law enforcers, as they try to protect innocent citizens, are at war with criminals of all descriptions. In Somalia, famine has killed thousands because food from other countries is prohibited by warring tribes. Everywhere, there are the homeless, even in America, testifying to economic imbalance and lack of help for the underprivileged and refugees from tyranny.

During the 1980s, exportation of terrorism drew Europe and America into the quagmire of Middle East politics in a new way. That is, in previous years, it was confined to the Israeli Palestinian territorial dispute. It then became linked with other Arab nations while "moderates" were opposed to radicalism It is the latter group that has brought that land to the peace table.

The United Nations partitioned Palestine in 1948 with boundaries to define the two nations. But war broke out between them, and since Israel prevailed, the Arabian people never acquired their land. Instead, they took the area of Jordan, east of Palestine. During the 1980s the crux of the unrest remained: Israeli occupation in Palestine. Bitter war has continued between rock-throwing Palestinian youth and Israeli soldiers in the streets where both groups claim is their homeland from biblical times. "There are 900,000 Palestinians living in squalor on the West Bank; some 500,000 in the Gaza strip, and about 550,000 in Israel."[52a]

Other countries have tried over decades to bring peace to the Middle East. Under President Carter, the Camp David peace talks in 1981 were joined by Great Britain, Israel, and Egypt—the only Arab nation to participate. Its leader, Anwar Sadat, was subsequently assassinated as a "traitor" to the Arab world.

Egypt is in the middle of the trauma, and, according to Cayce and ancient belief, the Great Pyramid marks the center of the earth. It is central, not only geographically but also culturally, to both East and West, past and present. It is seen as a monument of spiritual progress through time. Appropriately, Egypt's influence is important in the peace effort. But with the stepping up of hostilities, territorial and religious, and the cycle of revenge and hatred from past terrorist attacks, peace remains ever elusive.

As we find in these accounts, the world was learning that diplomacy rather than bullets is the wiser answer to conflict. The year 1991 drew to a close with many problems in the world scene closer to being resolved, as if there was a timetable at work. Solutions to long problems of the past everywhere were nearing reality, while others had to be put on hold.

In October 1991, hope for peace in the Middle East was

given the best chance ever yet possible for the centuries-long rivalry between Arabs and Jews. It was due principally to the shuttle diplomacy of James A. Baker, United States secretary of state, carrying out President Bush's continued peacemaking policy inherited from past U.S. efforts, highlighted by the Camp David talks led by President Carter.

Over a period of eight months, Secretary Baker traveled to Syria, Jordan, Lebanon, as well as to Israel, to persuade those countries to make peace. Baker's work led finally to agreement on both sides for a peace conference to be held on October 30, 1991. Long-standing major obstacles are the status of Jerusalem related to claims by both Palestinians and Jews and Jewish settlements in the occupied territories. Few expectations were held that peace would break out immediately, given the many decades—yes, centuries—of the many factions. It was seen as only the first step in a long process toward cooperation and brotherhood that is the standard sought.[52b]

Fresh in the minds of delegates at the historic meeting in Madrid were victories over the cold war and the Gulf War. The world had changed. Hope for peace was expressed in spite of hard-line attitudes by some, including Prime Minister Yitzhak Shamir, and in spite of terrorist activity by some factions.

The Palestinian delegation was led by Dr. Haider Abdul-Shafi, seventy-one, a physician from occupied Gaza.

We recall that in 1989, the Russian professor Dr. Shmarov had suggested that Russia and the United States should seek Mideastern peace. In April 1991, the Soviets announced that they would join the United States in sponsoring the Israeli-Arab talks.

Compromise on both sides was not typical, but Faisal Husseini, who negotiated with Baker, led a group of Jerusalem moderates who became key figures with the Palestinian delegation to the conference. He was able to persuade the PLO to compromise on a step-by-step process of freeing the West Bank and Gaza from Israeli control. It was an important element later in the talks. He was further able to convince the

Palestinians that they have little choice but to cooperate with new world politics dominated by the United States. He is reported to have said, "Now new regimes have come, and there is a new world order. We must understand the rules of the new game so that we can face the challenge and reach our goal."[53]

As President Bush and President Gorbachev presented their preliminary views in a press conference at the Soviet Embassy in Madrid the day before the talks were to start, they agreed that their influence remained as catalysts in the peace talks. "We are not imposing settlement at the conference. We are here to be a catalyst." Bush emphasized that it was a historic event: "they are sitting down to talk to each other for the first time."[54] In agreement with Bush, Gorbachev said that there should be "proper respect for the negotiating parties for final, positive conclusions" to the talks. "We are not going to simply stand on the side," said Gorbachev, ". . . but we need a new climate of relations between nations." The talks should not be entered into "without taking into account everybody's needs."[55]

Other issues as well were on the minds of reporters from both the Russian TV and American news media. The Russian republics' economy was one topic questioned, to which Gorbachev assured the world that the memorandum facilitating the economic reform movement was being signed by all twelve republics, evincing their solidarity. He said that in the Soviet Parliament, 284 were for signing the treaty, only 30 against. "We are beginning to make steps in the marketplace . . . speeding up the process." He added that there were many complex decisions to be made yet.[56]

As the peace conference progressed, the world marveled as once more television presented one of the most meaningful events of these times, as delegates on both sides delivered their histories of the conflict and their visions of peace.

Touchingly, olive branches were offered by the Palestinians. Their goal is self-rule and statehood. The Israelis' goal is that they keep the land captured in the 1967 war. At this point, they refused to accept only limited Palestinian self-rule.

The hope was to keep them talking long enough to get them

past their antagonisms. Bush warned that there's a long way to go before we have agreement for peace.[57] Although Bush was saying that peace must come "from within," the differences seemed insurmountable. For the Arabs, peace was conditional on Israeli willingness to give up the captured territories. But Shamir said, "The issue is not territory but our existence."[58] Talks were held in Washington on December 11 to 13 with little progress but expressions of hope from both sides. For twenty years, Arabs had insisted that talks with Israel would have to be through international mediation. Now they agreed to speak directly, brokered by the United States and Russia. Palestinians pressed for U.S. intervention in order to realize concessions. Israelis saw personal contacts as basis for trust.[59] After six days of attempts to negotiate, marred by recriminations about terrorism on both sides, they acknowledged a temporary setback. Territorial issues were carried on not only between Israelis and Palestinians but also between Syria and Israel; among the Palestinians, Jordanians, and Israelis; between Lebanon and Israel.[60]

The new year started off on a sour note: Israel had decided to expel twelve Palestinian activists. Talks that were scheduled to resume in early January in Washington were delayed by Jordanian, Syrian, and Lebanese delegates in protest. The U.S. State Department sharply criticized Israel. Although Egyptian President Hosni Mubarak requested Israeli Prime Minister Yitzhak Shamir to overturn the expulsion order, he refused. The Palestinian Liberation Organization was considering a boycott.[61]

Shortly after, two right-wing parties in the Israeli government opposed the Arab-Israeli peace talks and withdrew, making early general elections necessary. The talks posed a mortal danger to Israel, said Science Minister Yuval Neeman, leader of Tehiya, who hoped American elections would produce leaders more favorable to Israel. They thought self-rule, agreed by both Palestinians and Israelis to be an interim settlement, will inevitably lead to a Palestinian state.[62]

In 1997, the talks between Israelis and Palestinians continued very much on the same level, with no resolution leading to real peace. It was Israel's Netanyahu who met with President Clinton, Palestine's Arafat, and Russia's Yeltsin. Because of the impasse over Israeli construction of new homes in Gaza, the Palestinians were again accused of terrorism. And because the Israeli police have often been abusive to Palestinian youth, the impasse remained. Therefore, by spring 1997, Clinton was advised to take a stronger stand than before, stronger than that of "catalyst."

The ongoing attempt over the years to make peace has exacted its price. Many lives have been lost in Palestine, on both sides. Anwar Sadat's widow, Jehan, interviewed by William Ruelmann, stated in December 1985 that, "My husband started the peace initiative and he paid his life for it." She added that "we still have relations with Israel." In spite of all the political differences, she has hope that there will be ultimate amity between Egypt and Israel. "As a Moslem, because I believe in faith in God . . . with God we will carry on. . . . It is the mission of everyone on earth."[63]

International terrorism held sway from 1973 to 1989 as the Iran-Iraq war went on for eight years, and the other radical Arab countries acted chiefly against their moderate brothers and Arabs friendly to the Israelis. The United States was determined to keep open the highly strategic passage through which oil and other commodities of the Gulf countries are transported to the rest of the world. This is the Strait of Hormuz, a narrow inlet leading to the Arabian Sea and thence the Indian Ocean. Then, as now, the United States was committed to keeping the stability of the Gulf countries.

As for our "good judgment" of which Cayce spoke, and wisdom to know how to deal with hostile elements, our leaders are often sorely challenged. A notorious example is the terrorism perpetrated by Libya's President Muammar Qaddafi in the 1980s, bent on destroying those persons with specific interests in the United States. In 1985, President Ronald Reagan held to a policy of restraint, even after Qaddafi was accused of harboring and possibly arming terrorists who attacked Rome and Vienna airports. Reagan used sanctions against Libya but with little change. Finally, he ordered the air raid on Tripoli and Benghazi. He was criticized, but when seven industrial democracies met in an economic summit in Tokyo a few weeks later, Reagan found he had their support together with strong support from Americans.

Israeli experts later stated that the air strike deterred international terrorism as a welcome trend. Certainly terrorism was markedly decreased, generally. We do not forget the loss of many innocent civilians, or the 250 marines killed when the U.S. Embassy in Beirut was bombed. Or Lieutenant Col. William R. Higgins, kidnapped and later hanged in early 1988 by a pro-Iranian group.

For the first time, terrorism came to America at the New York World Trade Center; we can never forget that, or the bombing in Oklahoma City with innocent men, women, and children dead or injured.

"NEGOTIATION, NOT INSURRECTION": DEMOCRACY WINS IN LATIN AMERICA

The seeking of democracy and peace in the southern regions of the Americas has been a study of conflict. Revolution in Nicaragua began in 1978 with the assassination of Joaquim Chamorro because he openly waged verbal warfare against the dictator Anastasio Somoza through his newspaper, *La Prenza.* The Sandinistas came to power in 1979, toppling the Somoza family, which had been in control since 1936. Daniel Ortega took power in 1985, his government ruled by hard-line Marxism.[64]

James Wallace points out that in late April 1985, after being refused help by the House, Ortega visited Moscow to seek aid from the Soviets, "which added weight to Reagan's arguments that Nicaragua already is a Soviet outpost on the mainland of the Western Hemisphere."[65]

Tom Wells reported that heavy fighting was taking place along the borders of Honduras and Nicaragua. Guerrillas seeking to topple the leftist Sandinista government in Managua were based in Honduras. There was fighting where Nicaraguan troops crossed into Costa Rica on May 31, 1985, and were beaten back.[66]

Since 1930 the United States promoted a "Good Neighbor

Policy'' in keeping friendly relations with Latin America. Much of international relations depended then, as now, on trade and the economic well being of all concerned. The Roosevelt administration opposed our intervention with Latin American affairs, but there was aggression by Rome and Berlin that was troubling because of the presence of many Germans and Italians in South America.[68]

Anastasio Somoza Debayle was the third member of the Somoza family to be president. In addition to his brutal treatment of his opponents, he made himself rich, acquiring a ''half-billion dollars worth of investments and 8,260 square miles of Nicaragua, while two hundred thousand peasants were landless.'' After he had Chamarro murdered, there followed three days during which the National Guard scourged five major cities, killing three thousand people.[69]

Not happy enough, Somoza ordered heavy shelling of civilian areas and the execution of suspected opponents, many of whom were youths. But his own supporters fled the country now, and he, too, took refuge in another dictatorship: Paraguay. There he was gunned down by three men said to be Argentines.[70]

The Nicaraguans united under the name *Sandinista*, a famed guerrilla leader of the 1930s. They were a strange mix of Marxists, Roman Catholics, and spiritist cults. Even nuns and priests supported them. In 1962 Vatican II initiated unprecedented reform for meeting social needs. Catholics developed a ''theology of liberation'', based on their new perspective of how to interpret the liberating teachings of Christ.[71]

The United States had renounced a policy of unilateral intervention in Central American affairs. But it helped create multilateral intervention through the Rio Pact of 1947 and the formation of the Organization of American States in 1948. By 1954 the United States decided that political control by the international communist movement was a threat to peace in the hemisphere and called for collective intervention. The OAS promoted a policy of intervention in cases of communist revolutionary threats. There were fears that the Cuban revolution would escalate throughout the other Latin American nations. It didn't happen.[72]

Tiny Nicaragua was a poor country under dictatorship for most of its history. It became a symbol, however, in the Catholic church for both progressives and conservatives because it was the center for struggle between Christianity and revolutionary politics.[73] "They saw no contradiction between being Christians and being revolutionaries," states Peter Winn. They were united in rebellion against the brutal Somoza dictatorship. When a coalition government was formed in 1979, priests were named to cabinet positions; others took over economic planning and a literacy program. But they soon saw their revolution as a "Marxist wolf in Christian sheep's clothing." Therefore, the Church could not support it; only a peace based on human rights and social justice would do.[74]

The U.S. Southern Command's task under General Fred Werner was to safeguard U.S. access to raw materials and energy resources, stated Tom Wells. He sought peaceful solutions and was sensitive to the poverty and victimization of the people there. He thought the drug cartels may have blocked democratic progress in Central and South America.[78]

Now the war between democracy and communism in Latin America brought efforts by its leaders to make peace. In 1985, when Ortega came to power, Belisario Betancur, president of Colombia, announced that work on a peace plan was in the final stages. He sought a team from eight nations—the Contadora—to oversee a peace pact. It consisted of Colombia, Venezuela, Mexico, Panama, Argentina, Brazil, Peru, and Uruguay.[76]

AID FROM THE SUPERPOWERS

Help was offered by both the United States and the Soviet Union; thus, communist influence contended with the growing trend toward democracy. In 1987 the United States sent Central American nations $196 million in military aid and $862.6 million in economic and humanitarian assistance. The refugee camp in Honduras was operated by the United Nations, putting the aid largely under the heading of "humanitarian.''[77] Honduras, poorest of the six Central American nations, harbored thousands who fled El Salvador and Guatemala. Twenty-six thousand Indian and non-Indian Nicaraguans lived in the camps. Seventy-five thousand Nicaraguans were under United Nations protection there. But in Nicaragua, prisoners were tortured. Her citizens feared to go home. Most refugees lived without hope.[78]

At best, life is harsh in impoverished countries of Central and South America, according to reports by Americans who have been there. There is typically one ten-by-twelve-foot hut to a family. Tropical disease, gynecological problems, rabies, tetanus, pneumonia, and diarrhea are common. The people lack fresh milk, meat, and produce. Water and firewood are rationed, and there is no sanitation. But it's better than a life of terror.

PRESIDENT OSCAR ARIAS' PEACE PLAN

President Oscar Arias of Costa Rica did not believe, however, in helping the Contras, whose counterattacks he said only proved to prolong the war. He hoped, instead, to bring about peaceful accord through negotiation among the nations.

In 1987 he introduced a historic Central American Peace Plan. Leaders of Costa Rica, El Salvador, Honduras, Guatemala, and Nicaragua signed it at Guatemala City, August 7, 1987. It ordered a cease-fire by the Sandinistas with the Contras, freedom of the press and other media, an end to political repression, and free democratic elections.[79]

President Reagan believed it was best to help the Contras, but at home, he was criticized for his stand and had little support from Congress. Meanwhile, the Sandinistas were getting help from Moscow. He termed support for the Contras partly a religious issue because there had been religious persecution by the Sandinistas.

But in March 1988, Arias persuaded the Marxist Sandinistas in Nicaragua and the Contras to keep a cease-fire indefinitely. Then he organized negotiations for peace.

For his ongoing work for peace accord, he won the 1987 Nobel Peace Prize. He then criticized the United States for its Contra aid, including nonmilitary. At a summit held in San José, Costa Rica, on January 15, 1988, the five Central American presidents met to decide whether the failing peace initiative should continue. Arias told the group, "If we don't have the capacity to reach this day the agreements our people demand of us, there is much to lose and nothing to gain."[80]

It seemed, however, that success would depend on the combination of Arias's insistence on diplomacy and Reagan's insistence on material supplies, including bullets.

THE REAGAN DOCTRINE

Centerpiece for United States action was established by law as the Reagan Doctrine. In June 1988, Senator Paul Trible introduced the Freedom Fighter Assistance Act: "A bill to ensure the provision of effective military and economic assistance to anti-Communist freedom fighter movements, to prohibit certain direct and indirect assistance to Communist countries."

It was to "promote freedom in the world by writing the Reagan doctrine into law." It "authorized economic and military assistance to anti-Communist insurgent movements that are indigenous and that respect human rights. This measure also makes it more difficult for any President to give assistance to Communist governments," authorizing the secretary of defense and the secretary of state "to provide assistance—military, humanitarian, economic, and political—to freedom fighter movements and to promote democratic training programs and democratic institution building. Such assistance can only be given to those movements that are indigenous, anti-Communist, and that respect human rights."[81]

It urged the president to suspend trade and diplomatic relations with governments in whose countries the United States was aiding an insurgent movement. It covered human rights practices accounting by those groups receiving United States aid and the presence of Soviet and Eastern bloc advisers in foreign countries and the amount of Soviet and Eastern bloc aid they receive; stricter standards in financial credits to a communist government.[82]

Mr. President, the Reagan doctrine works. By providing assistance to freedom fighters, America has moved country after country closer to freedom. We have brought hope to distant lands where Communist rule had all but extinguished hope . . .

The Soviets are now withdrawing their military forces from Afghanistan. The Sandinista government in Nicaragua has signed a peace accord and has taken halting steps toward a freer society and negotiated peace. In Angola, the Communist government has announced a willingness to send home 35,000 Cuban troops. The Communist government in Cambodia has agreed to direct talks with its opponents. Our purpose is to insure that the Reagan doctrine lives on. America must stand with those people who are risking their lives throughout the world—from Afghanistan to Angola to Nicaragua—to defy Marxist aggression and to secure basic human rights. Our law should reflect what President Reagan has said to the world's freedom fighters: "America will support with moral and material assistance your right not just to fight and die for freedom, but to fight and win freedom."

Now if we are to assist freedom fighters abroad, we must ensure that we do not help the Communist government they are fighting. Too often the United States has found itself in this untenable position.

For the past 6 years, we have maintained diplomatic relations with the Sandinista regime, while aiding the Contras. We have repealed the ban on aid to Angola's rebels during the same period that our Export-Import Bank pumped $200 million in credits into the oil fields that sustain the Communist government.

Our Ex-Im Bank has given over $50 million in credits to finance Ethiopia's purchase of aircraft and its expansion of the Addis Hilton Hotel, during the same time that our citizens were paying to ease a famine which Ethiopia's Communist government helped to cause. And until 2 years ago, the Soviet puppet regime in Afghanistan enjoyed most-favored-nation trade status with the United States.

Enough is enough, Mr. President . . . [83]

Signing on with Trible were five Republican senators: Kansas's Robert Dole, North Carolina's Jesse Helms, Utah's Jake Garn, Idaho's Steve Symms, and South Carolina's Strom Thurmond.[84]

* * *

Nicaragua was so important to the United States that the Reagan administration challenged a congressional ban against supporting the Contras. To continue that support, the Reagan administration suffered scandal when it secretly and illegally sold arms to Iran in order to finance the Contras with the profits.

Despite Arias's objection to further aid, on October 1, 1988, Reagan signed into law a new $27 million six-month package for the Contras that called for aid for food, clothing, medical services, and shelter, with flexibility in how to distribute the money. It was to help in providing training camps and ammunition for the rebels.[85]

In 1987 the United States sent Central American nations $196 million in military aid and $862.6 million in economic and humanitarian assistance. The refugee camp was operated by the United Nations, putting the aid largely under the heading of "humanitarian."[87] In February 1988, President Reagan termed support for the Contras partly a religious issue because there had been religious persecution by the Sandinistas, persistent and often brutal for people of all faiths, those who proclaimed freedom in the context of the struggle in Latin America. Among them are the Central American leaders who sided with Arias.

In an interview with Tad Szulc, Arias pointed out that Costa Rica has the same social indicators today as Cuba, but without the *paredon* (execution wall) . . . without thousands of citizens in exile.''[88] He drew the line clearly as to which philosophy was conducive to the welfare of the people. Dictators achieve their power by rigging elections, assassination, allowing bribery and corruption to thrive, and using military might to control the dissenters. When the Fidel Castros, Anastasio Somozas, and Francois Duvaliers thrive, they may do so for a while, but they ultimately fall of their own weight.

Fidel Castro rose to power in 1953 when he organized

other young men who sought to counteract the corrupted rule of their time. Dictator Fulgencio Batista had disrupted free elections with a military coup. When he allowed all political prisoners to go free, among them was Castro, who landed an expedition on the eastern end of the island. It placed him at an advantage at a time when Batista was doomed by corruption and a debauched military. At first, Castro's own inclination to violence and absolute power was not recognized by the people who applauded him as a hero with promise to bring back democracy to Cuba. They found later that he used his heroic persona and charisma as a "weapon to crush his opponents." As he needed financial help for Cuba, he became dependent on the Soviet communists, to whom by the 1970s he owed $2 billion annually, to more than $5 billion.[89]

Since Columbus found these shores, Latin American countries have undergone wide contrasts in the kinds of government they attract. The difference in recent years has become sharply evident between the two extremes, as leaders have risen out of diverse leadership styles ranging from political integrity to political adventurism.

Tad Szulc interviewed Arias in Costa Rica in mid-1988. He wrote that Arias was the only mediator acceptable to all sides in the Central American conflicts. He brought about the first lasting cease-fire between the Sandinistas and United States-backed rebels. He led peace negotiations between the two hostile bands—"an event that was unthinkable even a few months earlier."[90] The talks bogged down because the Sandinistas and the *contras* could not agree on a political settlement. As a result of the Arias plan, the Nicaraguan battlefields were still silent that summer after seven years of war, except for scattered clashes, "but the civil war next door in El Salvador between the U.S.-supported government and Marxist guerrillas went on unabated . . ."[91]

Szulc states that Arias and his fellow Costa Ricans are vigorously pro-United States—possibly more so than most other Latin Americans.[92] Costa Rica is important to the United States, said Arias, because it is an example to other small nations of how well a small country can thrive and grow, free and secure, if its neighbors and the rest of the world will give it a chance.[93]

As reported on February 13, 1989: The presidents of five Central American countries are to begin a regional summit today that is described by their aides as a "showdown" with Nicaragua's Sandinista government. "The question is whether or not the Sandinistas are ready for immediate moves towards democratization," said an aide to the Costa Rican president. Aides to Arias said he believed that since the accord had removed the Contra threat, it was incumbent on Nicaragua to lead the way in compliance.[94]

Pressure was put by the Bush administration on the Sandinistas to keep their promises about political freedoms in the election due in February 1990. But by December 1989, flow of Soviet arms to leftists in Central America continued. Leftist guerrillas in El Salvador were presumed to be receiving aid from Cuba and Nicaragua. This was despite assurances from Moscow that it would use its influence to stop the flow. It was the "biggest obstacle" to an overall improvement in superpower relations, at the time of the Malta talks between Bush and Gorbachev.[95]

The ten-year-old communist Sandinista revolution ended in Nicaragua on April 25, 1990, with the upset victory of Violeta Chamorro over Daniel Ortega. She formed a coalition government.

However, the Sandinistas, who had been voted down in February, did not fully cooperate. Although she is defense minister, she had no staff. Instead, the Sandinista army chief Humberto Ortega had been given full power over the army. It had weakened the economy: The former government had used up all the nation's budget on cars, farms, houses, and trips abroad for officials, with added overexpenditures. Not surprising, whereas the Contras surrendered their weapons to the UN peacekeeping forces, the Sandinistas turned in few arms.[96]

By July 1990, Ortega proved he could not keep his promise: He kept President Chamorro from carrying out her benign plan to make permanent peace for her country. She found certain groups, such as the labor unions, influenced against her; the city's utilities were shut off. The police ignored her calls to bring about order. She knew the people wanted to keep trying to negotiate rather than continue to fight. They were tired of insurrection, tired of the old rule but encouraged by the meager steps that were leading to freedom. They were aided by the fall of communism around the world.

Typical and germane to the ideological chasm that divided the world, the democracy of El Salvador under President Alfredo Christiani was courted by both the U.S.- and the Russian-backed Marti National Liberation Front, led by President Alfredo Christiani. He was opposed by the democratic forces and was no longer backed by the Russians after the Soviet decline.

Finally, those oppressive leaders who had obstructed democracy and freedom by death and destruction found their influence no longer felt. When the showdowns came, by democratic processes, by the aid of friends, the people of South America and Central America, as elsewhere, found they could create their own autonomy.

Though not as visible as Gorbachev and Mandela, Americans like General Woerner and the Latin American leaders—followers of Oscar Arias Sanchez—who struggled to free their countries are surely among those Cayce said would "proclaim the day of freedom." As in Europe, Africa, and Asia, there were those in Latin America who proclaimed freedom in the midst of longtime Marxist ideology. They are the Central American leaders who sided with President Arias, heroes in the drive for freedom in the Americas.

In their roles in Europe and many third world countries, presidents of the United States—Carter, Reagan, and Bush—worked each from his own position and viewpoint to help win the war. The American General Woerner is a man who sought peaceful solutions for his Southern Command, who was sensitive to the poverty and victimization of the people there. As he observed, the drug cartels may have been blocking evolution to democratic government in Central and South America, and they still could be. Cayce seems to have seen an end to all wrong conditions: "For all stand as ONE before

Him. For the Lord is not a respecter of persons, and these things (oppression for many in the 1930s) cannot long exist" (3976-19).

Compounding the conditions of war and poverty in third world countries is the drug trade. It begins with the poor who can find no other means of making a living. In South America, farmers raise the native coca plant to sell to drug dealers, who make millions of dollars on the world market. It is a war between them and the authorities who try to keep drug dealers from coming into the United States across our southern borders, due to demand for drugs at all levels of society.

The drug trade is closely allied with terrorism, especially evident in South America. It has been connected with dictators of the past and those who still linger even after the democratization of many countries in Latin America in recent years. Drug cartels were believed to be used to topple the government of Colombia.[97]

The new president by the 1990s, César Gaviria, hoped to bring back the former criminal justice system that was destroyed by the drug barons. He planned to make judges and their families safe against terrorists in the drug war, to sequester them in high-security compounds using tribunals rather than lone judges in drug cases. Of the killing that claimed eleven thousand lives in 1989 alone by terrorists, he came to office declaring, "It is impossible to think of five more years like the last one."[98]

The powerful cartels were the Medellín, which is responsible for most of the murders; one in Cali; and perhaps another in Bogotá. The United States continued to cooperate with Colombia in its drug war, but it was considered an international issue. The European Community planned to lift all tariffs on Colombian tropical products, and a similar break was expected from Washington. Otherwise, without such help, "Colombia's new government may be forced to abandon the front lines of an unpopular war."

U.S. civilian helicopter pilots who were part of the antidrug effort at a Peruvian jungle base took part in firefight with guerrillas supporting coca growers. U.S. antidrug advisers moved into the new Peruvian jungle base in the upper Huallaga valley, source of the raw material for about half of the world's cocaine.

Colombia is reportedly responsible for 80 percent of the cocaine sent to the United States. The United States pledged $65 million in military aid and another $5 million to protect threatened judges there. Other Latin American countries are part of the cocaine trail to both U.S. users and those in Europe. They include Peru, the main supplier of coca to Colombian producers; Bolivia; and Ecuador, an important money-laundering center. Police estimated that up to $400 million was laundered or invested in Ecuador in 1989. The United States provides Ecuador with $1 million a year to help fight drugs.

In Latin America, not only drug trafficking has held back progress but "the economies are sagging and the voters are defecting. The average Latin is poorer now than he was in 1980. Most Latin governments have prescribed, with varying consistency, painful economic medicine. The voters are turning to left-wingers who promise sweeter drugs."[99]

The pursuit of peace and freedom in South and Central America is slow, despite the cold war thaw and Reagan's wise military stance. Years of dictatorship, which have been the norm, are difficult to overcome in the minds of the dictators and those who have lived in their shadow for generations.

In Paraguay, General Andrés Rodríguez, who led a bloody coup that ended the thirty-four-year reign of President Alfredo Stroessner, was considered by law enforcement authorities to be the country's number-one drug trafficker, according to a classified State Department report published February 5, 1989. Quick elections were planned after the coup. An estimated three hundred soldiers and police were killed. As Rodriguez was sworn in, he promised to make democracy and human rights a reality. There was a lack of demonstrations or euphoria, indicating the public's doubt that things would be any different.[100]

In Chile, General Augusto Pinochet was defeated at the polls in October 1988, ending a twenty-five-year-old dictatorship. He had seized power in a violent coup in 1973 and defied those who said a dictator never would submit to the free election process. His defeat paved the way for multiparty elections for president and a new congress. Yet, according to reports, he kept his constitution, which held him in office for seventeen more months.[101]

In Burma, a brave woman—Aung San Suu Kyi—led the National League for Democracy in nonviolent opposition to oppressive government there. Democratic forces overwhelmingly won in parliamentary elections in May 1990. As the daughter of Burmese independence hero Aung San, she insisted on nonviolence. In spite of the election, Burma's generals refused to let the party take power. Still under house arrest after two years, Aung San Suu Kyi had not seen her husband, Michael Aris, of England, a visiting professor at Harvard University in Cambridge, Massachusetts, or their two sons since Christmas 1989.

On October 14, 1991, she was awarded the Nobel Peace Prize.[102]

The economies of many Latin American countries suffered in the decade that led to political freedom. In 1989, typical was that of Argentina. President Carlos Menem found inflation at 200 percent and thousands out of work, leading to looting and food riots. He imposed austerity measures to stem inflation, which brought interest rates down to 15 percent. His personal troubles, which were considerable, he thought were "God's will." "When one has faith, he believes in God and these events should serve to strengthen the spirit."[103]

The United States had helped El Salvador along with many other nations, as the people of elected President Alfredo Christiani were gravely stricken in war against Marxist forces. In November 1989, aid was debated in Congress, but President Bush thought that El Salvador should not be further weakened by denying the Salvadorans help.[104] Two years later, a peace treaty was signed on January 16, 1992, ending twelve years of civil war. The country rejoiced in its new peace. The people who had fled began coming back right away to try to heal the wounds of the torture, bloodshed, and killing they had endured for so long. There was the risk that, just as in Haiti, there would be those trying to retain their former positions of self-serving power.

America's involvement in helping people everywhere free themselves from such power over their very lives has proved dramatically effective. Said Cayce, speaking for the time when Franklin D. Roosevelt dealt with the growing crisis in Europe in 1940, America's counsel should be that "all are brethren . . . : not merely as a pacifist attitude of peace at any cost, but rather as that of equity . . . brother as with brother . . ." (3976-20).

CHINA

Of China's future, Cayce stated in 1944 that China "will one day be the cradle of Christianity as applied in the lives of men. Yea, it is far off as man counts time, but only a day in the heart of God—for tomorrow China will awake. Let each and every soul as they come to those understandings do something, then, in his or her own heart" (3976-29).

It doesn't seem today as though China is ever likely to be the cradle of Christianity. She is persecuting thousands of Christians. Her leaders have outraged the free world by holding to communist ideology, which always negates the interests of the people when they defy the government. In spring 1989, thousands of pro-democracy student protesters were killed, jailed, or injured when police put down the demonstrators with tanks and guns. Many more students attending foreign universities refused to return to China.

It is a matter of fact that the young communists of Mao's day now have become the old communists, themselves challenged by the new generation that is critical of a government that tries to control them by force and ideology. China began in 1990 to end her traditional isolation by seeking to normalize relations with South Korea, Indonesia, Saudi Arabia, and Singapore—even Tibet, which had been taken over by China in the 1950s and put under martial law in 1989 because of anti-Chinese riots there. In the 1950s, China overran Tibet, destroying its temples and threatening the life of the Dalai Lama. In April 1997, the Dalai Lama, spiritual leader of Tibet, appeared on television to say in an interview that he was seeking dialogue and understanding with China.[105]

Communism's appeal in China was for much the same reason as that in Russia. Dr. A. K. Reischauer wrote that in Russia, the movement was led by the intelligentsia. In China, however, by the peasantry. Although the older generation still clung to glorification of China's past, the younger people of the mid-1900s had seen glimpses of the Western world and realized their backwardness. China's religions, especially Confucianism, had always kept their minds on the past and were geared to the privileged class.[106]

Today, however, we must deal with China and all other nations as they are now! Today, due to a lack of trust among us, nations including China and the United States continue to build up strong military defense. As diplomats and prime ministers, presidents and kings meet to offset the many differences between countries, as always they must trust each other. But is it enough to control the arms race?

Just how important arms control has become is chilling fare. States James Adams, many nations, both developed and undeveloped, are still producing, selling, and buying arms of all kinds—and the chemical warfare industry is not far behind. Arms suppliers, says Adams, include, besides the United States, Europe, Britain, France, West Germany, Latin America, South Africa, China. They find ready markets in the Middle East, the largest buyer being Saudi Arabia. Chemical weapons produced in Libya have involved Japanese and West German firms. Adams declares that the real challenge facing the world in the aftermath of the Gulf War and the cold war is how to break out of the arms cycle that puts ever more advanced weapons into circulation.[107]

Adams continues: "While the exact terms of President George Bush's new world order have never been articulated, the major Western allies have understood the phrase to mean that the United States will lead the way in breaking out of the arms race that has dominated so much of international trade since the end of the Second World War. Yet already the focus of the struggle in the arms race is once again on the competition for sales and not on the fight to reduce the traffic.

If much more time is allowed to pass, it will be clear that national security policy in the Bush administration is still being dictated by the traditional unholy trinity of defense-industry lobbyists, die-hards in the Pentagon, and State Department policy makers who see arms as a tool of foreign policy."[108]

In early 1997, seventy-five nations including the United States ratified a treaty banning chemical weapons around the globe, putting pressure on renegade nations producing poison gas.

Against the background of worldwide arms trade of which Adams spoke, the search for peace was heightened in the Middle East in spring 1997, when Islamic extremists made more suicide bombings and Palestinian youth threw stones and bottles at Israeli troops. On March 21, three women in Tel Aviv were killed and others injured by Islamic Hamas bomb terrorists. It was the Jewish holiday of Purim.[109]

"There cannot be peace if this goes on," stated Prime Minister Benjamin Netanyahu. Yasser Arafat told a conference of Islamic leaders in Islamabad, Pakistan, that "Israel was bowing to extremist religious parties who we know are hostile to the peace process and to the rights of the Palestinian people." Talks were deadlocked. "It seems Netanyahu closed all doors tonight," said Saeb Erekat, a member of Arafat's cabinet.[110]

At a meeting in Washington on April 7, President Clinton and Prime Minister Netanyahu tried to find a peaceful solution. Clinton wanted to "explore any reasonable opportunity" to end the impasse. He urged the Palestinian leader to issue a statement of "zero tolerance" for terrorism.[111] Israelis demanded that the Palestinian authority led by Arafat crack down on the extremists. Israel's government blamed him directly for having given the go-ahead.

Netanyahu affirmed that new homes for Palestinians should be built in Jerusalem, to offset harsh criticism of Israel's new project of six thousand five hundred new Jewish housing units on the West Bank and Gaza. He pledged a pullback on the West Bank whether or not the Palestinians accepted his proposal for immediate negotiations over Jerusalem, refugees, and other tough issues.[112]

But Hassan Abdel-Rahman, chief Palestine Liberation Organization representative in Washington, stated that the Palestinian position remained: Talks would not be resumed until Israel stopped construction of the Har Homa project.[113]

Again, Hebron on the West Bank was the scene of "the worst violence in months." Netanyahu warned that one more major terrorist attack could scuttle the peace process.[114]

A few days later, gates of the West Bank and Gaza where twenty thousand Palestinians lived were opened to allow them to reach jobs in the Jewish state. Clashes continued between Palestinian rioters and Jewish settlers. Palestinian police kept the rioters from reaching Israeli-controlled downtown Hebron.[115]

Clashes continued in August. The peace process needed more time.

What must we think of the Israeli-Palestinian stand-off that goes on year after year? In November 1995, Israel's prime minister Yitzhak Rabin was assassinated by one of his own kind who acted from the old barbaric mindset of violence and hatred. Rabin had called for more tolerance from Israel by granting land for peace to the Palestinians. Nor do terrorist attacks by Arabs belong to this day of enlightenment. The explanation for their enmity goes back to the Biblical account that they descend from Abraham and two different women, and have been blood rivals ever since. Such rivalry after many generations has caused untold suffering among other cultures such as that in Bosnia and the wars between the Tutsis and the Hutus in Africa.

It's time for Israel and the Palestinians to put aside events several thousand years old, and move ahead to amity and peace.

8

"HE IS THY BROTHER!"

> . . . all ARE brethren. For these must bring and
> keep peace one with another. (3976-19, June 24,
> 1938)

EDGAR CAYCE ENJOYED WALKING along the boardwalk,
meeting people and talking with them. Many times tourists
he encountered had no idea who he was. He just liked people,
and they liked him back.

The broad promenade has been greatly beautified since
then, for the enjoyment of the thousands of families who
make it their vacation mecca. Although most of his readings
were given in his home on Fourteenth Street where congresses were held, some events were hosted by a few hotels.
Now replaced by high-rise modern structures, the old hotels,
as do the new ones, overlooked the ocean across broad lawns
and the boardwalk.

What is changing along with the Virginia Beach skyline is
racial attitudes, generally from confrontation to collaboration,
to opportunities for healing. The cooperation that both blacks
and whites have begun to exhibit in the 1980s and 1990s was
exactly what Cayce meant as he gave an especially significant
reading on ideals, principles, and purposes of America. In
imagination, we return to that day in 1939.

A hush fell on the group of people sitting around Edgar
Cayce as he prepared to give a reading for the Eighth Annual
A.R.E. Congress. The scene was the Warner Hotel, Virginia
Beach. It was June 16, and the world of turmoil and oppres-

sion seemed far away, as they contemplated the vast expanse of the Atlantic Ocean, or adjusted electric fans to augment ocean breezes.

"You will have before you the mass thought of the American nation," began Gertrude Cayce, conductor of the reading, "its ideals, principles and purposes. You will give at this time a discourse on the major problems which confront the American people, indicating their basic causes and suggesting what attitudes we may hold and procedures we may take individually and collectively to help correct and balance these conditions. You will answer the questions as I ask them."

Yes, we have those suggestions here as to problems which confront American people today, and what individuals or groups may do as respecting same.

The ideals, the purposes that called the nation into being are well. It might be answered by saying that there needs to be on the part of each man, each woman, the adhering to those principles that caused the formulating of the American thought.

Yet in the present there are seen many complex problems, many conditions that are at variance to the first cause or first principles; not only among groups and individuals in high places, both from the political and the economic situations, but the problems of labor-capital as well. All of these are problems in America today, as well as that of religious thought, religious principles, racial concern,—which are mass as well as individual and group thought. . . .

(3976-24)

"What should be our attitude toward the Negro, and how may we best work out the karma created in relations with him?"

The answer was: "He is thy brother! They that produced, they that brought servitude without thought or purpose have created that which they must meet within their own principles, their own selves. . . ."

"Is there," asked the conductor, Gertrude Cayce, "a racial or social problem facing America?"

"As indicated, these all depend upon the effort of individuals to all live as brothers one with another!"

The following pages continue this reading as it applies to prophecies and statements pertinent to those problems and conditions, particularly those relating to racial and social justice.

Cayce foresaw the racial revolution in America of the 1960s twenty-five years before it happened: "Unless there is brought about a more universal unity of purpose on the part of all, this will one day bring—here—in America—revolution!" (3976-24). The revolution that Cayce foretold did happen in 1964–1967 with much real bloodshed in the streets and much confusion as to who was behind it. So there were investigations. Taking a leading role was journalist Gary Allen, a graduate of Stanford University and one of the nation's top authorities on civil turmoil and the New Left.

Allen is author of *Communist Revolution in the Streets,* a book "highly praised as definitive on revolutionary tactics and strategies."

In a magazine article he said that, "In the long hot summer of 1967 a total of 110 American cities were subjected to severe rioting, looting, and civil insurrection. Within the last three years, such guerrilla warfare in American cities has killed 130, and injured 1,897; there have been 16,389 arrested at the scene of these holocausts, and the damage to property now approaches one *billion* dollars . . . we are now being asked to believe that what happened in Watts and Newark, Detroit and Chicago and Milwaukee and Kansas City, Nashville and Boston,—and in more than a hundred other American cities last year was a product of the terrible poverty in America."[1]

Rather, he said that the country then was enjoying a boom market for labor, with employment at an all-time high. Even during the Great Depression no such riots had occurred.[2]

In the article he documents many names, places, dates, and incidents attesting to wide influence of communism among leaders: from black militants to student organizations to white people known as communists. Caches of guns and ammunition were found in communist-front locations; blacks chanted slogans of hatred against "whitey," and riots were instigated. In his investigations, Allen was given assurances that the riots were not spontaneous but were related to the United States War on Poverty.[3]

That is, the billions of dollars allocated for that war were found to be *used to finance revolution.* To learn just where the money was coming from, Allen toured the nation extensively, interviewing law enforcement officers, civil officials, blacks, riot victims, and concerned citizens. The trail led always to the federal Office of Economic Opportunity, the general staff and paymaster for the War on Poverty. From all that we can learn it is Shriver's OEO that is being used to finance that revolution. As OEO Director R. Sargent Shriver put it, "You are in the midst of a revolution."[4]

Said Allen, it was the revolutionaries who profited. But behind them were theorists who provided the ideology: "Michael Harrington, the Trotskyite Communist whose book *The Other America* supplied the basis for the War on Poverty, "had in a speech to the Conference of Socialist Scholars September ninth and tenth, 1967, argued for 'evolutionary Marxism.' " Four days before the Watts uprising in 1965, Allen stated, phony "hearings" were held there that proved to be a mere cover for what amounted to a pep-rally for riot. . . . Stated an unnamed West coast Congressman: "I (have) little doubt but that the hearing is what triggered the riots in Watts . . . giving those people the idea that they were being mistreated was the spark that set off the blast."[5]

Knowledge of communist involvement with the War on Poverty has been submerged if not forgotten in today's swiftly paced events, but is worth being measured by what the Cayce readings had to say regarding American racial problems.

Cayce was characteristically sympathetic with any group that was a victim of human rights abuse. Hence we are moved by his championing both blacks and Jews, the Russian people of Stalin's tyranny, and any others who suffer at the hands of oppressors. He would today have had something to say no doubt about the Chinese leadership for which Tiananmen Square has become both scene and symbol of China's crime against its own. Nevertheless, it is the ideology of the misguided—Marxist communism—that has managed to create an environment of social unrest much worse than was the case in the first place. Cayce denied the wisdom of any "cult or ism." "Any movement that is other than that of the brotherhood of man and the Fatherhood of God is dangerous!" (3976-24)

In that same reading it was asked how fascism could be combated. "By that same purpose or principle as has been indicated," he replied. In this reading he had stated the principle: "If there is the turning of every man and woman to the thought of God, then we may solve every problem."

Of course, Cayce had in his many discourses given us the principles by which we could heal all our ills, but that seems to sum them up. In this reading he continued: ". . . social order, social justice shall be ever NOT of any individual, but as just indicated—that all are free, all are equal before God. The social order, the religious order, the economic order must all be for ONE God! For, know that the Lord thy God is ONE!"

Nor did Cayce mean to put down good leaders in their positions where they found themselves "by the grace of God."

"Is there a racial or social problem facing America?" was asked.

"As indicated, these all depend upon the effort of *individuals* to all live as brothers one with another!"

"How can it be met for the protection of democracy?" was then asked.

"Raise not democracy nor any other name above the brotherhood of man, the Fatherhood of God!" (3976-24)

It is noteworthy that Cayce phrased his prediction of revolution with the words "unless there is a more universal oneness of purpose on the part of all . . ." Was the country of one purpose in the 1960s? Or is it even now? Were there not many more divisions among us than before? We are allegedly "one nation under God," but dissention rules. Our leadership fails often to reflect our wishes; there are opposing forces. Surely communism might not have been able to woo the have-nots, both minorities and whites, in this country if there had been more compassion among those with power to heal economic ills.

As Cayce stated, "not as that of sometimes termed the Communist, the Bolshevistic, no. But freedom! Freedom!" He made it clear that communism was *not* the answer to economic, political, or social problems.

In 1942 he was asked for "the basic principles upon which constructive attitudes may be based on economic inequalities of nations." These are all answered, he replied, "in that question asked, 'Art thou the Christ, or must we look for another?' What was the answer? Not 'Yes, I am he that ye announced some three and a half years ago at Jordan.' No. 'Tell him the sick are healed, the blind see—' This is the answer for meeting EVERY problem, every question as to the economic condition of the nations. For He gave, 'Let him that hath two coats give one to another. Let him that is forced to do this or that go the whole length.' These are the basic principles upon which world order, world economic and social relations may be established, manifested among men" (2936-27).

Americans understand generosity. Giving to those less fortunate than ourselves has been a characteristic we may be proud of. Such attitudes of helpfulness and sacrifice are based on the biblical principles Cayce saw as practical everywhere.

But because there still is division among Americans in attitudes toward minorities, whether Indians, Asians, Vietnamese, Hispanics, because some Americans "don't like having them here" to compete for jobs, housing, educational advantages, we must deal with our own failure to prove our brotherhood.

So, whether against these, or blacks, in some parts of the world, racism dies hard. Why? We forget that the white race is not the only one to have discovered God or evolved by our long experience over millennia. We can't deny that the five races are equal to each other in their common spiritual origin.

No race has more access to that source than any other, for, unlike man, it allows no racial barriers.

To find political and economic strength, the various races must work within their own ranks to demand rights in the nations where they live. They therefore organize. Such is the Continental Encounters of Indigenous Peoples. In 1992 they met in Guatemala to plan Indians' response to the celebrations of the five hundredth anniversary of Christopher Columbus's voyage to the Americas. But land rights and preservation of Indian culture were addressed as well. More than 200,000 people joined the conference to demonstrate for native rights in Guatemala, despite fear of government reprisals. They planned to meet again in Nicaragua.[6]

However, they feared that if they worked with the Roman Catholic church and other non-Indian organizations, their needs would be ignored.[7]

In the United States, the Pueblo Indians have lived in our far West for at least eight hundred years, perhaps longer. In the West Indies, native people were put to forced labor by the Spanish and died out. The Plains Indians suffered starvation because in the nineteenth century their food supply was depleted by the white man. "Still others like the Carib and a good part of the Algonkin (as in our day many of the Polynesians) were destroyed by the religion and vices and diseases of white men who wished them well. . . . Anthropologists have ascertained that if we wish to conserve a people of lower culture, we must respect their religion and folkways, and not attempt to clothe their bodies or dethrone their gods. . . ."[8]

According to new archaeological discoveries, probably the Pueblos have lived in our western region much longer than eight hundred years. Other tribes lived throughout the continent with relative peace among themselves and would have lived accordingly with the white man as well. But in the American wilderness of the late eighteenth century, the gods of the Indians weren't dethroned. Instead, the Indians were caught up between the American conflict with Britain, choosing to be on the side of the British. At the Battle of the Fallen Timbers, at Fort Defiance in Ohio, several thousand Indians were defeated, suffering loss of life, and scattered in less than forty minutes.[9]

But the ultimate solution to the Indian "problem" was "the removal of all Indian tribes to the Far West, when, between 1829 and 1837, ninety-four Indian treaties were concluded, several million acres relinquished, and many thousand redskins more or less forcibly transferred to the trans-Mississippi West." Now in the Missouri Territory, the Indians underwent famine. The starving Indians were pursued by the Illinois militia into Wisconsin. Indians were massacred, including women and children.[10]

The difference between the Indian experience and the black experience is obvious. The Indians were early shuttled away onto reservations where they could never enjoy the privileges of the rest of the American culture. The blacks were enslaved but found the advantages of freedom when it finally came— freedom to be educated and take their part in the system. The difference has been the important factor of economics. The Indians remain poor; the blacks have a high percentage of professionals who are financially well off. As for their gods, the Indians hold to their ancient beliefs in the spirit world in nature, as real to them as any other great religion is to its adherents. The blacks hold to the Christian belief. To those who care, it is the same God we all worship.

AN EXPERIMENT OF THE SPIRIT

Sadly, in spite of the progress made, racial tensions still take violent form. Today, experts are reported seeing a rise in racism across the United States. It is increasingly evident in other countries. Unfortunately, racial incidents are occurring throughout the nation. Gangs of black teenage boys attack white people; individual incidents between teenage boys are less defined as racial.

It is most prevalent among the young, who are beleaguered by the code of the streets in big cities. They strive to deal with not only racial prejudice but also with the need to find their own reasons for living. As are all young people, young blacks are more motivated by their peers than they are by adult society. So they apparently conclude that in order to deal with their problems, they should confront the people who represent to them all their inner anger, confusion, and hatred.

But there are ways to prevent further racial conflict, as the people of Virginia Beach learned in 1990.

Attracting national attention were the Labor Day riots of 1989 in Virginia Beach. Thousands of black college students descended on the family resort city for their annual "Greekfest" celebration, which turned into a weekend of terror in the streets. The celebration first became ugly as some black youths smashed store windows and looted merchandise, damaging city property as well. Police were called on, and as the violence continued, strong police action was required. The National Guard was called in to help. Thousands of dollars were lost by Beach businesspeople.

Neither residents nor tourists could walk the streets because of the roaming visitors who destroyed hotel property and small business stores. Virginia Beach residents living near the "strip" reported watching as they approached in the dark, hearing them trashing businesses. Few assaults were by whites attacking blacks.

Beach leaders determined to avoid a repetition of the 1989 riots. To plan for the expected crowds in 1990, a summit was held of about seventy black students and local civic, police, and business leaders—the Interracial Business and Civic Coalition. The group met weekly thereafter with the Labor Day Community Coordination Committee for candid discussion and debate toward a peaceful "Laborfest" 1990. Leaders and students pledged to work together for its success in the years ahead. They planned attractive entertainment for the droves of students who were expected to be checking in at Virginia Beach hotels, then taking to the streets and boardwalk. They would help the citizens to make them welcome.

But beginning in April 1990, bands of South Hampton Roads black teens assaulted groups of whites. A curfew helped keep them off the streets.

Officials of the National Association for the Advancement of Colored People deplored the gang assaults and led in persuading Virginia Beach blacks to help solve the problem. Leaders of Hampton Roads chapters urged the Virginia Beach City Council to form a permanent human relations commission to bring about better race relations. They asked the U.S. attorney to prosecute blacks and whites who are caught provoking racial confrontations at the Oceanfront.

In late June 1990, the black clergy entered with their "God Squad," working with Virginia Beach police as chaplains. They had been trained by the Rev. Larry Edwards, of Daytona Beach, who had been successful in bringing resolution to similar situations in that city. A number of black police officers joined them from the National Black Police Association in Washington, D.C., Maryland, and Virginia. Samuel Dewitt Proctor, minister of a Baptist church in New York City and professor emeritus at Rutgers University, pointed out that spiritual values and prayer were needed to meet racial conflicts.

Although the city had provided concerts and had gone out of its way to make the weekend a happy one for everybody, thousands of blacks went to other places. Only a relatively small number showed up for the concerts staged in Redwing Park. The city lost money, as did shopkeepers, hotels, and restaurants. However, peaceful water battles and dancing in the streets took the place of looting and assaults.

The NAACP expressed concern that the violence threatened to drive a wedge between blacks and whites. Officials of Hampton Roads chapters urged the Virginia Beach City Council to form a permanent human relations commission to improve the city's racial climate. That was heartily accepted by the council, which then asked the U.S. attorney to prosecute blacks and whites caught stirring up racial conflict.

Mayor Meyera Oberndorf said the success of 1990 Laborfest was an important social experiment for the country. She added that its success was not measured in money, but in creating better human relations.[11]

Along with all the progress, there still remains racial unrest throughout the world, and freedom is not complete. Differences of skin color, or even language and ethnic differences, divide us because we cannot accept them. We are blind to the real person we see before us. When I see a person, whether black, white, or of whatever makes us "different," I look behind the physical and cultural aspects and try to see, instead, that spark of divinity that is in each one of us. That is, we sense more than physical attributes in others as we encounter them. We receive impressions and even thoughts more than spoken words, at times. It's the inner person that speaks louder than we might expect. But we're learning that it's good to get together and talk.

What has been the case in the past? Hostility between the races, the fear it creates, where there should be the love and brotherhood all major religions espouse but often forget. It's the emotions of hatred and fear that fuel racial violence. We can't be at peace when the hearts rage, however silently, when some people believe in their superiority over the rest of mankind. Peace can come to us only when the vibrations of anger and hate are transmuted to vibrations of love.

In recent years, due to materialistic influences, many people have grown more secular and fail to look behind the events in our lives for clues as to meaning and right living. At the time I met Edgar Cayce, years ago, I didn't understand much of what I read in the Bible. I began studying his readings and found assurance that religious concepts are the answer to our social problems. The amazing, unprecedented events of recent decades throughout the world speak of help from a higher Source, of the timing at work in world events, cosmic cause and effect as opposed to coincidence.

I believe that His spirit is moving in the major political, economic, and racial changes we are witnessing as we enter the third millennium after centuries of little progress. It is the timing that intrigues us: the beginning of the Aquarian Age of brotherhood and a new order of conditions not before thought would come about. Not only world government leaders but leaders at every level are the instruments of that power at work: those enlightened leaders raised for a purpose. They must contend, however, with the forces of darkness among us that cause the havoc we see.

*   *   *

When today's white Americans are confronted with expo-
nents of bigotry, they can express deep outrage. On *Donahue*
on June 6, 1990, were two members of the Ku Klux Klan,
one hooded, the other wearing a T-shirt depicting approval of
Martin Luther King's assassination. Alongside these guests
was a black minister of the gospel. They had it out, in verbal
confrontation, right there, and who was being cheered by the
mostly white audience? The black man. When the robed
Klansman claimed—and he claimed it with great belliger-
ency—that the Klan stood for "the love of Jesus Christ" in
their attitude toward blacks and Jews, the audience laughed
him down.

"Why," asked one young white man from the audience,
"can't we all live in peace? Why do you people have to make
trouble?"[12]

It was the question of the ages.

As Cayce advised when asked about racial tensions, we
should "do something about it." There have been many
movements, great and small, on the part of white people in
America, and in South Africa as well, who have made justice
an issue and then found ways to do something about the injustice they found in their cultures.

After Martin Luther King, Jr.'s assassination, there was fear
and anger. In a grassroots movement, some white women in
the South collected in small groups to meet with black women
in an attempt to bridge the gap that had existed for so long.
The attempts were awkward and tentative, as I found in joining just such a project in my Virginia Beach neighborhood.
But they were better than no attempt at all.

We collected in twos and threes, greeting one another as
we entered Wycliffe Presbyterian Church in Virginia Beach.
Fifteen of the group of forty were black. They came from
various churches and backgrounds.

One of the leaders, a white woman, explained that the
movement began "when a group of girls got together after
the death of Martin Luther King to try to do something" to
alleviate tension between black and white people. "It just
seemed to happen," she said, and "each two in the little

group interested two more and they began meeting in their homes to talk." A mature, soft-spoken black woman with great dignity then said that the movement had as its purpose "to bring about understanding between the two races. "The death of Martin Luther King caused a lot of violence and if there had been an understanding on the part of our people, of the white society, the looting and other violence would not have happened." She expressed concern "that the extreme militants such as Carmichael will influence our youngsters." She pointed out that if the movement could spread, and there was a mutual interchange of ideas and goodwill between the women of both races, "we would know how to brief them so that they would not follow advocators of crime. If they understood that it is for the human race that both races are working, they would not be led into wrongdoing." She added, "I'm not worried about myself. I'm worried about the youngsters."

Another black woman, the wife of a Norfolk State University professor, said, "We Negroes moved into a neighborhood and found that white neighbors didn't come to visit. We've been called names, and we had to face the question, 'Should we get angry?' We found that children can play together better than adults, and with no color consciousness. When they don't, it's because the parents tell them."

Although she lived in a mixed neighborhood, most of the people at the meeting were from segregated areas.

Halting questions came from the floor, long-cherished misconceptions were clarified in exchanges marked by genuine, honest, and mutual respect. Stated a white woman, "We [black and white women] have been meeting in different homes and have been discussing the problems and have found we have no problems—the problems are all on the outside. . . ." We had to agree that problems are created by superficial attitudes about color of skin, not considering the quality of heart and mind within.

In 1977, there appeared a book by John Howard Griffin, a record of his personal experience: that of a white journalist who changed his skin color to black in order to experience firsthand the life of blacks in the Deep South. It was 1959, a time in which black anger was brewing against white oppression that was more blatant than any white people who were not a part of it could have known. Because he was taken as black by dint of his excellent disguise, he was able to mingle among "Negroes," as the term was still used then. He suffered the humiliating arrogance of white supremacists, the poverty, the denial of work because of his color. He found black friends who were kind to him as they were to each other, in a world vastly alien to that of the white man in America.

Griffin lived for six weeks in the climate of America's own apartheid: the white man's ugliness, from lynchings that went unpunished to petty denial of a drink of water at a cafe. It went along with the face white people reserved only for blacks, in that time and place, at least: the "hate look" that withered the soul. He was appalled at the hatred and prejudice white people in the south heaped upon blacks. Sick at heart, following his ordeal as a black man, Griffin was unwilling any longer to live in the degrading conditions he had experienced. He changed his skin color back to white.[13]

He visited briefly the campus of Tuskegee University in Alabama. As the guest of a Trappist monastery near Atlanta he found genuine love of God and fellowman. He welcomed the peace and healing of chapel prayer services.

Among other disciplines, Griffin had studied philosophy with the Dominicans in Paris under the guidance of Jacques Maritain. He quotes Maritain's *Scholasticism and Politics*, in which he found an answer to the enigma of the religiosity of racists: "God is invoked . . . and He is invoked against the God of the Spirit, of intelligence and love—excluding and hating this God. What an extraordinary spiritual phenomenon this is: people believe in God and yet do not know God. The idea of God is affirmed and at the same time disfigured and perverted."[14]

We compare that with Cayce, who, as we have quoted in Chapter One, stated, "He that saith he loveth God and seeth his neighbor in need of food or a coat and saith 'Go in peace—God be with thee' and does nothing about same, is a liar and a thief, wherever he may be; is false to self and will one day create those things that will bring discontent and disputation in the earth" (3976-28).

Discontent and disputation have indeed been created in the earth, as history has shown, as Cayce warned in our time.

However, blacks have been denied the very *means* for material well-being: freedom of equal opportunity, and with it, human dignity. Cayce spoke in this reading of the "soul life" of a nation that must be founded upon fundamental principles if it is to be true to that which is the birthright of every soul: to pursue as an individual the right "to manifest that (which) it would worship in its Creator." When men deprive others of that birthright, to live their life in freedom according to their concept of God, there arises "fruits of the evil influences that are in the earth, such as hate, jealousy, avarice. These make for the creating of those conditions in all walks of life for power, for position, for the love of money. . . ."

Christians everywhere pray to God for peace. But Cayce reminded those seeking the way to peace in 1942: "Ye cannot pray 'Peace-Peace' when there is no peace in thine own heart and soul! but by knowing (for His Spirit answers with thy Spirit) that each day, each person ye meet is GLAD that you are alive! Glad that you have come in touch with them; for you have brought—and bring—hope to their lives, just in the passing!" (3976-27)

> . . . Only as ye use that birthright, that purpose, that WILL within thine own consciousness to do justice, to do right, to love good, to eschew evil, may ye as individuals, as a group, as a nation, stand between the living and the dead—and stay the sin that maketh man make war—of any nature—against his brother.
>
> Thou art thy brother's keeper! Act that in thine own heart. Who is thy brother? 'Who is my mother? They that do the will of the Father, the same is my mother, my sister, my brother.'

"Who is the representative of the Father in the earth?" Cayce asked in the Depression year of 1933.

Hath not He committed unto mankind the keeping of his
brother? Hast thou answered that question that has been
of old in thine experience—"Am I my brother's keeper?"
The answer that should ring in the heart and soul of every
individual is: "Know ye not that the blood of your brother
crieth unto me from the ground!"

So, in the experience of those that have sent and made
the conditions are greed, selfishness; that has been practiced in the minds, in the lives, in the experience of the
nation. Think not any soul, 'Yea, that is true for the other
fellow. But it applies to Jim, to Tom, to those in ordinary
walks of life, to those who have been given those powers
in high places, those that have wealth about them; *they*
are the oppressors; yea, look within thine own heart! Hast
thou not practiced the same? For, as it has been given,
'Yea, though there be only ten just men, they may save
the city; they may save the nation; they may save the
world' if they will but *practice* in their daily experience
that which has been the command from the first: "Thou
shalt love the Lord thy God with all thine heart, and thy
neighbor as thyself."

(3976-14)

In his book, Griffin has contributed to the white community
everywhere the gift of rare insight into such degradation in a
nation that prides itself on equality and fair play. The book
reflects conditions that were to change a few years later with
the civil rights revolution that occurred in the late 1960s.

The Thirteenth Amendment of 1865 ended slavery and in-
voluntary servitude in the United States. But after Reconstruction in much of the Old South, laws were passed that got
around the Constitution, that actually bound blacks to white
domination. They were not allowed to hold jobs, to be educated, or to be free to walk the streets without first receiving
permission. Public facilities were excluded to them. They
were "kept in their place" by unlawful lynchings, by denial
of jobs based solely on color, by segregation.

Griffin, who spoke of his own family with pride, saw the
plight of black children who were, like children everywhere,

full of promise and hope, doomed to a life of poverty and hopelessness. Their freedom was the goal of Reverend King and the many others who conducted the marches, the sit-ins, the peaceful demonstrations, vowing to overcome the barriers to their God-given right to be free—"some day."

Since Griffin's report on civil rights in the South of 1959, much improvement has been realized. States sociologist Reynolds Farley: "For seventy years following the Civil War, blacks were concentrated in the rural South, where they were politically and economically powerless. Demographic changes in the 1940's and 1950's—especially the black migration to cities in the North and West—and the civil rights laws of the 1960's made blacks an important force in the political arena. Black voters increasingly influence elections, and the number of black officeholders continues to rise. . . ."[15]

In 1965 the Voting Rights Act allowed all southern blacks to vote. By that time, blacks had become more educated due to more and better schools. By the 1970s "the racial discrepancy in enrollment through the high school ages disappeared." Farley quotes President Johnson: "Freedom is not enough. You do not wipe away the scars of centuries by saying: 'Now you are free . . .' You do not take a person who, for years, has been hobbled by chains and liberate him, bring him up to the starting line of a race" and then tell him he is free to compete with all the others and still believe you are fair. . . ."[16]

In spite of his report of undeniable progress, Farley's research had ambiguous results in answering the question of whether there has occurred a narrowing of the gap between the two races. He finds progress in the earnings of workers. Occupations of employed workers have become better in prestige as well as income. In education, racial differences in both secondary and college schooling have decreased. However, in 1980, about 85 percent of white youth but only 70 percent of blacks had finished high school.[17]

In his "scorecard" at the end of the book, Farley reiterates that three different opinions surfaced in his extensive survey. Optimists think that racial progress has been great, that the practice of discrimination has declined or even been elimi-nated, and that skin color now has little to do with any phase of black experience. Pessimists consider many changes to be superficial and progress minimal. A third group thinks "blacks are increasingly polarized into a successful elite group and a downtrodden underclass."[18]

As late as 1985, opinion in the United States and throughout the world brought demonstrations by pressure groups not only against apartheid in South Africa but in the United States as well. A key issue was housing for blacks, notoriously inad-equate in America's Deep South especially, but just as dismal in the cities' ghettos throughout the nation. Much has been said regarding white racism, but the truth is, blacks have shown their own brand of racism in retaliation to historic human rights violations. In an epilogue to his book, Griffin says, "On the streets young black men would call out, 'Take ten!' to one another. Whites thought they were talking about a ten-minute coffee break. What they were really saying was that this country was moving toward the destruction of black people, and since the proportion was ten whites to every black, then black men should take ten white lives for every black life taken by white men."[19]

Even today, some blacks assume that the Confederate flag denotes the owner as a white supremacist.

Cayce had much to say in other readings about the power of thought and how it influences our destinies for good or ill. He said that the "power of thought is created by the very mass of the thought itself" and that the power of many minds concentrated on the problems actually makes them worse. Conversely, the power of prayer and positive thinking throughout a large number of people, anywhere, has its influence for untold good.

"Yet, as we find, if there is the turning of every man and woman to the thought of God, then we may solve every prob-lem. For it is not by mere thought, not by any activity other than the moving force within each entity, each body; and when more of patience, more tolerance, more thought of others is advanced and kept in the heart of the individual, this lends that power, that influence, that force for good'' (3976-24). He then said, ''there is the need more for world thought, for every soul turning to the power within, and giving GOD a chance with their lives, their purposes, their desires one with His!''

He added that man has use of that power for destruction as man himself gives it power.

> But just as has been given of old, ONE with the strength, the power of the Lord, may put the thousands to flight.
>   Then it behooves EACH soul—here, everywhere—to seek more and more for the strength, the direction, the might of that promise in, 'If ye will call, I will hear.'
>
>   (3976-24)

In foretelling the turmoils of this century, strife between capital and labor, and the division of America before the third of the presidents who would not live through his office—a mob rule—he advised that people not look to their own strength alone but to meet the troubles in such a way that there would be an awakening to the principles the nation was founded upon.

The events he spoke of in June 1939 did happen in the 1960s—the troubles caused by division between blacks and whites despite peaceful demonstrations for human rights. Troubles were compounded by the communist influence in America, by assassinations of the two Kennedys, and that of the Reverend King, inflaming the emotions of both races.

Said Cayce, the problems political, economic, religious, racial, were due to conditions ''at variance to the first cause or first principles.'' They were exacerbated by negative mass, individual, and group thought.

''That such is, and to be, a part of the experience of America is because of unbelief!'' (3976-24)

In our increasingly secularized society, some church leaders have pointed out that there has been rule more by unbelief, rather than belief, in the laws and principles this nation was founded on. Over the decades, have we not witnessed those beliefs give way to pseudosophisticated cant of those who say they are "outdated"? "Irrelevant to the modern world"? There have been fewer and fewer voices to champion belief in the ageless wisdom handed down by word of mouth and by Scripture.

Evidently, Cayce's readings have been given us for this very age, to remind us of the need we have for a return to our belief. It was in this context: belief in the power for great change a person or a nation is afforded in returning to God and His principles. In this context, Cayce approached all problems, international or personal.

The World Affairs readings we quoted have dealt mainly with the worldview. However, thousands of readings gave help for individual seekers, based on the same principles. It was, after all, he said, the individual who is the determining factor in all events, whether in financial situations, policy among nations, religious disputes, or race relations.

So it was not ritual that was needed, "or this form or the other, for any given peoples or any nation, but rather that the individuals in each nation, EVERYWHERE, are to turn again TO the God of the fathers "and not in self-indulgence, self-aggrandizement, but more self-effacement" (3976-24).

Obviously, there are extreme and complex sides to the acounts of race relations. As we have stated, Gary Allen stressed the prosperity America was experiencing in the early 1960s, suggesting that there could be no real reason for riots except inflammatory rhetoric of communists of both races. Griffin said that white and black alike were subject to reprisals if they spoke out against injustice against blacks and feared above all the character assassination for those standing up for civil rights. In a word, he had lived as a black man and saw reason enough from living the experience of being black.

As was Gary Allen's exposé of communist agitation in the 1960s, Griffin's depiction of conditions in the Deep South was like holding up a mirror to the things white Americans would just as soon not look at. This was much-needed reporting—as is the book on South Africa by Richard Manning, *They Cannot Kill Us All*. Each has brought out the truth as fairly and as accurately as was possible, reported from incontestable sources.

HUMAN RIGHTS FOR ALL

There have been still different viewpoints from government. Under President Carter, one of the major cornerstones of U.S. foreign policy was human rights, with denunciations of nations that were violating those basic rights. Not only South Africa but also Israel, Iran, and the Soviet Union were condemned, along with South American countries. Critics of this policy held, however, that such condemnation would alienate America's political friends. Disagreement among U.S. leaders was particularly evident regarding El Salvador and Nicaragua.[20]

No direct intervention was called for. Under Reagan, the policy of "constructive engagement" toward South Africa was expressed by withholding sanctions, despite growing demand by many, including South African blacks who were increasing their fight for liberation.[21]

In a pluralistic society such as the United States, no one group rules, but the nation's mores are reflected in its representatives and the laws they make. At times the influence of American ideals of justice and equality for all is compromised. Such problems as housing for the poor and discrimination against American minorities have in recent years been addressed. The government also must deal with the growing Hispanic population, which is reported to be rapidly approaching that of the black population. Issues of education, social services, and employment are added to problems of poverty and racism.[22]

Many minorities without early privileges in youth have been winners. They might have had parents who worked hard and raised them with "tough love" to excel. They might have had no father or mother, or were raised by grandparents. Others might have been given no education at all but became outstanding citizens. Those who earn an education rise to become professional doctors and lawyers, businesspeople, educators, by scholarships or sheer stamina. These self-made giants are admired, or should be, because there was something in them that urged them forward out of poverty and hopelessness. Such self-reliance is the stuff many minorities are showing today. It has been the norm for immigrants of the past: the Horatio Alger story.

Not all American Indians live on reservations, but they suffer the white man's callous disregard for their ancestry. It is their custom, however, to conduct sacred ceremonies in appropriate secluded forest settings for re-burial of the skeletal remains of their forebears, which were excavated at construction and archeological sites and kept in cardboard boxes by official state custodians.[22] The sacred ceremony they conduct means much to them because their ancestors are finally buried with dignity. It is generally known that the bones of Indians found in fields and woodlands where they were killed in battle or died from other causes have been bought and sold on the market.

This points up the mostly shabby treatment of Indians in America since the white man first stepped ashore. The long history of keeping American Indians on reservations and denying them the rights other Americans enjoy, is well-known and deplored by fair-minded Americans. Yet the rich heritage of native Indian belief remains. We are aware of it throughout the country in many ways, particularly in the sacred sites of the Midwest and Far West still honored and visited by people of all faiths.

Edgar Cayce advised that all humans seek to know God better through working with nature. The Indians have understood that, perhaps since the time of Atlantis.

The Cayce concepts of our divine affinity to the natural world were shared with visitors from throughout the world in October 1998, when A.R.E. cosponsored "A Gathering of Indigenous Peoples" including native Americans and other nonindigenous spiritual groups. They met to share ancient wisdom to encourage the healing of humankind and the nourishment and survival of Mother Earth. Cosponsors were the Institute of Global Education and Radio for Peace International, in partnership with many indigenous nations and Native American tribes representing every part of the world. A central feature was the "Mending of the Hoop of All Nations," ritual led by Dr. Arvol Looking Horse, who is the nineteenth-generation Keeper of the Sacred Buffalo Calf Pipe of the Lakota nation.

America is richer for the Indians and their spirituality. They have honored the Great Father by keeping their ceremonies and their sacred lands from desecration. We can learn much from them as they meet with us and share their special knowledge. It is expressed in their ritual and their numinous shrines such as the Sun Temple in Colorado and Rainbow Bridge in Utah, as beloved to them as a church or synagogue is to other Americans. The Serpent Mound State Memorial in Ohio is a mysterious structure 1,348 feet long facing west and overlooking a deep gorge. When I visited it with my husband and two children some years ago, there were few answers to explain who built it or why it was constructed. It's considered to be perhaps several thousand years old. It seemed to me to be a guidepost for travelers in the air, from its high vantage, pointing west as well as a message of high spiritual import perhaps related to the Feathered Serpent of the Mayas. It is considered by the Indian population to be a place of worship.

Perhaps the most mysterious of all is Mount Shasta, where legends tell of ancient beings who live in its hollow regions, survivors of the sunken continent of Lemuria in the Pacific. It is a spiritual center for the Indians and for many metaphysical groups, one of which is I Am, founded by the Ascended Master St. Germaine. The mountain is over 14,000 feet high and has many trails leading through its wilderness. People throughout the world are drawn to it for its peace and beauty, but the Indians of the region have revered it for generations.

FREEDOM FOR AFRICA

Violent revolution took place in Africa in the 1980s, which has led to humanitarian changes in laws and attitudes. For years, many reports came out of Africa of police brutality against blacks, of unjust laws that denied them equal educaon, decent housing, and self-respect as human beings. Degrading conditions over long years of apartheid created among them determination to overthrow the South African government.

Under the African National Congress, (ANC), which was banned in 1960, the leadership—Nelson Mandela and others—sought to bring about equality under law through peaceful dialogue. However, the National party (NP), which came into power in 1948, had never admitted black representation. It was not ready for a change in the status quo. The blacks had no alternative but to try to wrest their freedom by violent means.

Even then, the ANC ruled out attacks on civilians, limiting destruction to government installations. But the NP retaliated by arrests and torture.[23]

Three million whites have dominated twenty-three million blacks since 1948. The extent to which white supremacy has moved in South Africa seems to Americans something from a world of two hundred years ago, when, as in Africa today, virtual slavery and white supremacy were practiced without compunction. In lagging South Africa, blacks could not own land or a business, legally form unions, or use the same stairways, elevators, and washrooms used by whites. By law, blacks were taught nothing of usefulness in the modern world. Learning was a privilege reserved for whites only.[24]

Cayce had little to say about Africa. It was probably because no one asked him to discourse on the continent. The world was more aware of what was going on in Europe and America, of economic depression and global warfare, of John Steinbeck's *Grapes of Wrath* than the inequalities of life between blacks and whites in Africa. So many problems and issues pressed in that needed answers in the immediate time and place of those around Cayce, that much was left unasked.

But we have his statements on race problems in America. He would say of the black man in Africa, "he, too, is thy brother," in that time or this. Racial prejudice, labor-capital relations were not confined to America or to Germany. Nor did these injustices end with the passing of the 1940s but are with us still. So we can take our lesson on today's world

problems from his passages quoted throughout this book.
When you "dishonor your fellow man, you dishonor you
God" (3976-28).

In reading those words today, we find they are no less
applicable to issues demanding our attention. Has humanity
changed for the better? We could say it's waking up, as Cayce
predicted. Has human nature changed? What a disturbing
question to ask ourselves, as we look at historic and present
examples of human greatness, human courage, human beauty
of spirit; for in spite of examples of heinous crimes in high
places and low, we are hopefully evolving. The freedom won
throughout the world at about the same moment in time came
to Africa as well. It seems to be more than a subtle indication
that the world is divinely led. But the rules stay the same
throughout time, and what some souls are learning is that they
apply to *all* the people of the earth.

For Afrikaners, any reform of those unjust laws was a sign
that the NP was "going soft" on the preservation of white
privilege. President P. W. Botha had caved in to pressures
from the right wing, and that hardening of the lines on the
right surely meant that the country was headed for bloody
civil war.[25]

Richard Manning, an editor of *Newsweek,* spent nine
months in South Africa before being expelled in June 1986,
by the South African government for his pieces critical of
apartheid and the attendant hatred it engenders. He had eye-
witness knowledge about life in South Africa in the 1980s for
both black and white. He wrote with painful clarity about both
races.

It is not possible to tell in this brief space the complete
history of South Africa's ongoing ordeal in the cities where
blacks work for low wages and the townships where they live.
But through the eyes of writers who filed their reports from
such places as Johannesburg, Cape Town, and Pretoria, we
learned much about what took place.

In the early 1980s, to force black compliance with white
domination, South African commando raids were carried out
against black civilian populations, not necessarily guerrillas.
One raid in 1982 was made on Maseru, capital of Lesotho,

eaving forty-two people dead. South African military units it alleged targets in Mozambique twice in four years, once with warplanes.[26]

Since that time, blacks have rioted in the cities. In May 983, twenty people were killed and more than two hundred wounded by a guerrilla car bomb attack in Pretoria.[27] In June 984, a South African commando team crossed into Zimbabwe to strike at least ten houses that allegedly were used by ANC guerrillas, killing twelve people.[28]

In July 1988, black guerrillas planted a land mine in Zimbabwe, killing six white people, including four children, when their truck blew apart. The ANC declared, however, it had no bases in that country and was not responsible for the tragedy.[29]

In his revealing book, Manning describes the people he came to know and love, those youths who carried out "Black Consciousness" demonstrations and raids; leaders on both sides; white people who expressed their various emotions— from tolerance of blacks to fear or disdain or outright white supremacy. He marveled that the white population lived so far apart from the blacks that they never saw the squalor, illness, police arrests, and brutality that were the daily life in the townships where they lived.

The uprising continued, in spite of police gunfire, beatings with rubber whips, and dogs used to disperse crowds. In 1985 the fighting increased with coup attempts in Liberia and guerrilla rocket attacks on oil refineries south of Johannesburg. In the hands of blacks, firearms were beginning to replace stones and gasoline bombs.[30]

A state of emergency was declared on July 21, 1985, giving the police virtual martial law powers that only served to increase the division between whites and blacks. Anarchy was feared by many. The black youth became more radicalized, more violent. While National party supporters intensified their hostility toward blacks, black opposition groups such as the ANC and the United Democratic Front were targeted for roundups by a government dragnet.[31]

By August 1985, months of racial violence caused the

South African government to consider negotiations between blacks and whites. President Pieter Botha was said to be studying four proposals: to offer blacks a role in the central government, leading to the end of apartheid; to declare that South Africa is a single, unitary state; to grant common citizenship to all thirty million people in South Africa, regardless of race; to hold a national meeting of the country's main black, white, colored, and Indian leaders to agree on a new power-sharing constitutional structure for the country. The reform here outlined was accompanied by a more realistic understanding by whites of the country's situation, heightened by pressure from other countries against apartheid. The possibilities of economic sanctions were threatened by the U.S. Congress, amid fears the country would slide into anarchy if such a plan was not adopted. But if the reform were to become reality, apartheid, the white supremacy policy since 1948, would be brought down.[32]

The reform hoped for did not materialize. Riots and fighting resumed. By November 3, added to the list of human rights denied in Africa was freedom of the press: It was announced that the South African government was imposing severe controls of news coverage of the country's continuing unrest. "All anti-apartheid riots and protests," scenes of police and soldiers shooting and beating blacks, would no longer be viewed by the outside world. It was an indication that the government could not control the violence.[33]

Observed one man: "They believe that if those awful pictures of policemen beating little children and old women and shooting down kids on their way to the store are no longer published, that the outside world will forget about the situation here and that the blacks, without this backing, will stop fighting apartheid."[34]

In September 1990, after Nelson Mandela had been released from prison, he and President F. W. de Klerk concluded that a "hidden hand" was orchestrating the black township fighting to undermine peace talks aimed at black-white power sharing. The fighting was still going on. "We are dealing with highly professional killers," said Mandela at a Johannesburg news conference.[40]

In Liberia, an attempted coup was made against the government of General Samuel K. Doe, in which a "substantial loss of life" was reported. Concerned about reports of executions of the opposition leaders, the United States told the Liberian government that it was important that "due process is afforded to all those taken into custody." It hinted that "continued aid to the West African nation will depend on its government's observance of human rights."[41]

The issue of human rights in Africa, despite new rule, has been ignored in some pockets of the continent. In Rwanda, 500,000 people were slaughtered in 1993–1994, states General Romeo Dallaire of Canada. As commander of the UN peacekeeping mission in Rwanda, he witnessed a genocide planned by Hutu extremists against the minority Tutsis and moderate Hutus, with other crimes against humanity.[42]

A particularly shocking account is told of heroism and courage on the part of seventy-one Catholics including thirty-nine children and eight nuns in 1988. As they were making a pilgrimage to Maseru, Lesotho, on the eve of Pope John Paul II's visit, four terrorists highjacked their bus, demanding to see the pope, Lesotho's King Moshoeshoe II, and the British ambassador. The pilgrims refused. Before the terrorists could set off their homemade bomb, South Africa's anti-terrorist unit killed three of the highjackers. Two of the hostages were killed.[43]

Not all violence is directed at whites. In the nation of Burundi, a savage tribal massacre took place resulting in twenty thousand deaths, with fifty thousand Burundians fleeing to bordering Rwanda. "Most of those who died were of the majority tribe, the Hutu, and evidence suggests most of them were killed by government soldiers. . . . Burundi's government is controlled by the minority Tutsi tribe, and nearly every government soldier is a Tutsi. . . ."[44]

A study of 49 political assassinations, 160 assassination attempts, and 10 abductions since 1977 was made known in a report on November 5, 1989: "The U.S. government joined anti-apartheid figures Thursday in calling for an inquiry into allegations by Butana Almond Nofomela that he and other black undercover police officers took part in at least nine assassinations and 'numerous' kidnappings of African National Congress members under orders from police Security Branch officers.'' A lawyer was stabbed to death in 1981; his wife was killed three years later. Another victim was Dr. David Webster, an activist university professor, shot to death in May 1989. The assassinations, attempts, and abductions all remained unsolved. The South African Council of Churches officials urged that the solution of such murders is "vital to the creation of a climate conducive to genuine negotiations.'' A police investigation was ordered.[45]

A terrorist campaign by right-wing extremists started in April 1990 in the form of bombings and attacks. The terrorists hoped to preserve white rule at any price. It was feared that the attacks would be a major threat to peace negotiations. Nine right-wing terrorists were detained indefinitely without trial. White conservatives were demanding a state for whites only. At that time, the African National Congress had all but abandoned violence.[46]

Human rights lawyers in Nairobi, Kenya, had to go into hiding when they protested Kenya's one-party government. Trucks carrying scores of armed troops moved in, and club-bearing riot police roamed about the neighborhoods breaking up groups.[47]

Now, President F. W. Botha was freeing political prisoners as the NP government promised reform (again) after more protests and turmoil accompanying an election on September 8, 1989. The Nationalists received less than 50 percent of the vote and lost nearly a quarter of their seats to an antiapartheid party and to a far-right group that favored strict racial segregation. ''Police used shotguns, tear gas, and whips on anti-election protesters in black and mixed-race townships outside Cape Town.'' Twenty-five people were reported killed.[48]

In October, de Klerk was reported ready for talks on giving blacks a vote. Meeting with him were Anglican Archbishop Desmond Tutu; the Rev. Allan Boesak, president of the World Alliance of Reformed Churches; and the Rev. Frank Chikane, general secretary of the South African Council of Churches. They demanded lifting the state of emergency, le-

galization of the ANC and other banned groups, release of all
detainees and political prisoners, lifting of restrictions on political activity, and clemency for prisoners on death row. They
said they would press for tougher economic sanctions against
South Africa unless de Klerk complied with their demands.[49]

In November 1989, President de Klerk opened all beaches
to blacks and promised to end racial segregation of public
facilities. Blacks had been barred from parks, libraries, swim-
ming pools, civic centers, buses, public toilets, and even hospitals.[50]

Repeal of the law—the Separate Amenities Act—was
termed by conservatives as "the beginning of the end of a
separate white community life." Conservatives feared that
black freedom would bring about an end to their rule, that
blacks would take over. De Klerk declared that he did not
want a one-man, one-vote system. Repeal of the Separate
Amenities Act was given official approval by the United
States. Whites could still keep to their segregated neighborhoods.

Nelson Mandela had been imprisoned in the maximum-
security cell in Johannesburg for twenty-seven years. He was
serving a life sentence for helping plan the start of the ANC's
antigovernment sabotage campaign. South African authorities
had discussed with him the possibility of release four years
before. But President Botha's word was sent that that was
only rumor.[51]

Throughout his imprisonment, not only his countrymen but
also his friends around the world rallied to his defense. He is
looked on as a symbol of the hope of freedom for millions
of blacks. Despite his Marxist philosophy, among his friends
are powerful leaders of democratic governments including the
United States and international figures in business and banking. Many nations have urged his release to help bring about
a peaceful resolution of South Africa's inhumane hold on
black citizens.[52]

As people around the world were celebrating Mandela's
seventieth birthday on July 18, 1988, Johannesburg police set
up roadblocks and guarded private homes, schools, and sports

fields to break up black African observances. Stated Winnie Mandela, "This day turned out into what the government wanted to be made of it. We had every intention of conveying messages of good will in the country."[53]

In London, "Christians, Buddhist monks, a rabbi and a Moslem scholar led prayers for Mandela at the St. James Piccadilly Church. Among the worshipers were 25 activists who had marched about 600 miles from Glasgow, Scotland."[54]

Birthday events were scheduled in London and Amsterdam, Hungary, Paris, Santiago, and New Delhi. One event not banned was a call by clergymen for Mandela's release in a service at Francis Roman Catholic Church near Cape Town.[55]

Stated Reverend Boesak, "In spite of all the intimidation, in spite of the obvious fear of the government, our decision is clear: we will celebrate."[56]

On February 11, 1990, Mandela was released from prison. Before huge crowds he appeared at a rally at the Cape Town city hall at noon, his first public appearance in thirty years. He appeared on television. "I greet you all," he began, "in the name of democracy and peace and freedom for all." He called for the cooperation of the world. "I have fought white domination but wish to end it in peace, harmony. But I am prepared to die [for the cause of freedom]."[57]

As he has maintained since the 1960s, Mandela affirmed that he still is against either black or white domination. He appealed for calm, for self-control for everyone. "Don't do anything to make people say we don't have control over our own people."

He had practiced law before his incarceration, which says something about his respect for legal channels rather than anarchy. In his rising above bitterness against those who had denied him his freedom for twenty-seven years, he presented a peaceful demeanor (albeit he agreed that violence has been neccessary in that fight). In it was the spirit Cayce recommended: "Whose spirit, what manner of peace, then, seek ye as individuals? That ye may gratify the appetites of thy body? That ye may satisfy the lust of the eye? That ye may know fame or fortune? These fade, these pass away. Only that which enables the individual also to bear the cross, even as

He, will enable that individual to know that peace which encompassed Him . . .'' (3976-27).

On his world tour visiting fourteen nations, he continued to receive acclamation from freedom-loving people everywhere. In Washington, D.C., and other cities throughout America, he was hailed as a hero, a modern-day Moses leading his people out of modern-day slavery. Many Westerners, and those people who have lived and suffered from terrorism or tyranny under those leaders, were incensed at his declaration of alliance with Muammar Qaddafi, Yasser Arafat, and Fidel Castro. It was because, he told Ted Koppel's television audience, those leaders had supported his cause of freedom ''one hundred percent'' when the Western nations gave no moral support. When challenged that the ANC should sit down and talk with the Pretoria government, Mandela replied, ''It's the A.N.C. and not the government that has wanted to sit down and discuss. I've made that call not once but several times.'' He urged intensified U.S. sanctions against the Pretoria government.[57]

Meeting with President Bush on June 25, the two leaders discussed negotiations between the African government and the ANC. He addressed Congress as the third foreign non–head of state to do so.[58]

Continuing the policy of Carter and Reagan, Bush has never favored sanctions but conceded that U.S. sanctions may have helped pressure the reforms by South Africa. Such sanctions number more than two hundred by American firms. In 1990, 120 more remained acccording to reports, but trade between the two countries continues. The European Economic Community and Great Britain have also kept sanctions there, but the latter ended its ban on voluntary investment after de Klerk announced his reforms and released Mandela from prison.[59]

Since February 1990, blacks who were imprisoned by the South African government for their protests against apartheid were released in growing numbers, due to pressure not only by sanctions but also by the Roman Catholic church, as well as Protestant churches.[60]

In Atlanta, he was cheered by about five thousand people

in a historic section of black businesses and civil rights land-marks as he arrived at the Martin Luther King Jr. Center for Nonviolent Social Change.[61]

During his visit he received honorary doctorate degrees from forty predominantly black colleges at a convocation at Morehouse College.[62] Martin Luther King III thought Mandela's visit to the center showed that he did not support violence. Mandela was quick to say that black South Africa faces a different battle from that led by King. "Unlike you, we are still under the grip of white supremacy. Non-violence is a good policy when conditions permit."[63]

In the world community, Mandela asked not only for intensified sanctions but resources as well. He is reported to have received generous contributions. His goal is to bring complete freedom to all minorities in South Africa.

Though of another time, and in a different setting, what Cayce had to say about how we treat our fellowman seems mighty pertinent here. The problems of human relations can be met by honoring and worshiping God. "For this may only be done in the manner in which individuals, states, nations treat their fellow man. For as ye do unto others, ye do to thy Maker. And when these activities are such as to dishonor thy fellow man, ye dishonor thy God and it brings all of those forms of disturbance that exist in the world today" (3976-28).

Cayce's words have been heeded in the last decades of the twentieth century by millions of people around the globe. As he declared, though, it's the Spirit that moves in these times to work God's will. Many people who might or might not have heard of Cayce have taken it on themselves—been moved by the Spirit?—to "do something about" problems confronting us. As in Europe, there are those in the Americas, the Middle East, the Far East, and Africa who fit the Cayce standard as "proclaimers of the day of freedom." Revolutions by diplomacy and peacemaking as well as by bullets led to freedom and a better life in much of the world under those brave leaders we have named.

Among a number of both black and white proclaimers, the named and the nameless took up the cry, "I have a dream!"

The Reverend Martin Luther King inspired his people and others around the world to adopt nonviolent means to achieve equality. He was one of the first to be assassinated among those leading the freedom movement everywhere, while many others suffered character assassination, imprisonment, and physical injury. As the walls came down, symbolized by the infamous Berlin Wall in 1989, all within a span of three or four years, the light of freedom shone bright for the first time in thousands of years.

A key adage of the Cayce readings is "Mind is the Builder." No condition or thing exists without first the mind bringing it into existence, the thoughts that lead to their manifestation. Thus, societies and conditions are created by the power of consciousness, both collective and individual. What kind of society depends on what kind of consciousness it entertains. In the explosive 1960s, for instance, it was the mass mind that led us for good or ill as thousands of people protested—or defended!—injustice. The inspired leadership of Dr. King lifted the consciousness of his followers to see themselves as brothers and sisters, regardless of color. The Great Society of President Lyndon Johnson attempted similar goals.

As Cayce said, leaders are raised for a purpose, with great power to carry out their own ideas of what is best for society. But to do so, the people can create their milieu by their thought. We·have the power of judgment to be certain whom we follow and where we are led. The eternal foundation, our best protection, is the understanding, acceptance, and practice of the Fatherhood of God, the Brotherhood of Man, which Christ exemplified.

I'm certain that had Cayce lived at this time of change in both the earth and its ideologies, he would have given ·guidance as good as he gave long ago. He anticipated events just now taking place. He pointed to the two conflicting forces among us: "the prince of this world and that Principle that says to every soul, 'Fear not, I have overcome the world' and the prince of the world hath nothing in Me'" (3976-29).

On March 18, 1992, President F. W. de Klerk finally realized his goal to abolish apartheid. In a 90 percent turnout, the South African white population voted to end their centuries-long rule over the black provinces. It was a land-slide victory of 68.6 percent of the 2.9 million whites who voted. The blacks celebrated in the streets, dancing and sing-ing "Welcome to the new South Africa!"[64]

However, as happy as Nelson Mandela, president of the African National Congress, was at learning of the election results, he is quoted as saying, "Apartheid is still very much alive. I still cannot vote in my own country."[65]

Barry Renfrew of the Associated Press observed that the world has probably never before seen a people vote to give up power, especially when they still dominate a nation. He called the vote a "political miracle."[66]

For the whites, "although the lifestyles have not changed much, the certainties they grew up with crumbled. Whites were no longer assured of advantages setting them apart as the ruling class." He added that many whites still are blinded by prejudice and do not see blacks as equals.[67]

But those of us who have never condoned apartheid, much less its partner, oppression, reacted with approval and relief, because if the vote had gone the other way, dire predictions had been made of more violence and bloodshed.

Let there be no more shackles of the heart, mind, or soul, among any of us, but rather those purposes in the hearts Cayce claimed: "Then the mind and the spirit, in accord with . . . hope, faith, and understanding in the minds and the hearts of men EVERYWHERE will bring into the experiences of all that relationship one to another wherein that all ARE brethren. For these must bring and keep peace one with another" (3976-19).

"So long as ye turn thy thoughts to the manners and means for meeting and overcoming those destructive forces, ye show forth that which may bring to the world that day of the Lord. For the promise is that in the latter days there shall be the purposes in the HEARTS of men, everywhere!" (3976-23)

The message for us all is, from Cayce, "Hence each would ask, then: 'What must *I* do about it; not what shall this, that or the other ruler, other office holder, or the other individual do' but each should ask, 'What must *I* do about the economic conditions in which we find ourselves?' " (3976-14)

And these latter days find us, as no people before us, seeking to overcome destructive forces of the past. In the hearts of people everywhere, we share the dream, and the vow, "We shall overcome, someday."

9

"Why Then the Turmoil?"

*Nations have said, "Send help, for man's heritage
of freedom would be taken away." By whom? He
that hath said, "Surely ye will not die." (Genesis
3:4) (3976-25, June 22, 1944)*

ACCORDING TO THE BIBLE story, in the Garden of Eden,
Adam and Eve were told by God not to eat of the tree of
knowledge of good and evil, lest they die. But the serpent
(Satan) told Eve, "Ye will not die" (Gen.3:4). Ever since the
original couple, and today, opposing voices seem to be com-
peting for our very souls.

It is a different world from that of even fifty years ago. In
past centuries, many issues troubling us today we have not
known in such devastating numbers. They affect millions of
people: drug abuse, sexual promiscuity, abortion rights. Due
to widespread divorce, children are separated from their bi-
ological parents. Gang violence and murder take place in the
streets and homes when often the children are the victims.
Moreover, even the police are unable to help in some places,
as crime becomes more prevalent.

Cayce pointed to "mass, individual, and group thought"
at a time when half the world was ruled under atheism, and
the people were enabled to worship God only in secret. Op-
positely, in democracies of the West, belief in God's rules is
the means for man's salvation and a better life. So mass beliefs and thinking based on those beliefs are a powerful force
today, as people march or organize for one cause or another,

often conflicting with each other. It is mass thought upon which the Bill of Rights was produced at the founding of our country, because the people, aware of the English constitutional documents of 1689 that provided those rights, demanded them in their new homeland.[1] In France, mass consciousness demanding freedom from the old rule brought down the monarchy.

However, even in a democratic country such as America, where our nation was founded on religious principles, the new climate of division is all too obvious: There are those who would keep the eternal spiritual values that provide stability and peace. There are others vehemently opposed to those values.

What a cacophony of voices jangle in this brave, new world of unexpected change, unleashed drives, prejudices, desires, and grievances! Indeed, we have for some years not shared the same code of morality or religious faith of our forefathers. Desert Storm, however, changed our view of ourselves in relation to our country, and once more, patriotism was in. We were surprised to find we could feel so deeply about the American flag and what it stands for. It created a revival of the oneness that characterized our earlier history, giving us pride again. But we see examples of division, lack of one law of morality: Since the Gulf War of 1991, there have been reports of another side to our military personnel. In the last decade of the twentieth century, we learned of brutal hazing in the military, of both men and women, and sexual harassment of women in the armed forces. Such behavior is evidently directly in proportion to our lowered standards and decline in morals.

In recent years, many concerned people have wondered where the oneness of ideals that once characterized America has gone. Many wonder where our national moral certitude, our faith, and values have gone.

It is certain Cayce would agree that our morally flaccid sex attitudes are destructive. The entertainment world strives to titillate us with its appeal to our lower instincts. It's a deplorable comment on our society, to say the least, when it welcomes decadent ideas. The young are led to think such entertainment is acceptable in a nation that professes to live "under God" and all the high idealism that implies. The idealism, dear ones, includes chastity and purity before marriage, and all the rules in the Ten Commandments. Entertainment seen on television and in the movies has been a powerful allure to the young and impressionable minds that seek models to emulate. Once, such entertainment did not have to attract us by a steady dose of sex, foul language, and violence. The stories were wonderful, family-oriented.

Today, the media—television or movies—give us a message of less than what is our value: the true value of our lives that has nothing to do with fame, fortune, or immediate gratification. Such entertainment was not acceptable or tolerated in previous decades. It should not be now.

As a friend of Hugh Lynn Cayce pointed out in 1963, there is at work a divisive force in the world that opposes family values, the God-inspired reality that is their foundation. Based on his view of the sanctity of life, Edgar Cayce would say that abortion is wrong. It is indeed a matter of moral concern if abortion is used as a means of birth control. However, women are disturbingly affected by abortion mores. We see abortion rights differently from men, especially if we are victims of rape or health problems to ourselves or to the child. But in the case of a child found by physicians to be born disabled in some way, the physician holds to his oath to save it.

Cayce agreed. Sometimes a child is born blind or crippled or otherwise disabled, unable to function normally, in need of constant care. Is he or she any less dear to the parents? Cayce said that the child's soul is present, responding to love and caring; parents and their progeny are living out karmic conditions, blessings to each other.

Cayce was asked often about child care. In his readings, he advised that parents and not anyone else should nurture their children, because they are continuing a relationship from a past life and they have things to work out. Parents have just what their children need. Seen in that light, parenting is an awesome responsibility and an even greater joy.

But as our children venture into the world that awaits them, what is out there? Because of what we hear of death and injury in the very streets near our homes, parents today are often terrified. What new drug fad or cigarette is possibly being offered the children? Today's permissiveness and the dilemmas it creates have proven disastrous to our youth. Once, premarital sex was looked on as folly. Today, many leaders and parents alike condone it "if it's safe." And we ask, "Why the turmoil among our youth?"

Just when we thought our society couldn't have sunk much lower, particularly in the arts, we have the blatant obscenity cases involving explicit sex and degradation of women—as we can purchase music albums that incite brutalization of women, and children can turn to the Internet to be subject to strangers of questionable character.

It was not government, it was the people, the founding fathers thought, who are sovereign. Yet we are increasingly aware of government's encroachment on our personal lives, in every phase. It wants to control our constitutional rights, meddle in such situations as teenage pregnancy, prayer in schools, the display of religious symbols. I can remember when I was a child, prayer and Bible reading in school were daily practices that tended to center children for their studies. Children are deprived of that benevolent advantage by law. The reason is given that the schools might be caught committing "religious indoctrination."

Yet few restraints have been evident in the world of entertainment, in the arts, to the detriment of decency and morality. In mid-1990, Congress rejected grants for four controversial works of "art" by gays and lesbians, and "avant-garde" stage performances that were puerile because they seemed to be meant to shock the culturally mature like naughty children who want to provoke their elders. States David Gergen of *U.S. News & World Report,* leading artistic figures are angrily protesting any and all restrictions on federal moneys. However, he says, "If artists insist upon a wholesale denial of any standards, they will wind up wrecking the very institution they claim they need. Some congressmen have indicated an inclination to cut off National Endowment for the Arts, he explains. But Gergen points out the NEA's work in encouraging tremendous growth of the arts since the 1960s, which offsets the few controversies. "Congress should keep current rules against funding obscene works but avoid imposing new restrictions that would handcuff the NEA. . . . It knows where to draw the line."[2]

About irresponsible moral attitudes, including use of drugs and alcohol that destroy lives, when Cayce was asked if prohibition would be lost in America, he said, in effect, you can't legislate morality: "No one may ever legislate GOODNESS into the heart or the soul of anyone!" Prohibition must be from the choices people make. It "only awaits the decisions of Americans as to whether the peoples will stand as a law abiding, or a law breaking peoples" (3976-8, January 12, 1932).

The world into which we send our children is fraught by other factors—the economy, crime, and, lately, not any easier to control, the weather. But I think the weather is trying to tell us something. In 1967, when I was writing *Edgar Cayce on Prophecy,* Hugh Lynn Cayce told me that his father had predicted more than I was then aware of. I had stated in that book what Edgar Cayce had said about earthquakes and volcanoes. But Hugh Lynn said to me in passing, just two words: *"The weather!"* I thought that by comparison with earthquakes and volcanoes, the weather was tame fare. And in that era, it was certainly a problem at times, but there had been no great activity of El Niño. So I never tried to follow up that tip.

Throughout known history, great storms, hurricanes, and tornadoes have caused massive destruction. To the turmoil of international politics, economic and cultural conditions, we are being clobbered with roaring weather patterns. They have tested the mettle of thousands of people caught in floods, landslides, avalanches, and wind-driven fires. Half a century after Cayce, El Niño has borne out Hugh Lynn's allusion to the weather being a problem unknown and unanticipated before now.

According to Cayce, it's a matter of consciousness. What kind of mind rules the universe? It's a combination of the great Mind that made the laws and the minds of everyone on earth, and perhaps on a million planets throughout the universe itself, whether positive, or negative/destructive ones. For "Souls are atoms in the body of God" (S L 900) and "The earth is only an atom in the universe of worlds!" (5753-1) Said Cayce, our thoughts even affect the planet and its weather, for good or ill. Could be true.

On June 23, 1940, members of the Ninth Annual Congress asked for "a discourse on world affairs for understanding what is taking place today and in meeting the conditions which are to come in America." Cayce began by reminding them that:

In the early days of man's development on earth (Atlantean?) in his attempts to understand his relationships to his Maker, warnings were given again and again as to what would happen to people who professed one thing and lived another, or who attempted to use amiss that which was given them.

Then there came that period in man's activity in which it was proclaimed that no longer it would be in this temple or in this mountain that there would go out the message to the people, or to their gatherings here or there, but lo it would be written upon their hearts—so that the old men should dream dreams, the young men should see visions, the maidens should proclaim the acceptable years of the Lord.

And then there came into the experience of the world HE who was rejected of man.

Only here and there, apparently for the little while, has there been that peace, that harmony which apparently was the promise of those, or to those, who would live or accept that promise He gave, "I will come and abide with you always."

Why then the turmoil in the world today?

They have forgotten God! Not that it is merely a karmic condition of a nation, of a people; for, know ye not that the prayer of one man saved a city?

Thinkest thou that the arm of God is shorter today than in days of yore?

Then, as to the needs for those things and conditions which are to come to pass in America:

When many of the isles of the sea, many of the lands, have come under the subjugation of those who fear not man nor the devil, but rather would associate with that in which they may proclaim MIGHT and power as being right in that of the superman, that would be of the generations as would be established—then shall thine own land see the blood flow as in those periods when brother fought against brother . . .

(3976-25)

In that same letter to Hugh Lynn Cayce mentioned earlier, a thoughtful and perceptive friend wrote of the events of the decade of the 1960s. The thoughts he conveyed were received in accord with what many people acquainted with the readings were saying. The letter began:

How far man has come, in some ways. In others we are nearing the end of an era, and the death struggle of this age is not an easy thing to watch. During the past few years this country has seen many of the Cayce predictions fulfilled—turmoil, strife, riots, rule by men and mobs instead of rule by law, a great division in our land, and now the death of a second president (John F. Kennedy). (3976-24)

Although for those of us who have been watching with concern the great opposing forces in this country grow stronger daily, these tragedies cause no surprise—only horror and sadness that they are finally happening . . .

The writer pointed out Cayce's predictions about racial conflicts found scattered throughout the readings: "Unless these truths are considered, a revolution must eventually come in this country . . . This is almost upon us, Hugh Lynn. Many of us see it being precipitated and coming to a head. But too many people have had their thinking processed by managed

news and remain blissfully brainwashed and unaware."
He emphasized the value of

> both understanding and *using* the Cayce predictions in
> this very crucial time in history, when A.R.E. work is so
> desperately needed and so terribly important, and its
> leaders need to understand the problem in order to be of
> help.
>   Hugh Lynn, you and I have talked many times on "The
> Shadow of Atlantis on America," history repeating itself,
> old problems rising again. It is the understanding of man's
> past in relation to his present that helps him to grow . . .

The writer compared what is happening in the twentieth
century with that of Atlantis of twelve thousand years ago
when there was great division between the forces of light and
darkness—the Children of the Law of One and the Sons of
Belial. "The Sons of Belial were without a standard of morality. The other group—those who followed the Law of
One—had a standard" (877-26).
  Then the writer suggested that the great division Cayce had
predicted "before the second of the presidents dies in office"
(John F. Kennedy) was a continuation of the division of
forces in Atlantis, which finally brought down that great civilization described by Cayce.

> The parallels between these days and our past in Atlantis
> match point for point, but only if the present is seen from
> the point of view I am asking you to consider.
>   I think the Cayce readings say, Hugh Lynn, that the
> same forces who warred in Atlantis and caused its de-
> struction are at it again today, in this present war. Only
> if we recognize this can we be effective in doing some-
> thing about it. And isn't that why the history of Atlantis is
> important—why your father brought it into the life read-
> ings? . . . If history repeats itself, Hugh Lynn, then that
> shadow of Atlantis, that problem, would be again be-
> tween those forces of light and darkness, between good
> and evil, Christ and antiChrist,—a war between those

who have declared the Law of One God and those who proclaim, "There is no God—the State is supreme"—a war between men who want to keep the freedom God gave each soul as its most precious gift from Him and a few men who want to enslave all other men.

This writer saw the polarity between those serving atheistic and amoral tenets of communism and those serving God as the religious war Cayce foretold for this century.

As in Atlantis, those who would control and enslave men . . . opposed those who would fight for their God-given freedoms.
   And that which has made and does make the people of America afraid is the fear of servitude in any form!
                                                        (3976-19)

Continued the writer:

Today, over óne billion people, over one-third of the human race, is enslaved by that tyranny that proclaims as its first principle, "There is no God!" . . . Is it any wonder then that thousands of these captive people have risked their lives trying to escape over mine-fields, over barbed wire, over machine-gun barricades like the Berlin Wall—rather than live in slavery under the horror of a Godless system?
   (Said Cayce) Nations have said, "Send help, for man's heritage of freedom would be taken away." Taken away by whom? By that one who hath said of old, "Surely ye will not die, if ye eat." There are these two principles and two conflicting forces in the earth today.
                                                        (3976-29)

"Communism," wrote this Cayce supporter,

is the dark force which Lenin said must conquer and enslave the world if it is to survive. It is the dark force that denies God, that is based on hate, not love, on force and brutality, not free will . . .

Some of our leaders have decided it is wrong for children to learn of God, or even mention Him, in schools. Yet Cayce reading 3976-25 said, "Why is there turmoil in the world today? People have forgotten God!" Is it any wonder with our leaders making mention of Him "unconstitutional"? No wonder Cayce spoke of "corruption in high places." If America goes down, he said, it will be from forces working *within*.

THE TURMOIL CONTINUES

Since this writer wrote Hugh Lynn Cayce in 1963, the turmoil has worsened. The decline has increased in religious worship, of remembering who we are as Americans with respect and love of education *for the whole person*. Concurrently, for thirty years there has been denied young people prayer and Bible reading in school. There has been at the same time increase in drug and alcohol use by young people, which has, as throughout the world, led to their own deaths or disablement. Does there not seem to be a grim logical connection?

A report in June 1990 by a panel of medical and education leaders stated that America is raising a generation of adolescents plagued by pregnancies, illegal drug use, suicide, and violence.

"We are absolutely convinced that if we don't take action immediately, we're going to find ourselves with a failing economy and social unrest," said Roseann Bentley of the National Association of State Boards of Education. The commission's report concluded that "young people are less healthy and less-prepared to take their places in society than were their parents. Inattention to these problems has left thousands of young people doomed to failure which for many will be a precursor to an adult life of crime, unemployment or welfare dependency."[3]

The commission was formed by the National Association of State Boards of Education and the American Medical Association to make recommendations on the role of the school and community in improving adolescent health.

The report is accompanied by the following statistics:

One million teenage girls, nearly one in ten, get pregnant each year.

Thirty-nine percent of high school seniors reported they had gotten drunk within the two previous weeks.

Alcohol-related accidents are the leading cause of death among teenagers.

The suicide rate for teens has doubled since 1968, making it the second leading cause of death among adolescents. Ten percent of teenage boys and 18 percent of girls have attempted suicide.

Teenage arrests are up thirtyfold since 1950.[4]

Since that time, as a result of stronger police work and otherwise unknown causes, such statistics have looked better, and crime in general, including murder, is down in 1998. Is it the rise in consciousness working? The Spirit moving us in spite of ourselves? Would it not be even easier to attain the Great Society if we put more emphasis on good conversation, for instance, about our purpose on this planet? We could pose the notion that maybe earth is a school where we are supposed to be learning how to really succeed at living our lives. We evidently have a direct connection indeed between the nation's religious principles—or its failure to honor them—and what happens to its children.

If we look back to the founding of America, we are told that George Washington was a deeply religious man. He is said to have prayed fervently at Valley Forge, where he and his men were fighting the Revolution in the middle of winter of 1777. All were suffering. He saw a vision at that time of America's future: Villages and towns and cities springing up one after the other, and the angel bringing him his vision told him, "Remember, ye are brethren."[5]

This nation's success has been seen by many sober-minded people as the result of our acknowledging God and realizing His power to guide us. If the first president of the United States was so led by the Spirit, it was for a purpose. He was to lead us to greatness.

Such greatness was realized since that prayer at Valley Forge, for America fulfilled its mission. It was because America prayed, worked hard, and built churches.

Edgar Cayce prophesied in the 1930s a religious awakening ahead. In 1991, the Reverend Jerry Falwell thought that such an awakening was imminent. In February of 1998, Pat Robertson called for fasting to bring it about because he believes the world is ripe for a religious revival. It is again a matter of consciousness—as Edgar Cayce said: "prayer and more prayer" was needed. In May 1940, he spoke of the need to be "planted in Him who is the *true* light." So we send our prayers and light out to accomplish whatever good we know is of God. "And as ye live (in righteousness) so may the Christian light of love encompass the earth . . ." (3936-25).

Both Edgar Cayce and C. G. Jung taught that man is naturally endowed with an inborn collective unconscious which is, in Jung's words, "identical in all men." It is the link with man's spiritual life, common therefore to all religions. Free expression of our relationship to God is therefore an inalienable right.

But over the years, Bible study has been denied public school students because it conflicts with separation of church and state. Kids who want to meet after school to study the Bible have been told they must avoid religious speech. Speech like such treasured Bible teachings as "Do unto others as you would have them do unto you," "Love one another," or perhaps "A good man out of the good treasure of his heart bringeth forth that which is good; and an evil man out of the evil treasure of his heart bringeth forth that which is evil: for of the abundance of the heart his mouth speaketh" (Luke 6: 45). Wise speech such as this might change the consciousness of our youth! It might turn them from their hopeless dependencies to a wonderful life of the spirit, of turning their lives around and becoming what they have a right to be: happy, productive human beings. Watch out! Such speech is powerful!

However, the basic human right to worship God, to receive comfort, healing, and inspiration from the Source within, has also been denied in the ruling against prayer in the schools.

Haven't we learned from observing for many years the godless society in communist countries where freedom to worship God and pray was prohibited? No matter what country you're in, denying free religious speech has similar results.

Worship is not confined to church or synagogue, for God lets us commune with Him anytime. Separation of church and state must be respected but need not prevent us from learning and praying together. If we are denied that under law, we have neither freedom nor justice.

As various religious groups protest that prayer in the schools does not allow them to pray the way *they* do, Supreme Court ruling has forbidden prayer at all. Only silent prayer is accepted, to protect children of different faiths from feeling excluded. Religious differences, Cayce stated, "are the swords He brought into man's material understanding. And more wars, more bloodshed have been shed over the racial and religious differences than over any other problem! These, too, must go the way of all others; and man must learn—if he will know the peace as promised by Him—that God loveth those who love Him, whether they be called of this or that sect or schism or ism or cult! The Lord is ONE!" (3976-27)

Why not teach that to the children?

Why not teach it to the leaders in charge of the public good? Heaven knows we need all the help we can get. Neither prayer among people of different faiths should be denied nor religious discussion be feared. They should be a vital part of our public life, our education. The study of comparative religion keeps the faiths from being closed away, for it enlightens us; it gives us perspective that bridges the chasms of prejudice. As well, prayer should be understood as direct connection with God, as natural to all people as breathing.

In 1938 Cayce was asked what President Roosevelt should do in the international situations. He replied:

it is brother against brother in the disputes. And know that all stand as one before the judgment bar of the Creator.

Hence, prayer, and more prayer; and as we have given, LIVE toward one another as a nation, as a brother nation to the others—on EITHER side—as ye pray!

> Do not pray one way and live another! Be consistent,
> be persistent.
>
> (3976-20)

If presidents are advised to go to the Lord for answers to the questions of international issues, should the general population do without the same spiritual guidance? Cayce didn't think so. Those people, who helped him to present his readings to the public, asked how they might start a world organization of benefit to mankind. He urged that as they met as a body, they be "praying, offering service . . ." (3976-7). All of us might take a cue from that advice in our own needs, or help us in our efforts to help others.

It's interesting that both Cayce and the great psychiatrist C. G. Jung taught that man is naturally endowed with an inborn collective unconscious which is, in Jung's words, "identical in all men." In Russia, or in the Latin American countries before Marxist governments were brought down, the people sought freedom, which, religion teaches, is the natural condition of the human soul. So even before the fall of communism, the people there challenged the rules against religious life. They thronged to hear church representatives from the rest of the world. Foremost of these was the Reverend Billy Graham, who toured sixty-three countries and spoke to more that 100 million people in his forty years of ministry. In 1984 he toured the Soviet Union. He wrote: "Religious faith in the U.S.S.R. is livelier than most people in the West realize. Although full statistics are not kept by the churches, it is estimated that 100 million people in the Soviet Union profess belief in God. . . ."[6] This report by the very beloved American spiritual leader reminds us Cayce predicted that Russia was to be "born again." The term means the same, we think, as that used in churches teaching the kind of religious experience that brings rebirth of a spiritual kind.

In America, belief in God has always been the norm for most people, because our ancestors brought that belief with them. Free speech gave us the option to express our faith in the values it offers. So our flag represents more than American military power, or our prestige in the world community: It represents as well what our faith provides—God's grace, peace among all, which is consensual prayer that He "crown our good with brotherhood from sea to shining sea."

But in the spring of 1990, the issue of flag burning prompted debate as to its being tolerated as means of communicating dissatisfaction with American policies. Why, I wondered, was flag burning considered by some, including the Supreme Court, a form of speech? What the First Amendment was talking about was the spoken word, a powerful force in itself. If the framers of the Constitution had thought speech included destruction of property and national symbols, they would have said so.

After all, the framers of the Constitution expected that criticism of any kind would be by articulate, literate citizens, not by those who had no other means of expression except physical violence like flag burning. Such action is tantamount to shouting, using bad language, with clenched fist. It does not bring up the notion of reasoned discourse.

The framers also mandated "the right of the people peaceably to assemble." The key word is "peaceably," which they evidently expected to characterize public meetings and demonstrations. Is flag burning a peaceable work? It's quite violent.

The flag has continued to be honored for more than two hundred years. It is still honored by most citizens for those who died for it, by all who appreciate what America means to the rest of the world, much of which has lived under tyranny for ages past. Because America was created as a Christian nation, the flag is a symbol of the brotherhood of man, the Fatherhood of God, in which credo is included peace, justice, and the blessing of God's grace.

So let the flag speak for itself!

10

Oneness of All Faiths

In all of these (religions), then, there is that same impelling spirit. (364-9)

"Where there is no vision," said Solomon, wise king of the Hebrews, "the people perish" (Proverbs 29:18). Over the ages, there have been leaders without vision for their people. But the Hebrews have a history of great leaders such as Moses, whose vision led them to receive the Ten Commandments from God, to be passed down to all the world.

Vision is gained from the inner spiritual experience and, by its nature as a universal gift to the human psyche, cannot be the exclusive property of one group. Concerning the Cayce concept of accepting the major religions that recognize the one God—Jewish, Buddhist, Muslim, Hindu—I believe that the Christian is no less a Christian because he or she accepts these and honors those who so believe. Nor should any religion reject the others: They all have a common belief in God, with its attendant motivation Jesus Christ taught to strive for Godlike attributes of mastery over the lower consciousness, of showing the compassion and love to others that we have received from God. Before we cast stones at other God-fearing people, we had better be sure we are showing as much love as they do!

Cayce's principles, based on the Christian experience, help to clarify much of the confusion. We emphasize his message of "One Ideal" all religions can accept: one God and brotherhood among all of us.

Too often, religious groups express intolerance of other religions that worship God! Swami Sri Yukteswar, recognized as a Christlike master and teacher of Hindu religious insights, speaks of this problem this way: "... there is an essential unity in all religions; ... there is no difference in the truths inculcated by the various faiths; ... there is but one method by which the world, both external and internal, has evolved; and ... there is but one Goal admitted by all scriptures." The method of which he speaks, he states, is the same as that practiced by devout Christians: penance, deep study (of the Holy Science), and the practice of meditation. The lives of the great spiritual leaders, of which he is one, is attested to by just such a leader, founder of Self-Realization Fellowship, Paramahansa Yogananda. Says Sri Yukteswar further: "This basic truth [the unity of all God-centered faiths] is not comprehended. The discord existing between the different religions, and the ignorance of men, make it almost impossible to lift the veil and have a look at this grand verity. The creeds foster a spirit of hostility and dissension; ignorance widens the gulf that separates one creed from another. Only a few specially gifted persons can rise superior to the influence of their professed creeds and find absolute unanimity in the truths propagated by all great faiths." [1]

We recall Cayce said there were more wars caused by religion than any other reason. Sadly, history bears this out. Up to and including the present time, the shameful story is that one faith is often pitted against another in violent clashes. In the name of God, members of one major group are hostile against another, just as are races. Are even holy wars justified in the sight of a God of peace? It is a difficult question. As Archbishop Mahoney stated on November 12, 1990, he thought war is justified "if there is just cause." [2]

History tells us of such prejudice on a wide and violent scale. The Crusades were a series of holy wars, begun in 1096 to free the Holy Land from the Muslim Turks who were persecuting the Christians there. They were begun with the cry, "God wills it!" But they were stained with the excesses of Christian warriors who massacred the Turks in Jerusalem in 1099. A positive result of the Crusades that lasted for two centuries is that they opened up the world to cultures un-known before, which, according to historians, led eventually to the Renaissance.

In the past, also, religion has usually been used by despots for their own purposes, rather than the good of their subjects. Henry VIII broke with the pope in order to divorce Catherine and marry Anne Boleyn, making himself "supreme Head of the Church of England" by an act of Parliament. He then persecuted the Catholics loyal to the government at Rome, as well as Protestants.

From the thirteenth century to the nineteenth, inquisitions were carried out by the Church of Rome to stop people from revolting against religious rule. Heretics were hauled before courts to "confess," often only after torture or by threat of burning at the stake. Political advantage was often taken against those accused of heresy because church and state collaborated in power over their subjects.

Curiously, with the spread of freedom, religious prejudice has taken on worldwide proportions in recent decades. As in former centuries, religion is often the cause for division and combat rather than a fulfillment of the founders' purpose of peace and love.

In Ireland, Catholics and Protestants have fought each other for several decades but have resolved their enmity at last.

As in Jerusalem where both Jews and Palestinians claim the same sacred ground, so do the Muslims and Hindus of India at one contested site at Ayodhya. The Hindus believe the god Rama was born under the present Muslim mosque.

In India, 82 percent of the people are Hindu and only 12 percent Muslim. In October and November 1990, Muslims contended with Hindus in another "holy war" as the Hindus attempted to seize the sixteenth-century Islamic mosque. The riots that followed brought the death toll to more than two hundred.[3]

Secessionists in Muslim Kashmir and the Sikhs in Punjab caused the loss of thousands of lives there and in New Delhi. The strife caused serious political upheaval because India's secular government had to cope with the Bharatiya Janata party, which pulled out of its support of Prime Minister V. P. Singh's regime. As a result, Singh was certain to be replaced.[4]

During the 1980s, the time of Iran's bloody war of eight years with Iraq, Iran's supreme religious leader, Ayatollah Khomeini, called America the "great Satan." He commanded all Muslims to join Iraq in a holy war against U.S. troops. In 1991, Saddam Hussein as well attempted to appeal to the Islamic tradition of such war against "unbelievers" but was condemned for this by the Muslim religious leaders.

That condemnation lends hope. Will the faiths—whether Muslim, Christian, or other—that have traditionally closed themselves to each other, persist or finally admit their common origin?

In the new world order, are we growing toward a time when we will no longer resort to war, either religious or political? The standard given by Edgar Cayce states: "And as ye live, so may the Christian light of LOVE encompass the earth; not that of hate, selfishness, money, power, or fame!" (3976-25)

Regarding fears of an aggressive Germany made powerful after reunification, Dr. Ralf Brinkman declared, "Those fears are unfounded. West Germany has been a member of NATO. Forty years of living next to West German democracy have inclined us to adopt the values of the West. Friendship with France and other cultures has brought prosperity so that it would be impossible to be hostile against Germany's neighbors. She depends on them. . . . A unified Germany will be European. Anything else will generate catastrophe."[5]

I asked him what the German people thought about Gorbachev. "We can't tell what he thinks," he replied, "but he has done much to benefit the people. He is very popular in Germany."

I asked if East and West Germany would share a united but neutral Germany. "I think it's a bit unrealistic to think that the East Germans can be not neutral. After World War I, Germany was part neutral."[6]

I recalled the Holocaust under Hitler. Among other European countries there was fear of a resurgent Nazi Germany.

asked him what Germans felt about that and if he thought the Nazis would become a threat.

"In America you have people such as the Ku Klux Klan and other troublesome groups. There are such people in every country but they are not a great threat."[7]

Regarding nationalism, Cayce said that there should be regard and concern for one's self, but not to the detriment of others. "For, though He were the Son, He took upon Himself the form of man, became as naught, subject to all the trials, all the sorrows of thine own self.

"Then, what right has any man to set state or nation above the principle of brotherly love?

"But always 'Render unto Caesar the things that are Caesar's and unto God the things that are God's.' " (3976-27) (Luke 20:25)

While reunification of Germany was taking place, Soviet bloc and Eastern bloc nations sought to regain their national independence. Nations around the world asserted their own sovereignty under democratic leadership.

However, in her article "Pogroms and Peristroika" Karla Goldman says Russia herself found her own brand of nationalism which has led to racism, "with little moral fiber in the Russian culture." She deplores the revival of ugly ethnic emotions. "Jews in the Soviet Union today are scared. They are scared that the anti-Semitic forces that have always been present in their nation will find expression in widespread violence . . . As in the past, ultra-Semitic forces that have always been present in their nation will find expression in widespread violence . . . As in the past, ultra-nationalists are making Jews the scapegoats for deteriorating social and economic conditions. Leaflets indicting Jews for all the Soviet Union's current ills and proclaiming 'death to the Jews' have been distributed in major Soviet cities and have appeared in many Jewish mailboxes."[8]

Goldman cites Pamyat, one of the organizations thought to be behind these threats. She describes it as an organization dedicated to preserving Russian monuments and artifacts but is now considered "one of the most viciously racist of Soviet right-wing groups. Nostalgic nationalism has translated into ethnic hatred.''⁹

She says that today, in contrast to the past when Hebrew teachers were sent to Siberia, ''the Moscow synagogue echoes with the sounds of young children studying Hebrew and English. . . . The acquisition of Jewish knowledge, like the study of English, seems directed toward the expectation of emigrating. . . .''¹⁰

Said Cayce regarding the persecution of Jews under Hitler: ''those peoples—though they were called—have wandered far afield, and (this) has rather brought them into their present position. . . . Hence the attitude that is assumed is rather a fulfilment of that (Biblical) prophecy that has been made, and is the beginning of the return that must come throughout the earth'' (3976-13; Jeremiah 44:12). ''The Jews are ''like any other individual . . . remember the first principle: *all* are equal before God!''

For decades, Cubans left their country to live in the United States rather than under Castro's communism. Their relatives and friends who stayed behind have been without freedom in many ways, most important, freedom of religion. Priests and nuns were expelled and their Cuban bishop prohibited from holding mass. Pope John Paul II's visit to Cuba in January 1998 brought a tremendous response from the people as they greeted him by the thousands in Havana and Santiago. Just as in Russia in 1990, they chanted ''Freedom!'', as we heard and saw on national television. Among them were children who had never known about the Catholic church or what it teaches, for as in Russia, such knowledge was banned.

That was not the first time Pope John Paul II had visited Latin America. According to Peter Winn, in October 1991 he paid his second visit to Brazil and his tenth to Latin America and the Caribbean in a little more than a decade. ''More Catholics live in Latin America and the Caribbean than in any other region on earth,'' states Winn. Membership dropped in recent years based on the issue of more democracy in the Church. During the revolution of the 1980s, Catholics moved from obedience and submission to more autonomy in their lives. The Contra-Sandinista revolution brought concern for human rights through social activism, which the Church has always emphasized. "But during recent decades, the Latin American Church has been at the storm center of change—and been transformed in the process." The numbers are growing.[11]

"The pope and a top Cuban prelate made appeals for greater freedom for the Roman Catholic Church, and for all Cubans. The pope's public appeal on behalf of Cuba's estimated 600 political prisoners came in the context of words of comfort to patients, including some suffering from AIDS and leprosy, at the Sanctuary of St. Lazarus, just outside Havana. 'There is also suffering of the soul,' the pope said, 'such as we see in those who are isolated, persecuted, imprisoned for various offenses or for reasons of conscience, for ideas which though dissident are nonetheless peaceful. . . .' The pope also called for a healing of pain caused by moral suffering—when people suffer in their soul, or when the soul of a nation suffers . . .' which he said should be a 'summons' to compassion and justice."[12]

THE AWAKENING NOW!

What people of all faiths do agree on is the power of prayer. It has no doubt played a part in many wars in history, in ways we can only surmise. During Desert Storm, the nation prayed. Religious leaders since then have marked the change, confirming Edgar Cayce's prophecy that there would be a world religious "awakening" in our time.

As we have given, Helene stated the Great Seal of the United States represents our leading the world toward the "New Order of the Ages." We have, for all our faults and our virtues, been given the responsibility to lead not only in democracy but what Cayce says is our highest ideal, that new order based on God's plan. Our status as the most powerful nation in the world tells us we are equal to the task: When we prevailed during Desert Storm, we were once more one nation.

Other wars in recent history have ended with millions of casualties, including both world wars, the Korean War, and the Vietnam War. As we noted in Chapter One, Cayce asserted that it was the prayers of the mothers and fathers of each nation involved in World War I that had a direct bearing on bringing about peace. Prayers from both democratic and totalitarian countries, he said, "caused the meeting" at Versailles that ended the war. During Desert Storm, prayers were offered for loved ones caught in the war zones. Millions of Americans and other Westerners prayed in churches, temples, homes, in cities and towns everywhere.

Just as devoutly, Muslims prayed in their mosques or in streets or in their homes. All faiths experienced the strange paradox of war: both sides supporting war and praying to God for special help. We wonder how God can answer both sides, for we recall He is no respecter of persons. As we prayed, we concentrated on protection for the men and women whose lives were at risk. We prayed for peace. We wanted it over with. Please, God, end the war.

But let *us* win!

As many people in the West declared, God had indeed answered our prayers: We did win, and there were few casualties on our side. Yet the Iraqis suffered horrendous losses of lives and property, complete defeat. We were appalled, for there was no hate on our part. Hussein's aggression against Kuwait was not condoned by all of Islam or by other faiths. Muslim leaders are reported to have told their congregations of the disparity between the actions of Saddam Hussein and the Muslim principles regarding peace. "*Salam,* or peace, is the signature of our religion," said Ahmed Noor, president of the Mosque and Islamic Center in Hampton Roads. "It is very sad to see that [in Iraq] Muslims start a crisis, invade other countries, and do not observe this concept of salam, or peace. Saddam Hussein has violated our principles many times and has no right to claim his acts of aggression in the name of the Muslim faith."[13]

"DIVISIONS AMONG YOU"

Cayce quoted Apostle Paul, who said to the gentiles: "I hear there are divisions among you. Some say I am Paul, another I am Apollos, another I am of Caiaphas. Paul may minister, Apollos may have watered, but it's God that gives the increase!'' (364-9)

The concept of the oneness of God is expressed in the Qur'an, and the terminology is much like our own: "He is God, One, God, the Everlasting refuge, who has not begotten, and has not been begotten, and equal to Him is not any one.''[14]

In the Christian concept, God is the Trinity of Father, Son, and Holy Ghost. Christ is the Son. Said Cayce, "Christ is the Power, Jesus is the pattern." In Galilee as the Bible teaches, He *became* the Christ. The Cayce readings indicated, along with the Bible, that the pattern and the power are meant for all mankind, as we each develop according to the pattern and power of His teachings.

However much we as a nation dreaded the war in the Gulf, most of us agreed with President Bush that it was a just war. Others did not, and demonstrations took place by pacifists. But the majority of Christians and Jews alike supported Bush. Early in the war, he is reported to have sought spiritual counsel from clergymen such as Billy Graham and Robert Schuller. The Jews conducted a small peace movement in the United States based on Jewish law and tradition that justify the war against Saddam Hussein.

I once asked a Japanese Buddhist who was visiting in America what the lotus meant to his people.

"It means," he told me, "the same as the Easter lily of Christianity." In Japan, there is a tradition of oneness in "that same impelling force" of which Cayce spoke. That is, there are many religions—the outer forms with their special ceremonies and emphases on various concepts—but the people acknowledge them as what the founder of Japanese Buddhism called "the composite whole of the nation's spiritual and moral life." Though there are many organized religions, those most prominent are Shinto, Confucianism, and Buddhism. Others have been introduced since these, which date from the founder, Prince Shotoku in the sixth century, and Shintoism in the eighth century. Christianity was introduced by Roman Catholic missionaries in the sixteenth century but was subjected to persecution due to the Japanese view that it was a foreign religion.

The national and cultural life of Japan is closely tied to its religions. Japanese customs and beliefs at the same time have mixed with Christian beliefs. Old Japanese religions blended with the people's ancient folk customs, whereas the Christian faith was exclusive of all others. The old ways were based on love and respect for nature and belief in the gods—either the *kami* of Shinto or the Buddhas—which denote the sacredness of high beings. Mortals, gods, and nature are seen in Japan as forming a relationship of harmony rather than division.[15]

It's not enough to rely on our mortal understanding, Cayce is telling us. Belief in the Power higher than ourselves does not settle for anything less.

Nor is it enough to be good without being good for something. Cayce urged us to "do something" about problems and take a stand for what is right.

By the very act of taking a stand on truth and righteousness, we set in motion a powerful, creative force that goes out into the world to accomplish more than we know, and we thereby slay dragons! Lately, small groups and masses of people have joined to take a stand and act to bring about better conditions from neighborhood safety to holistic living. World religious groups are uniting in this concept, have each from their various perceptions taken action in recent decades against oppression and for their belief. Buddhism is primarily a faith of quiet going within to worship God, a faith of liberation from earthly suffering through understanding religious principles. Its teachings lead "to peace, to discernment, to enlightenment, to Nirbbana." But it can be a faith of activism: Buddhist priests are known to join students in opposing political oppression.[16]

Despite the many many wrongs everywhere, on all levels, are the unprecedented events of these times leading the world toward a time we will be united in heart and mind? There are signs among Westerners and Easterners that true unity is a growing possibility: The world has matured and grown closer—"the global village"—through television, the print media, as well as evangelism around the world. The scornful have become a bit kinder; the subdued have become a bit bolder. In January 1991 a black sculptor exhibited a black figure with a wound showing red blood. The sculpture was a statement in truth, recalling Cayce who had declared, "For He hath made of one blood the nations of the earth" (3976-24).

In the chapter "The Awakening," Cayce stated regarding the appearance of Jesus Christ that He would not come to us "unless invited." In many ways, the minds of mankind have been opening to the promise in the New Testament that He will appear to us if we ask. Many people today give testimony of that event personally, as they seek communion with Him. It has made the way clear for the whole of humanity, as such presence of the Lord brings light to enlighten us all.

The centuries-long development of our consciousness to the present can be seen to spell closer "brotherhood" among people, despite lingering and even violent ethnic hostility.

Cayce pointed out the problem of denominationalism: "each church crying, 'Lo, here is Christ—Lo, this is the manner of approach—Lo, unless ye do this or that ye have no part in Him.' " He advised rather to subscribe to Christ's criterion: "He that loves me will keep my commandments."

"What are the commandments? 'Thou shalt have no other god before me.' And 'Love thy neighbor as thyself.' In this is builded the whole law and gospel of every age that has said, 'There is ONE God' " (364-9). Such advice to find unity among Christians was not confined to Christian belief and practice but was inclusive of all the major religions. In reading 364-9, the question was asked in 1932: "What part did Jesus play in any of His reincarnations in the development of the basic teachings of the following religions and philosophies?" The questions that followed mentioned Buddhism, Muhammadanism, Confucianism, Shintoism, Brahmanism, Platonism, Judaism. The answer was: "the entity—(Jesus)—influenced either directly or indirectly all those forms of philosophy or religious thought that taught God was One."

In fact, according to Cayce, much from the teachings of Jesus has been added to each of these religions. "In all of these, then, there is that same impelling spirit." He said that Jesus was directly associated with the one who guided the Buddha.

Moreover, it was not the mortal man Jesus who was the influence in all religions that taught God is one; rather, it was the universal Christ that He *became*. Therefore, distinction is made by Cayce that the Master Jesus was "the only one" to be the Son among world religious teachers such as Buddha and Muhammad. For such great souls "The Spirit of the Master, the Spirit of the Son, was manifested to each in their respective sphere." For them all, he said, it has been given: "Know, O Israel, the Lord thy God is One!" (364-9)

ONENESS OF FAITHS

Today, one sees persons of other races or religions as surprisingly like oneself. Just since Desert Storm, knowledge of Islam is of interest to many Christians, in a growing trend of the search for understanding. Before that, the people of the Middle East were unknown to Westerners except to those who have lived and worked there for decades. This new understanding can only be a step to recognition that we share the fatherhood of God. Such understanding is to be encouraged among all—our brothers around the world, regardless of their religious persuasion. Much of this new world understanding also is attributed to the prevalence of television, as well as the printed word. It plays, evidently, a part of the "awakening" Cayce spoke of, directly related to understanding one another, the way we perceive each other, for open communication is vital to peace among nations.

The "awakening" Cayce spoke of has to do with not only religion but a new perception of religion, to judge by the events of recent times. Whereas the American experience has been one of division among the many religions, of our national will that seems to have no central coordinating ideal, the world rejoiced as the Gulf crisis ended with the realization we are united in what is really the ideal of brotherhood.

The awakening is slow. Many nations are in chaos, as the transition takes place among us. But wisdom of the ages promises that there will be a new order of conditions long predicted that will be in favor of all humanity. The awakening is surely to be under the banners of all beliefs: Muslim, Christian, Catholic, Jew, the Eastern thought.

But religion, said Cayce, is more than a system, however honored. It is the "awakening of the individual to the truth of the divine heritage in each individual that may respond to that of creative energy in the universal forces" (254-48). The basic principles, he said, of all teachings are expressed in "Ye shall love the Lord." It is "at the core, the heart," of every major religious teaching. Thus he held that God does not favor one religious system over another, so long as it is God-centered.

To a Protestant woman concerned that her niece had married a Catholic, he said, "Is He not the God and Lord of the Catholic as well as of the Protestant and the Jew? Did He not make them all? Does He not love one the same as another? Know ye not that He is not a respecter of persons? Art thou?" (2783-1)

To a young woman debating whether she should marry her Catholic fiancé, although she was Protestant, he said, "What has been thy meditation? That ye may be a channel of blessings!" (1722-1)

And to a Methodist woman asking if she could be a channel for God's work as a Methodist, he said, "Magnify the Christ, not the method!" (2574-1)

11

IDEALS AND ECONOMICS

There must be first the return to a standard by which economics is to be judged, and then there may be gradually worked out a plausible, equitable, applicable situation in the affairs of the world. (3976-10, February 8, 1932)

"**THE LARGER LIFE, SPIRITUALLY**" was Cayce's thesis throughout the readings, meant for all of us. He applied it moreover to all facets of life, not merely organized religions or humanitarian efforts. The phrase embraces all *phases* of life—there is no human endeavor that is not in essence subject to spiritual laws. For instance, in answer to a question about impending serious strife between capital and labor in 1941, Cayce stated: "As we have indicated through these channels before, this depends upon whether or not those who have seen the light, those who understand the situations between labor and capital, the employee and the employer, pray and live consistent one with the other. . . ."

He was then asked: "What can we do to counteract such serious happenings [labor strikes]?"

Cayce's answer was: "Make known the trouble—*where it lies; that they who have forgotten God must right about face!*"

He added that a leader mentioned in the reading, through his series of conferences between the two factions, be aware of the disturbances, "that God must not be left out of the purposes of men! For, as indicated, point to the happenings as divine direction" (3976-26).

The world noted with much admiration the attitude of Walesa whose devotion to the Catholic church and his faith in God appeared to help in the labor disputes between Polish workers and their communist leaders.

Franklin Roosevelt saved many a family from want with his Works Progress Administration, in providing jobs where none had been before. But when Cayce was asked in 1938 about the unemployment situation in America, he replied that there must be "more return to the toil upon the land, and not so much of the makeshift of labor" (3976-19). He advocated in fact a return to the soil for this country, "for of dust the body is made and of dust the sustenance of same comes."

In 1939 Cayce also saw the problem between capital and labor in America. "Ye are to have strifes between capital and labor" (3976-24). Unless there is consideration of those that produce, so that they share more equitably profits from their labors, "there must be brought greater turmoils in the land." When Truman came into office following Roosevelt, America was experiencing communist infiltration, which Truman hoped to eliminate. Cayce warned that continuation of such "makeshift" labor would eventually lead to "disruption, turmoil, and strife." Was he referring to that strife that occurred under Lyndon Johnson in the 1960s—the War on Poverty, when revolution took place in many cities? It was, said Allen, a communist revolution.

It was, added Cayce, to be a part of the experience of America "because of unbelief!"

IDEALS AND ECONOMICS

Cayce's forecasts from the faraway time of 1932 seem to be even more remarkable in their description of what appears to be today's global economy. For it is a greatly changed world.

Cayce spoke of working toward "a plausible, equitable, applicable situation" in the future world economy. Evidently, that future is now, judging from progress on the part of governments and industry since 1950. It is seen as marked by cooperation (Cayce's first lesson in our search for God), multinational production of goods and trade, and third world development. Unhappily, severe debt crisis threatens large continents—Latin America, Africa, Asia—leading to possible political and economic breakdown. Old power politics held in place by military factions and banking institutions practicing corruption and fraud are the dark side of the 1990s. They are what Cayce meant by his assertion that war and social injustice have their roots in selfishness, greed, and immorality. It was present in the world of 1932 and it is with us still.

Economic inequality, particularly between strong nations and the third world, exists as a legacy of the past. With changes taking place toward freedom and democracy in the 1980s, however, the third world began to catch up. We saw humble minorities around the world running factories and businesses, taking their share of the power as they participated in local enterprise.

Cayce linked social and political factors with economic problems and their solutions. But the rules and reasons vary according to the mind-set of those leaders who control those factors. As Bill Still reminds us and many people have learned, the Bretton Woods Conference in 1944 was attended by representatives of forty nations. They created the World Bank and the International Federal Reserve System to centralize the monetary power of the entire world in a single entity.

As quoted, Cayce warned against that very power over world affairs: that it was not to be vested in the hands of a few. He said in effect we must remain as nations under our individual rule as such power on any level can be misused.

From his own words, such as "unit-making" to describe regionalism, we know Cayce would approve today's regional trading blocs, which all nations find attractive. Since 1970 we have seen global economic development as the world becomes a "village" where information and knowledge are exchanged with the swiftness of telecommunication, as well as trade and economic opportunity. Jan Dauman points out that the world is becoming increasingly interdependent, with economic nationalism giving way to economic regionalism.[1]

There are at least four such regional blocs now. The most striking examples of new international cooperation, states Raymond Vernon, is the twelve-nation European Community and the United States–Canada Free Trade Agreement of 1990.[2]

Vernon adds that the success of the four regional blocs is due to "the strong commitments and strong dispute settlement machinery which was difficult to conceive in 1950."

Another successful bloc, as Michael Smith reminds us, is the Pacific Rim—in which neither the United States nor Japan dominates but both cooperate in a benign fashion. The Pacific Rim is seen as a common market and includes many less powerful nations in the area. There are advantages of "a long-term agreement with the other Pacific Rim countries on trade, finance, development, education, and security."[3] Mexico is included in still another alliance with North America and Canada. And there are also inter-regional alliances such as Europe and Japan, North America and Asia.

The communication and trade advantages have brought the world much understanding about itself, and have helped bring about great social change today. But the change causes disruption, as well. In Puerto Rico, where the Telephone company, Telefonica, has been government-owned, strong resistance was reported in July 1998, to plans to privatize. Saboteurs exploded a bomb behind the company plant, but the sale of the company continued.[4]

Asia in 1998 experienced economic recession due to bad bank loans and the fall of the yen. Reform was slow, affecting the economies of countries to the west including Indochina, Korea, Malaysia, and Thailand. Japan was criticized for not having taken steps earlier to reform its economy, which was once highly successful and prosperous.

There have been many world orders in history, according to authors Anell and Nygren. During the eighteenth century, the philosophy was liberalism: "Ethics are thrown overboard. Man is selfish and must be so. The just price—which had been a preoccupation of earlier philosophers and economists—is settled by the world order. It functions up to the Great War, is passably restored by the 1920s, only to collapse after the stock market crash of 1929 in a tangle of bilateral agree-ments."[5]

The early 20th century was apparently in the midst of a general awakening to the transcending influence of Aquarius: Demand for a new economic order among third world coun-tries began early in the 20th century when demand was made also for political and racial equality.[6]

TODAY'S ECONOMIC IDEALS DEFINED

Just like America and Europe one hundred fifty years ago, newly freed nations today are becoming industrialized, real-izing *their* potential for growth and expansion. "The world is at a crossroads," states Dauman, "faced both politically and economically with volatility and uncertainty." He thinks the world economic situation could be stabilized by the year 2000 if governments reach the state of "competitive accom-modation," in order to have free trade and to manage the debt crisis.[7]

The third world countries each have their uniqueness of language, religious values, and history. They have resources, and skills, their "yearning to breathe free" within their own shores. So it is a time when they look to America's example. They, too, seek a Manifest Destiny, which includes a fair living for all, with benefit of a peaceful, prosperous culture ruled by ideals. But as all others in the world market, Dauman reminds us, they are subject to its vagaries such as population growth and demographics, environment, and even the weather. In addition, he says that the return in the 1980s to fundamentalist beliefs is among the many forces at work. He included among those forces the leadership of the major pow-ers, including Reagan, Gorbachev, Thatcher, and Lord Cock-field, architect of Europe '92.[8]

As early as 1927, the readings advised that although money is necessary, it should never be the first and foremost con-dition (reason?) to build a stable world economy. Rather, it was the principle of loving God and one's neighbor as one-self. However, when asked, advice was given that reflected understanding of macro- and microeconomics, and always with the purpose of upbuilding mankind (3976-5). It will be that fundamental belief that will determine how people rise up to challenge wrong ways in general, to promote brotherhood of mutual helpfulness.

Principles were established by Cayce in the 1930s for a world organization that would benefit everybody, as we have given. Those who had composed the central board of control of the parent holding corporation were told that they were to enter into their work realizing it was a "service to Him." As they came together, they should be "praying, offering service, then it shall be given thee in that selfsame hour what ye shall say and what ye shall do. Take no thought, but prepare thine self! . . . Laying aside, then, those things that so easily beset, purge thine heart as with clean water, and *then* the ways, the doors are open for those glories that may come to *others* through thine efforts!" (3976-7).

"When there are, then, the greater number that would *see* that the *Ideal* is again made the standard, then may conditions (of the Great Depression) be expected to improve. This not as men count improvement, in dollars and cents, but in contentment and understanding—and one is the fruit of the other!" (3976-8, January 15, 1932) That advice is just as valid today.

In 1933, Cayce again gave a reading requested to address the economics of the time:

In the very nature . . . of a nation, a people, there are some fundamental principles upon which the economic and the soul life of a nation must be founded, if such a people, such a nation, is to remain true to that which is the birthright of every soul: to pursue that which will give it as an individual the right to manifest that (which) it would worship in its Creator.

For, the first law that has been given to man from the beginning is: "Thou shalt have no other gods before me." And when man has faltered, has altered that, which has deprived others from giving expression to that birthright, that command that has come to man throughout the ages, then there arises that which creates those things that are the fruits of the evil influences that are in the earth. Such as: hate, jealousy, avarice. These make for the creating of those conditions in all walks of life for power, for position, for the love of money and what it will bring in its associations in the lives of individuals. . . .

Americans must turn within to find their relation to the Creative Forces and to ask themselves what they will do about it, said Cayce. "When conditions arise that make for distress, whether they be in body, in mind, in the economic influence, in the experience of any, sin lieth at thy door, not thy neighbor's!" (3976-14)

By 1937, questions were asked about the problems of capital and labor. Cayce pointed out that we are dependent upon each other. Cooperation and an attitude reflecting the ideal "We are our brother's keeper" were paramount. Whatever trends that lay ahead for the world in 1937 depended "upon that influence prompting actions of those in power. . . . If that ideal is kept by those who have been and are in power, there will be kept a general trend toward greater security, economic considerations, greater peace, greater harmony.

"Wherever selfishness is the prompting attitude there may be expected to be brought turmoils and strife.

"If there is still kept that attitude of peace and harmony," Cayce told this group, "if there are the considerations of the rights of others," the United States will not be involved in world war. The cause for such a war, he said, would be "*selfishness!*" (3976-17)[9]

It was selfishness, all right, in the form of war profiteering to the tune of billions of dollars paid by the American taxpayers.

In 1943 he said, "When there has been in the earth those groups that have sufficiently desired and sought peace, peace will begin. It must begin within self. The same is true in economic conditions. He that saith he loveth God and seeth his neighbor in need of food or a coat and saith 'Go in peace, God be with thee' and does nothing about same, is a liar and a thief, wherever he may be; is false to self and will one day create those things that will bring discontent and disputation

n the earth'' (3976-28). It's to Franklin D. Roosevelt's credit
hat he initiated the Works Progress Administration, which
provided jobs for many Americans during the Great Depression. In that respect, he did something about economic conditions, for which those involved were grateful. But it was far
from the ideal.

Certainly around the world in capitalist countries, including
America, Japan, and some European nations, there was ex-
posed in the 1990s large-scale business fraud and cheating.
Banking and business scandals have been reported ongoing
for years, the outrageous government spending for pork barrel
interests. Especially onerous is the misdirected allocation of
treasury funds for loans to questionable purposes. From our
daily media we learn of abuses of the capitalist system that
bring billions of dollars to the pockets of the manipulators of
that system while making financial hardship for the rest of
us. The ideal is, by contrast, capitalism under freedom in
which those in power over the nation's workers pay all employees living wages and benefits, honesty in dealings large
and small.

When the Asian economy faltered in 1998, the rest of the
world worried. We realized how interconnected the world
economy has become. Economist Lynn Reaser of Nations-
Bank stated the Asian situation would ultimately filter down;
meanwhile, prices and interest rates would remain low.[10]

But too many business companies throughout the world
prove unfair and greedy. It is especially evident among multinational companies. Latin American nations began industri-
alizing after World War II. They needed to replace the goods
they had been importing with their own products. With the
help given Latin American countries by the United Nations
Economic Commission, Brazilians added to their low-
technology products their first state-owned Volta Redonda
steelworks in 1946. They then began to make such high-tech
goods as motor vehicles. First world countries set up plants
in Brazil such as Volkswagen, Ford, General Motors, and
Toyota. Factories were built mostly in São Paulo, but in other
cities as well, as are most industries, located in the densely
populated cities of Rio de Janeiro and Belo Horizonte, in

southeast Brazil, and in Buenos Aires in Argentina.[11] Much funding was by foreign loans to the Brazilian government. The rest was from multinational companies or the Inter-American Development Bank. By 1980, Brazil became the world's tenth largest producer of steel—greater than the United Kingdom—exporting steel to the United States, Canada, and several third world countries.[12] That is a welcome success story.

Some South American countries, Peru, Chile, and Venezuela, nationalize their major industries. Others have reversed this, in order to be more successful, favoring free trade and the private sector.[13]

"Industrialization has not helped the poor. The wealth is concentrated in the cities, but there are hundreds of thousands of poor who must construct their own shanties because they cannot afford even modest housing."[14] Say authors D. F. and Ray Bromley, the problem is foreign domination in the industrial sector: "If the multinational companies were to play a lesser role in Latin America's industrial expansion, the people would be better off. The foreign companies there operate for their own interests, take greater profits, even have caused cut-offs in trade investment and economic aid for Latin American firms. Therefore, the Latin Americans gain very little from their investments."[15]

Although Latin American countries and others have been helped by loans from the IMF and the World Bank, they have had a difficult time paying them back. This has led to some restrictions.

Debt of all the less-developed countries rose from $130.1 billion to $1 trillion by 1985. The United States had to absorb an inordinate amount of the burden, and the sale of American goods to Latin America has been reduced by $20 billion a year. Such indebtedness of third world countries has contributed to the increasing inequality and stagnation between developed and undeveloped countries.[16]

All this took place against authoritarian communist rule until 1991, when democracy won out. The problems facing these developing countries call to mind Cayce's advice that there be a *standard* set in economic relations. Those multinational companies could use a higher standard of fair business practice—"the level playing field"—to give newly emerging trading partners both investment opportunity and greater profits. In South America the people wanted open markets for agricultural products, doing away with quotas. Of importance in a freer world was seen to be protection of intellectual property by patents and copyrights.

Judging from Cayce's urgent advice to seek a standard in world economics, the truth is that there has seemed to be no high level standard set forth. But late in October 1997, a standard was called for by Richard Trumka, secretary/treasurer for the AFL-CIO: "We need standard trade agreements: good labor, consumer, environment standards. It's a major issue. Seventy-five percent of the public think we need protection for workers, for the environment." He added that we need as well protection against child labor and slave labor that persist throughout the world. We are moving forward on the North American Free Trade Agreement, he said, but America seeking opportunities for a strong economy needs to show strong leadership under President Clinton. We won't make good deals with other countries if Clinton doesn't have the authority with Congress to hold it. Trumka feared that Congress might vote to lock in low wages.[17]

The word "standard" is a powerful one. It calls a halt to what is wrong, insufficient, or outgrown. Mindful of the power of "the word" in all life, we affirm that just proclaiming the new rallying point sets it in motion toward fulfillment. It calls for attention in all its ramifications. Once a higher standard is proclaimed, all that is less falls away because it is a matter of consciousness, and the former conditions must retreat into oblivion. The hope is that Trumka's call will set the pace.

"The world has undergone a radical transformation since 1945. It is so interdependent and complex that the United States can no longer create a policy to address one major economic issue without considering the effect that it will have on other issues . . . other nations. . . ."[18]

Some of those issues have long been there. Even as nations around the world shake off oppressive rule and shift to capitalism, they still contend with attempts at dictatorship, populist conflicts of nationalism, racism, and ethnicism; or civil war as in Yugoslavia and Albania, as in Cambodia where in 1997 the people's freedom was again threatened by the Pol Pot forces, as in Nicaragua where the Sandinistas continued to seek power.

However, many nations had been able to maintain their democratic autonomy won during the 1980s. Now they hoped for economic reform.

"They had changed from the old Marxist dependency theories. Now, instead, they were in debt," said Bruce Babbitt in 1991. But, he pointed out, some say that now that the cold war is over, Latin America simply doesn't matter anymore. As foreign aid and other forms of public investment continue to decline, trade at the regional level everywhere following the failure of the Uruguay Round, Brazil and the United States will possibly succeed in opening free markets. Babbitt called for "timely" international leadership" for South America.[19]

But in South America, democracy is too often linked with corruption of the system still in place from former Marxist leaders, characterized by inflation and economics favoring those in power. In those nations and throughout the world, millions of people live at poverty levels, according to reports by the United Nations Development Program. There is little faith among them in democracy's promise.

Such lack of faith is well founded when the people experience corruption and avarice for power and position among their leaders. Foreign domination in which the Latin Americans find profits are being unfairly taken from them has not helped. Both the people who conduct trade with other nations and their leaders, everywhere, should know about those fundamental principles Cayce spoke of, upon which the economic and the soul life of nations must be founded, if they will remain true to their birthright: "to manifest that which (a person) would worship in (his or her) Creator." When dishonest or selfish individuals cynically take power for their own advantage, at the expense of the people who trust and depend on them, either in politics or economics, they worship other gods. We should beware the danger for such nations to be forced by extreme economic pressures back into communism. Those without food or shelter care not who rescues them, as Cayce reminded us. So we should not ignore the third world's plight. Our own comparatively secure world is far from debt-free. But we can provide leadership to help those nations as we profess a higher consciousness of altruism and brotherhood.

In Western Europe there is general discontent in spite of the change in the ideological climate. And in Eastern Europe, democracy and perestroika remained only partially realized. Leonard Sussman quotes Gorbachev: "Changing peoples' minds is the most difficult thing. Perestroika depends on public opinion and it's conservative."[20] Europe is old in the ways of power and its influence, rivalries among nations, and inequality among classes.

Since the cold war, for years, we have heard, however, that Europeans look forward to a united Europe with stronger trade and business interests. Fear still lingered of the possibility of nuclear war. But that was before glasnost. Eastern European nations are now seen as potential investment and trade partners. NATO, the North Atlantic Treaty Organization, was formed by Europe and America as protection against the Russian military threat. In 1997 Russia's President Boris Yeltsin resisted joining because he now felt threatened by the former captive Eastern bloc nations! But on May 16, 1997, the sixteen NATO countries approved unanimously its accord with Russia, creating a new NATO-Russia Permanent Joint Council, enabling Russia a say in NATO plans but no veto power.

IS AMERICA FULFILLING HER DESTINY?

Along with other economists, David M. Abshire thinks America must lead the course of global economy. But America is now more vulnerable as other nations also become both military and economic powers. Reform in defense as well as its economic security is needed.[21] The key seems to be help through the UN. On August 25, 1990, the UN Security Council gave the world's navies the right to use force to stop violations of trade sanctions against Iraq. The UN vote marked the first time in its history that it authorized such military action without a UN flag or UN command and control to enforce its own sanctions. Moreover, the vote represented a major diplomatic victory for the United States. U.S. officials had worked strenuously to convince the Soviet Union, China, and third world countries, which were not as ready to agree that force was necessary, immediately to ensure that the trade embargo against Iraq would not be violated. All members voted for it except Cuba.[22]

Not only the UN but also individual nations can learn to help one another, for the good of all. "There is already ample evidence that American companies can and will exploit the opportunities for new business within the Soviet bloc," states Peter W. Ludlow.[23] In 1997, the prophecy of cooperation between the United States and Russia became a reality. American technology and know-how applied to Russia's vast natural oil resources resulted in a mutually workable business venture. (See Chapter five.)

South American leaders hosted President and Mrs. Clinton in October 1997 as they traveled to Brazil, Venezuela, and Argentina to reinforce U.S. trade partnership. National leaders and economists today seek answers to multiple new economic and cultural problems. Today, they could benefit from Cayce's worldview that calls for an enlightened electorate as well.

Throughout the readings, he spoke in terms of the heart, that we "go within" for help in all situations. He advised that we not look to others to solve our problems but seek help from our higher wisdom.

Especially emphasized in the "World Affairs" collection was faith in ourselves to find right solutions—God's solutions—for problems of whatever kind. There, he declared, we can find answers for ourselves. Right answers, he said, are "for every soul that seeks . . . Lo! ye shall find it in your own heart!" (3976-14)

He spoke of "the hearts of the nations" and "whether there is the arousing in the hearts, souls, and minds of a sufficient number of individuals—who will align, themselves with that that is right in *His* might or not!" (3976-8)

All nations today are in chaos. We are acutely aware of the misery, degradation, and hopelessness of millions of people throughout the world. In Africa, Asia, South America, and in the first world countries as well, the gulf between the affluent and the abjectly poor grows even as hopes for a better world are expressed.

Although the Bible teaches that the individual is the special concern of our Father in Heaven—"give us this day our daily bread; deliver us from evil"—He has spoken through His Old Testament prophets and his New Testament evangelists with equal emphasis on the importance of the consciousness of the entire national community. The message for all nations is clear throughout: "Blessed is the nation whose God is the Lord" (Psalms 33:12). "Righteousness exalteth a nation: but sin is a reproach to any people" (Proverbs 14:34). Paul in his letter to the Philippians advised them to be "blameless and harmless, the sons of God, without rebuke, in the midst of a crooked and perverse nation [Rome], among whom ye shine as lights in the world" (Philippians 2:15).

But who shapes the consciousness of a nation? Said Cayce, the consciousness of a nation is determined by the combined influence of what he calls the *universal* consciousness: all we are aware of, all influences on society at large—"conditions, thoughts, activities." But those in authority are the greater influence of a nation, the strongest influence for its particular character. So it's a combination of both the people's consciousness and their leaders, who together have the power to bring about their destruction or salvation (3976-16).

This was in answer to a question concerning the sources of his information. "Conditions, thoughts, activities of men in *every* clime are things, as thoughts are things. They make their impressions upon the skein of time and space. Thus, they become records that may be read by those in accord or *attuned* to such a condition." He likened such attunement to that made with radio waves and the consciousness to a "station.'' In this way, he tuned in to those nations he spoke about just as he tuned in to individuals. Upon that attunement of Cayce stands the veracity of the readings.

If the collective mass mind is made up of several opposing viewpoints, it is the stronger that rules. It seems we attract the leadership by our collective desires, opinions, wills, levels of spirituality, high and low. Thus, the collective consciousness of the people of the Soviet empire demanding reform and freedom brought it about through their new leaders. Roosevelt had the backing of almost the entire country, because he answered their needs then. But Wilson before him, although one of the greatest presidents America has ever had, was opposed by negative influential groups that were too strong for him.

After his landslide election in 1932, Roosevelt was the man for the times. He introduced plans to help banks, homeowners, and farmers with the words ''Try something!'' in response to the deepening Depression when twelve million men were reportedly out of work. For America as she tried to recover from the 1929 financial crash, his New Deal was the answer. After World War II, he met with Winston Churchill and Joseph Stalin in hopes for ''a world family of democratic nations.''

In answering questions about world leaders of the time, Cayce was able as well to enlighten us on their destinies. There was ''destiny for the man, Hitler, if he did not allow imperialism to enter in—and it is entering. Hence must be called into question'' (3976-15). It was June 1938. Three months later, Hitler marched his legions into Czechoslovakia.

In this same reading, when asked if America was fulfilling her destiny, Cayce put the responsibility on individual Americans to be fulfilling their own destinies! ''For each and every person, each and every nation, is led—even as in heaven.'' What we see in the earth is ''a shadow of spiritual truth, life and light.''

But he challenged America further: ''Is America fulfilling its destiny? Is it filling, rather, its place, that destined in the experience of peoples, of a nation? What have ye done with the knowledge that ye have respecting the relationships of thy

Creator to thy fellow man? and hast thou made known that
ye know of His ways, God's ways, among thy fellows?''
(3976-15)

As we are reminded by Frederick Merk, America in the
mid-nineteenth century was swiftly changing from a fledgling
nation to one feeling its new opportunities for growth. It was
the beginning of the Industrial Revolution, when machines
and technology were taking the place of horse and carriage,
of washboard and hoe. At about 1845, he says, a new phrase
was coined: "manifest destiny." It meant, "A free, confederated self-governed republic on a continental scale. It was
republicanism resting on a base of confederated states. Republicanism by definition meant freedom. It meant government by the people . . . of a classless society. . . .''[24]

Today, we can see a parallel between newly democratic
nations and America at that time of transition. As they are
doing, America was realizing her wealth of natural resources
and her freedom to exercise her choices in politics, economics, religion. So we surmise from the readings of Cayce, there
is a manifest destiny for *every* nation. For he said that nations
make their own destiny, just as do individuals. They create
their karma—their debts or their gifts—as the case might be.
It's a time when, like individuals, nations are evolving toward
a higher concept of their role in the evolution of mankind.

Franklin Roosevelt saved many a family from want with the
WPA in providing jobs where none had been before. But
when Cayce was asked in 1938 about the unemployment situation in America, he repled that there must be "more return
to toil upon the land and not so much of the makeshift of
labor" (3976-19). He advocated in fact a return to the *soil*
for this country.

In 1939 Cayce also saw the problem between capital and
labor in America: "Unless there is consideration of those that
produce—so that they share more equitably profits from their
labors, there must be brought greater turmoils in the land.''
Cayce warned that continuation of makeshift labor would
eventually lead to "disruption, turmoil, and strife" (3976-24).
It did. When Truman came to office following Roosevelt,

America was experiencing communist infiltration, which Truman inherited and hoped to eliminate.

Cayce's warning was validated. He was referring to that war that occurred under Lyndon Johnson in the 1960s when revolution took place in many American cities. It was, said Allen, a communist revolution. There was a problem, but communism was not the answer.

It was to be America's experience, Cayce had added, because of unbelief!

12

"THAT NATURAL EVOLUTION"

America . . . showing that natural *advancement or evolution of men's minds toward that of a* one God, one purpose, one IDEAL . . . *(3976-9, February 2, 1932)*

EDGAR CAYCE SPOKE OF "that natural evolution." He pointed evolution toward the First Cause, God as our holy destination, in "time, space, and patience." Evolution of all life takes place (hopefully with our patience) in what we call time and space, those great cycles of the millennia only lately rediscovered as the vehicles of our spiraling journey ever upward toward, as the Egyptians believed, the stars. Evolution is "natural" because it is part of the divine plan in which time is divided into great compartments to mark and measure the unfolding of both man and the universe. Just as we are aware of minutes, days, months, and years, we are realizing that the centuries, too, are part of infinite expanses of time, covering millennia, i.e., Kali Yugas, measured in thousands and millions of years. During those periods, just as spring brings back the sun, we find each age of about two thousand years brings its characteristic distinguishing quality. The twelve ages repeat their spiraled order throughout the vast and majestic drama, and those who understand them can know what the ages engender.

From Pisces, the age when the truth is hidden, we are coming into Aquarius, when the truth is made plain, that which has been well known by former advanced cultures. We are only now discovering by archeology and astronomy irrefutable evidence of high civilizations such as those in Central America and Egypt, of the antiquity of mankind and the universe itself. There is mystery yet. It dawns on us that we have much to learn.

The new Age of Aquarius began to influence human evolution several hundred years ago, in recent times speeding up as giant steps took place in science as well as in social reform. The twentieth century can be seen in retrospect as dynamic and mind-opening. But also the changes such as new weather patterns bring unprecedented havoc. Historically, such earth events as earthquakes and volcanic activity as we have seen in recent years do accompany transition from one two-thousand-year age to the next. According to legend and astrology, all such transitions are marked by tumultuous earth changes as well as changes in consciousness. Such are those ending the four- to five-thousand-year epochs calculated by the Maya, the twenty-five-thousand-year cycle of the Great Year. It is taking place in our present transition from Pisces to Aquarius, which some see as "the Day of the Lord."

Strangely analogous to these are the unsettling events described in Revelation in the Bible, of the dark forces contending for innocent souls of light; the four horsemen prophecies related to earth and sea cataclysm; sickness and death; of separation of "the sheep from the goats," the best and the worst of us. Cayce spoke of "teachers who would wage war in the air with those of darkness." Are they not the great white brotherhood, unseen by most of us, who are our teachers on higher planes to help us through these fearful times? However, many of us are not at all sure of such apocalyptic notions.

It looks as though the compassionate seer, Cayce, appeared in the early twentieth century to prepare us for Aquarius, the new Age of Enlightenment, itself placed in that special niche of time in which we find ourselves. Like all great souls, he was destined to show up at just the right moment. A Piscean by birth, he represents the positive Piscean traits: love and compassion for his fellowman, high spiritual development.

He, too, may return now, he was told by his readings, as a 'liberator.''

We realize that the Savior, Jesus Christ, was born just when He was needed to enlighten mankind when civilization was at its lowest point in known history, the beginning of the dark ages.

Christ would appear again, said Cayce, in 1998, ostensibly to help us make the troubling transition from chaos of centuries to the new and liberating consciousness of Aquarius, to guide us toward spiritual emancipation, which infers access to all knowledge, including science. Have there not been portents of that in recent decades? Suddenly, we have boldly gone where no man has gone before! Rogue archaeologists have gone lately where orthodox scientists fear to tread. Probes by astronomers to Mars and Jupiter lead us to think life is not confined to earth after all!

There are other new insights given us and received by many in recent years of the true nature of man and the time-space in which we find ourselves. Just lately informed, we see how ignorant we have been in the past. But why such ignorance? We are supposed to be children of God, inheritors of His attributes, who should never have suffered degradation of our claims to glory. But the fact is, we have evolved from primitive beginnings of the past. By some mysterious impetus of natural selection, we have grown to our space-age maturity, only in recent years, at the expense of confusion as to what Force impels us to evolve and search and grow in the first place!

But there are records of the distant past that scholars do not ignore. We should pay attention, one reason being that they are all we have. They include those "recent," such as the Bible; those from even older sources, such as the Sanskrit texts of *Sanatan Dharma,* of which Paramahansa Yogananda writes in his foreword to *The Holy Science*. He states that there is underlying unity between those holy Indian scriptures and Revelation.

My own question is, Why should man have ever been ignorant?

From ancient teachings of the sages of India, we have a

startling answer to the question, Why should man have ever been ignorant? The answer is based not on the disputed premise that we derived from monkeys and had to work our way up, but on the influence of those forces from God's universe the sun and stars. Which many Westerners might readily dispute but not necessarily disprove. What is suggested is that we have probably gone from primitive man to space exploration *many times*, every twenty-four thousand years, throughout millions of years. Again, Why? And, What happens to cause it?

"What happens to mankind," Swami Sri Yukteswar explains, "is due to influences of the movement of the sun as it revolves around *Brahma*, the grand center in the universe. When the sun is farthest away from that center, after 12,000 years," the mental virtue comes to such a reduced state that man cannot grasp anything beyond the gross material creation. Again, in the same manner, when the sun in its course of revolution begins to advance, this growth is gradually completed in another twelve thousand years.

"Each of these periods of 12,000 years brings a complete change, both externally in the material world and internally in the intellectual or electric world . . . thus the sun completes its 24,000 year cycle." So when the decline is in progress, man becomes ignorant, and "ignorance is the source of all other troubles."[1]

From our known history, we see how it works: a millennium, or Kali Yuga, is twelve hundred years, to allow one hundred years before and one hundred years after the precise date. The descent for the present cycle began in 11,501 B.C. The beginning of Pisces, A.D. 500, was at the bottom of the descent. "The period around A.D. 500 was thus the darkest part of the cycle or Kali Yuga. At that time, the sun began to advance in its orbit, bringing man's intellectual development once more."[2]

"From 499 A.D. onward, the sun began to advance toward the grand center, and the intellect of man started gradually to develop. During the 1100 years of the Ascending Kali Yuga, up to 1599 A.D., the human intellect was so dense that it could not comprehend the electricities . . . the fine matters of crea-

ion. In the political world also, generally speaking, there was
no peace in any kingdom.'' After that, scientific breakthroughs began with William Gilbert who discovered mag-
netic forces and observed the presence of electricity in all
material substances. There followed Kepler, Galileo, New-
ton.[3]

PISCES, AQUARIUS, AND US

Our comparatively brief written history of man testifies to
the accuracy of astrological prediction based on the effects of
the planets and signs at specific times in the past. We have
known for two thousand years the Piscean characteristics firsthand. We know what to expect as we enter the Age of Aquarius, if we know the Aquarian. Each age exerts its influence
for two thousand years. The contrast is greatest between Aries
and Pisces, beginning a new cycle of twenty-five thousand
years. At the end of Aries, philosophy and science flourished
in Greece, India, and Europe, where libraries and universities
spread intellectual knowledge. However, ''With the movement of the sun into Pisces, a significant change came over
the world,'' states Vera W. Reid. ''In India as in Europe, all
signs of creative activity disappeared. The rise of Brahmanism
in the East and Christianity in the west, on the one hand,
strengthened the caste system and on the other, introduced the
feudal systems from whose effects both India and Europe are
still suffering.'' The great transition came to a close and ush-
ered in the Dark Ages when the church, growing in power,
decreed learning confined to the privileged few. It was, we
realize, the darkest time of the cycle.[4]

States Reid: ''Traditionally, Pisces is the Age when the
truth is hidden.''[5] Pisces is marked by ''compassion, mysti-
cism, sacrifice, charity and seclusion'' with love in Venus, its
exalted planet.''[6]

As the sun moved into Pisces, these qualities were responsible for ''a general desire to retreat from the world, leading
to the extinction of the creative activity for which the last
centuries of the Age of Aries were famous.'' She cites barbarian invasions and the fall of Rome, which resulted in de-

cline of civilization. The Dark Ages followed from about 476 to 1000. Not until the fourteenth century did man begin to develop once again toward his ability to understand and use the laws that govern the universe. By the fifteenth century, he was on his way to the well-known achievements of the nineteenth and twentieth centuries, reflecting the early influence of approaching Aquarius. The Age of Leo and the Age of Aquarius are opposites. Leo's symbol is the lion, denoting kingship under which man must honor a hierarchy of power.

Aquarius is called the Age of Enlightenment. It is the sign of the Man, of Humanity, and of Brotherhood. Its characteristics are unity, vision, memory, cooperation, synthesis, and detachment, and through it the three aspects of mind—conscious, unconscious, and superconscious—seek simultaneous expression.[7]

"Aquarius is therefore the sign of the individual who, aware of himself and his relation to his fellows, participates consciously in the corporate life of the race. The true Aquarian knows no exclusive ties of race, colour, creed or family. To him, all men are brothers and to all alike he extends the hand of friendship and goodwill. His ideal of service is impersonal . . . and is dedicated to the cause of humanity."[8]

During the Age of Pisces, out of that suffering, man grew up, ready to take charge of his destiny. We recall Cayce said much the same of the Russian people: Because of their suffering, they have grown strong. They were to become "the hope of the world" demanding "freedom! that each man will live for his fellowman." The Russian experience of the eighteenth and nineteenth centuries illustrates the great changes taking place along with millions around the globe. People everywhere are throwing off the shackles of political and economic tyranny due to past Piscean tendency to secret strategies behind closed doors, truth hidden from the people, elitism of church and state. Today, we all are increasingly influenced by Aquarius.

However, Cayce teaches that "mind is the builder." Although the stars impel, they don't compel. We bring about our own conditions by the decisions and plans we make, the sires we entertain. Evidently, with the advent of Aquarius, will be a lot easier to rise up and claim our dominion in all control over the wealth and resources and administration of our earth, as Reid predicts.[9]

Our growing enlightenment of the past fifty years and more as taken place through knowledge gained from historic breakthroughs, especially in science and social issues. We have become enlightened by science to know how vast is the universe, the mysteries it holds regarding possible life on other planets. We have vicariously walked on the moon with the astronauts; we have sent robot investigators to Mars and Jupiter. We are becoming enlightened beyond any people in our known history in finding ways to overthrow social evils of the past, even as we recognize their presence in painful numbers. In retrospect, we can recognize the historic passage taking place in the earth throughout this century, primarily and essentially in consciousness.

When Cayce referred to "that natural evolution," he meant just that taking place. Presidents and kings, leaders of the masses, are raised by God for a purpose, he declared. But even God, he said, doesn't know what people will do. Of President Franklin D. Roosevelt, he said, "What will you do with this man?" Implying, it seems, that the influence of people of strong national resolve can supersede even the influence of the stars.

However, in the framework of astrology, leaders rise up in accordance with the influence of the planets. Some leaders in recent history have been precursors to the Aquarian Age, such as Abraham Lincoln, an Aquarian who freed the slaves in America, and Franklin D. Roosevelt who established the New Deal, which astrologer Goodavage sees as "forerunner of the Aquarian Age."[10]

Under the aegis of Aquarius, early in the twentieth century, we began to put much emphasis on educating the "common man," not just the elite. Only in recent times have we begun to educate every child. Only lately have we seen thousands of people realize that their minds are free to seek ways to help themselves rather than depend on kings and bureaucracies. Ethnic and racial minorities have risen in this century, along with women everywhere to be recognized for their abilities in business, the arts, government, and even the military forces.

The "million man march" and the "million woman march" in 1997 in Washington, D.C., gave evidence of the Aquarian trait of brotherhood (and sisterhood!). Magnificent and memorable demonstrations were attended by those with desire for personal growth and change. For Aquarius is also the sign of the individual who relates to the group, in cooperation and unity. Never before have we seen such demonstrations of earnest resolve on the part of people to change their lives around, to be better men and women. In the last days of the twentieth century, are we not also seeing signs of spiritual growth in the people we meet? There is reason to think that protecting our natural environment, the earth, affinity with the universe, affords healing and grace that can offset the materialism polluting our minds and souls. In the New Age literature that intrigues many and bemuses others, are lessons returning to us as knowledge we've known in the past? We find wisdom to appreciate more deeply the beauty and symbolism of the rose, the lotus, the lily of Easter. We find hope in experiencing the peace of the great forests, rivers, and mountains we visit for renewal. There is return to love of nature, heartfelt, vibrant. But there is renewal, too, generated from within by meditation and prayer. Many people now testify to their psychic gifts, their experience with spiritual perception such as the appearance of Mother Mary in many places, encounters with Jesus. Such gifts and renewal are recognized by the medical profession as authentic aids to healing; some physicians acknowledge that people who have faith, who live a life of prayer, live longer and are healthier than others. Doctors are now approving those unorthodox methods of healing such as acupuncture, herbal remedies, and massage.

Always in the past, as we have gone about the business of making a living, making whatever of our lives we call "success," we have tended not to be in touch with our spiritual connection with ourselves or the natural environment. But many people think it's time we did. From native Americans

native Europeans and all the Americas, to the Asiatic coun-
ries, traditions of honoring the earth, sun, and moon—after
ll, to us, God's special creations—have never quite left.

Reid compares the Age of Aquarius with its zodiacal op-
osite, Leo. While Aquarius is mental, the symbols of Leo
epresent "the spiritual aspiration which has ever been a guid-
ng principle in human evolution. . . . In the Age of Leo the
uman mind was stimulated by the upward surge of spiritual
orce. In the Age of Aquarius, spiritual awareness will not
rise through upsurge of spiritual forces but rather through
nental enlightenment."[11]

It seems this distinction is an example of Edgar Cayce's
ource prompting us not to judge the people of other ages by
he standards of the Piscean Age, for all twelve differ greatly
n emphasis. As mankind is much older than we have thought,
nany civilizations, many Golden Ages, are therefore said to
ave risen and fallen over vast passages of time. They have
appeared only to fade during cycles of ignorance and again
advanced to knowledge of "the electricities and their attributes which are the creating principles of the external
world."[12]

THE TRUE RELIGION

From legends of the past, it is thought that the zodiacal
journey through time is for our spiritual evolution. Knowledge gained throughout past epochs has never been lost.[13]

Is there any element of constancy throughout the twelve
ages of the great year cycle? Our orthodox religions are varied
and at times in conflict with one another, confusing the truth,
keeping the faithful apart. According to the teachings of ageless wisdom, they are only the outer shells of the "true religion." Reid points to St. Augustine, who stated: "What is
now called the Christian religion already existed among the
ancients and was not lacking from the beginning of the human
race. When Christ appeared in the flesh, the 'true religion'
already in existence received the name of Christian."[14] The
sign of Aquarius is the man. She states: "It was to the coming
Age of Aquarius that Jesus referred when He said: 'When the

Sign of the Man shall come he will enlighten you in al
things' " (Greek text).[15]

Could not the man in this quotation also refer to Christ
who is prophesied by Edgar Cayce to return to us in 1998?
Is He not to enlighten us in all things, as we understand Him?
The constant we look for is evidently that same "true religion" that RaTa sought and found in the south of Egypt when
he first came to bring enlightenment to the people there.

Whether one is Christian, Muslim, Jew, Buddhist, Hindu,
or, as Cayce added, "Hottentot," there are elements of the
true religion found in each. Whatever is true does not change,
no matter the form in which it appears, nor from one millennium to the next. Two plus two is always and everywhere
four.

RUDOLF STEINER ON EVOLUTION

Giving a view of evolution compatible to those of Reid,
Sri Yukteswar, and Cayce, speaking of "epochs" many
thousands of years, is the mystic Rudolf Steiner. In his *Occult
Science* he clarifies for us the form of evolution that has taken
place over the millennia, involving high beings of whom we
are quite unaware. As Cayce, Vera Reid, and Swami Sri Yukteswar speak of the great cycles of time or the zodiac, Steiner
emphasizes changes in mankind under the Initiates, influenced
by the moon, Uranus, the sun, the spiritual laws governing
everything: "Since the tremendous upheaval that brought the
life of old Atlantis to an end, there have been the successive
stages in man's development described in this book as the
ancient Indian, the ancient Persian, the Egypto-Chaldean and
the Graeco-Latin epochs. The fifth is the present—the epoch
man is going through today."

The fifth root race has been in preparation since the fourth
or fifth century A.D. "and began gradually about the twelfth,
thirteenth and fourteenth centuries, to emerge fully in the fifteenth. The preceding epoch—the Graeco-Latin—began
about the eighth century B.C. and included the Christ-
Event."[16]

However, according to the Cayce readings, preparation for

the fifth root race took place long before that, during the fourth root race epoch twelve thousand years ago. It was 10,500 B.C., the Age of Leo. At that time, humanity received knowledge through spiritual powers, according to both Cayce and Steiner, rather than intellectual understanding. At that time, part of the population had inherited animal appendages that made them outcasts. Under the high priest RaTa in the Temple of Sacrifice and Temple Beautiful, they partook of a successful physical and spiritual program to eliminate forever horns, feathers, fins, and hooves by operations, cleansing, and purification. It was understandably a major step in man's evolution, undertaken to benefit all people in an age when man's consciousness had been raised to a high level of spiritual growth. Acutely in touch with their intuitive powers, progenitors of 10,500 B.C. were even then aware they were taking part in the evolution of mankind.

Steiner speaks of the "Atlantean epoch" when, according to Cayce, a thriving civilization of at least 200,000 years ended with the sinking of Atlantis in 10,700 B.C. The ancient world even then, said Cayce, had records of an ancient world before that and was well aware of the great epochs of time as related to the zodiac.

Steiner relates that series of epochs to our present place on the evolutionary spiral: "With the transition from the Egypto-Chaldean into the Graeco-Latin epoch, the whole mode and disposition of man's soul and all his faculties had undergone an essential change. The kind of logical thinking and intellectual comprehension of the world with which we are now familiar did not exist in Egypto-Chaldean times." He states further that the way man acquires knowledge today by deliberate exercise of his intelligence, "he then received directly; it was given to him as an intuitive and inner—in some respects, supersensible—knowledge."[17]

The Graeco-Latin epoch was predominantly in Aries. But Aries is followed by a new great year or cycle beginning with Pisces. During the end of Aries and the beginning of Pisces, unusually extreme changes took place from 600 B.C. to A.D. 600, the transition from one great year or cycle of twenty-five thousand years to the next. It was, says Reid, a remarkable turning point in both human evolution and in world history. These years "covered the most brilliant epoch in history, the inauguration of the present world religions, the flowering of Greece and the rise and fall of Rome. . . . A fresh inspiration entered the human mind and continued to illuminate it until the third and fourth centuries A.D. when it began to fade and was finally extinguished in the sixth century A.D."[18]

Early in the first millennium A.D., the spread of Christianity began at the very time when "faculties of supersensible cognition were undeveloped in a large proportion of mankind," states Steiner. "This was intended. It was in harmony with the whole trend of mankind's evolution upon Earth, and it accounts for the overwhelming influence of tradition at that time. The strongest influence was needed to give men faith and trust when they had not the faculty of spiritual sight."[19] "For by the very laws of evolution," continues Steiner, "an older faculty of soul loses its full significance when new faculties develop."[20] When Christianity spread, without his faculty of spiritual sight, man had to depend on faith and trust in the supersensible world. However, "there were nearly always present on Earth some individuals who were able to lift themselves into the higher worlds of Imagination, Inspiration, and Intuition. These were the true successors in the Christian era of the Initiates who in pre-Christian times had guided and partaken in the old Mystery—wisdom. . . . To this they had to add the knowledge of the Christ-Event and its deeper meaning."[21]

CHANGES IN THE NEW MILLENNIUM

For our time, we are concerned with our known history and how we have evolved in that time. We're concerned with the transition from Pisces to Aquarius, which is full of change in how we will evolve during the next two thousand years. What changes are in store for us all? For one thing, we will change in how we understand Christianity, from what Steiner calls "the external view" of past centuries increasingly supplemented by the inner, esoteric aspect. "What man can come to know by dint of Imagination, Inspiration, and Intuition of the higher worlds in unison with the Mystery of Christ, will permeate men's thinking, their feeling, and their willing— ever increasingly as time goes on. The 'hidden knowledge of the Grail' will become manifest and grow to be a power in man's life, entering ever more fully into all the ways and walks of man.''[22]

Only the initiates themselves in our time have been said to have such inner knowledge just slightly apprehended by seekers and would-be initiates. Are we, in this early Aquarian stirring, awakening to that ancient mode of intuition of which Steiner speaks? He compares humanity of past and present: "What the soul knew of higher worlds in olden time was not yet permeated with her own human powers of intelligence and feeling . . . was given as a kind of spiritual inspiration. In future, man will not only be receiving 'inspirations' of this kind, but will understand them through and through, feeling them as his very own, the true expression of his inmost being. . . .''[23]

We already sense the Aquarian consciousness that is rising everywhere to express higher ideals, deeper religious experience, seeking good by large sections of humanity *for humanity,* a phenomenon not experienced on earth since 600 B.C. to judge from our recent past. As individuals, we do try to figure ourselves out. We know we must get along with one another if we are to survive. As nations, we seem never before in recent ages to have been so connected, communicating, thanks to ever-expanding technology, swift travel, and mobility. And in a mere two decades of the twentieth century, people everywhere have risen up to throw over the old order, demanding equality, justice, and freedom. Ancient regimes have been toppled, oppressors giving way to the disenfranchised. Spiritual values are sought with great sincerity, including those called "Promise Keepers." All of that is unprecedented in recent history. It is because we find ourselves outgrowing old patterns to move into a time in which we keep faith and hope but will discover, according to Steiner, "the Knowledge of the Grail."

Writing in the 1930s, he said there had been "an increasing

inflow of the higher knowledge, and will continue to develop
... As the cultural evolution of mankind absorbs the knowledge of the Grail, in the same measure will the spiritual im-
pulse of the Christ-Event become effective; its true
significance will be revealed and it will grow from strength
to strength."[24]

At about the same time, Cayce was on hand just at the
beginning of mass world revolution toward what he called the
"new order" of freedom and spiritual growth. It was fueled,
then, by the Aquarian influence toward, in Steiner's terms,
"the hidden knowledge, the 'Science of the Grail.' "[25]

When our orbiting sun comes near to Brahma, the grand
center, "*dharma,* the mental virtue, becomes so much developed that man can easily comprehend even the mysteries of
Spirit."[26]

We are heading back to the center after the long decline.
Such an epoch as Leo to Aquarius—12,500 years—of the
25,000-year cycle for the entire world, is just a fraction of
God's time but long enough for man to have grown as the
evolutionary spiral carries him always higher toward his goal.
During the Age of Aries, the Greeks gave us philosophy,
poetry, drama, and the healing arts. In contrast, by the end of
Aries and the beginning of Pisces and throughout, we were
obliged to depend on faith alone because man lacked inner
spiritual perception. As well, intellectual pursuits were denied
mankind by the church except for a few scientific philosophers.

But what of ourselves in the last years of the Piscean Age?
In the early twentieth century, H. G. Wells described elo-
quently our present state of consciousness: "We are beginning to understand something of what the world might be,
something of what our race might become, were it not for
our still raw humanity.... Make men and women only sufficiently jealous or fearful or drunken or angry, and the red
hot eyes of the cavemen will glare out at us today.... We
have tamed the beasts and schooled the lightning; but we are
still only shambling towards the light...."[27]

We still continue to shamble towards the light, with the
same "raw humanity" in many pockets of darkness around

the earth as political and religious factions carry out murder against innocent men, women, and children. Things haven't seemed to change since the days of Herod, who massacred all infant boys in Bethlehem in an attempt to eliminate the baby Jesus. Since then, we have wandered along with the sun in its orbit, far from the central Sun. But the good news is, we are turning back as we approach Aquarius, the second "month" of the great cycle. Despite the evidence of dark forces at work among us still, events of recent decades and our growing inner (Aquarian?) sense tell us we are truly progressing according to a larger plan. The great sidereal cycle that the Egyptians understood is recognized today by those groups that have kept the ancient teachings, such as the Freemasons, the spiritual gurus of India, the Theosophists, and our kind "elder brothers" known as the Ascended Masters of the Great White Brotherhood, of which Edgar Cayce is said to be a member. As a world spokesman for the beginning of the new two-thousand-year cycle, he stated on February 2, 1932: "The day approaches when 'neither in this mountain nor yet in Jerusalem,' but in each one's heart, will there be planted that truth that will bring the *world* out of chaos. . . ." (3976-9). See John 4:21-24.

NOTES

CHAPTER ONE: THE NEW ORDER

1. James Perloff, *The Shadows of Power: The Council on Foreign Relations and the American Decline* (Appleton, WI: Western Islands, 1988). Quoted in Bill Still, *On the Horns of the Beast* (Winchester, VA: Reinhardt and Still, 1995; E-mail: bstill@bigfoot.com.), p. 11.

2. *New York Times,* December 22, 1913, quoted in Still, *On the Horns of the Beast,* p. 151.

3. John Stormer, *None Dare Call It Treason* (Florisant, MO: Liberty Bell Press, 1964).

4. Still, *On the Horns of the Beast,* p. 7.

5. Ibid., p. 135.

6. Perloff quoted ibid., p. 16.

7. Still quoting Dwight L. Kinman, *The World's Last Dictator* (Woodburn, OR: Solid Rock Books, 1993), p. 159. Quoted ibid.

8. Still, *On the Horns of the Beast,* pp. 264, 265.

9. Mary Ellen Carter, *Edgar Cayce on Prophecy* (New York: Warner Books, 1968), p. 74.

10. Ibid., p. 75.

11. Still, *On the Horns of the Beast,* pp. 189, 190.

12. Cliff Kincaid, *Washington Post,* January 26, 1997.

13. James Harvey Robinson and Charles A. Beard, *History of Europe: Our Own Times* (Boston: Ginn and Company, 1921), p. 582.

14. Eduard A. Shevardnadze, interview with Tom Brokaw, *Meet the Press,* September 30, 1990.

15. Gary Allen, *None Dare Call it Conspiracy* (Rossmoor, CA: Concord

Press, 1972), quoted in Still, *On the Horns of the Beast*, p. 216.

16. Wire reports, June 4, 1990.

CHAPTER TWO: THE AWAKENING

1. Charles W. Meister, *The Founding Fathers* (Jefferson, NC: Farland and Co., 1987), pp. 16, 17.

2. Ibid.

3. Manly P. Hall, *The Lost Keys of Freemasonry* (Richmond, VA: McCoy Publishing and Masonic Supply Company).

4. Ibid., p. 121.

5. H. L. Haywood, *Famous Masons and Masonic Presidents* (Chicago: The Masonic History Co., 1944), p. 33.

6. Theodore Heline, *America's Destiny* (La Canada, CA: New Age Press, 1941), pp. 5, 6.

7. William Harman, Ph.D., *Global Mind Change* (Knowledge Systems, Inc., with Institute of Noetic Sciences, 1988). p. 117. 1976. pp. 11, 12.

8. John White, *Pole Shift* (Virginia Beach, VA: A.R.E. Press, 1987).

9. Heline, *America's Destiny*, p. 39.

10. Ibid., p. 121.

11. Harman, *Global Mind Change*, pp. 118–22.

12. Carter, *Edgar Cayce on Prophecy*, p. 79.

CHAPTER THREE: "FREEDOM! FREEDOM!"

1. *U.S. News & World Report*, December 2, 1985.

2. *Compton's Pictured Encyclopedia* (Chicago: F. E. Compton and Company, 1962).

3. Dr. Daniel Graf, History Professor, Virginia Wesleyan College, Virginia Beach, letter to the author.

4. Ibid.

5. Ibid.

6. *U.S. News & World Report*, December 25, 1989–January 1, 1990.

7. Steven V. Roberts, *U.S. News & World Report*, January 15, 1990.

8. Graf letter.

9. Dr. Yuri Shmarov, lecture at ODU/NSU Graduate Center, Virginia Beach, November 1989.

10. Ibid.

11. Ibid.

12. David Selbourne, *U.S. News & World Report,* December 11, 1989.

13. Stefan Heym, *U.S. News & World Report,* December 11, 1989.

14. David Satter, *Reader's Digest,* February 1990.

15. Ibid.

16. Ibid.

17. Ibid.

18. Ibid.

19. Ibid.

20. Lech Walesa, interview by Robert MacNeil, *MacNeil/Lehrer Nightly News Report,* November 1989.

21. Ibid.

22. Ibid.

23. Ibid.

24. Max Hayward, *Writers in Russia, 1917–1978,* ed. Patricia Blake (San Diego: Harcourt, 1983), p. 65.

25. Ibid., p. 72.

26. Ibid., p. 73.

27. Ibid., p. 80.

CHAPTER FOUR: "OUT OF RUSSIA"

1. Vladimer Solovyov and Elena Klepikova, *Behind the High Kremlin Walls* (New York: Dodd, Mead, 1986), p. 150.

2. Ibid., pp. 140–42.

3. Ibid.

4. Ibid., p. 153.

5. Ibid., pp 150–58.

6. Mikhail Gorbachev, *Perestroika: New Thinking for Our Country and the World* (New York: Harper, 1987), pp. 216, 217.

7. Ibid.

8. Alexander Solzhenitsyn, press report, 1979.

9. Nikita Struve, "Solzhenitsyn in Exile: An Interview on Literary Themes with Nikita Struve, March, 1976," in *Solzhenitsyn in Exile: Critical*

Essays and Documentary Material ed. John Dunlop, Richard S. Haugh, and Michael Nicholson (Stanford: Hoover Institution Press, 1985), p. 301.

10. John Dunlop, *"The Gulag Archipelago": Alternative to Ideology* p. 170.

11. Ibid., p. 173.

12. Ibid., p. 173.

13. Hayward, *Writers in Russia*, pp. 41–42.

14. Ibid., pp. 42–43.

15. Ibid., p. 54.

16. Ibid.

17. Alexander Solzhenitsyn, *A Day in the Life of Ivan Denisovich*, Explanatory Notes.

18. Richard Z. Chesnoff, "The Prisoner Who Took the Castle", *U.S. News & World Report*, February 26, 1990.

19. Ibid.

20. Vaclav Havel, speech before U.S. Congress, *U.S. News & World Report*, February 26, 1990.

21. *MacNeil/Lehrer Nightly News Report*, February 5, 1990.

22. Gorbachev, *Perestroika*, pp. 188, 189.

23. J. G. Garrard, "The Emergence of Modern Russian Literature and Thought," in *The Eighteenth Century in Russia*, ed. J. G. Garrard (Oxford: Oxford University Press, 1973), p. 3.

24. Nicholas V. Riasanovsky, *A History of Russia* (New York: Oxford University Press, 1984), pp. 72, 260.

25. Ibid., p. 107.

26. Ibid., p. 227.

27. Garrard, "Emergence of Modern Russian Literature," p. 3.

28. Alec Nove, *Glasnost in Action: Cultural Renaissance in Russia* (Boston: Unwin Hyman, 1989), pp. 62, 57.

29. Ibid., pp. 25–29.

30. Riasanovsky, *History of Russia*, p. 146–151.

31. Ibid., p. 151.

32. Marc Raeff, "The Enlightenment in Russia and Russian Thought in the Enlightenment," in Garrard, *Eighteenth Century in Russia*, p. 26.

33. Ibid., p. 28.

34. James Cracraft, "Feofan Prokopovich," in Garrard, *Eighteenth Century in Russia*, p. 75.

35. Raeff, "Enlightenment in Russia," pp. 42, 43.

36. Max J. Okenfuss, "The Jesuit Origins of Petrine Education," in Garrard, *Eighteenth Century in Russia*, pp. 109–13.

37. Cracraft, "Feofan Prokopovich," pp. 101–04.

38. Ibid., pp. 104, 105.

39. Quoted in Garrard, "Emergence of Modern Russian Literature," p. 20.

40. Arthur Wilson, "Diderot in Russia," in Garrard, *Eighteenth Century in Russia*, pp. 187, 188.

41. Garrard, "Emergence of Modern Russian Literature," p. 18.

42. Raeff, "Enlightenment in Russia," p. 38.

43. Riasanovsky, *History of Russia*, pp. 372–74.

44. Ibid., pp. 374–84.

45. Leonard Schapiro, *The Russian Revolution of 1917* (New York: Basic Books, 1984), pp. 1–5.

46. Riasanovsky, *History of Russia*, p. 185.

47. Ibid., p. 186.

48. Ibid., pp. 249, 250.

49. Graf letter.

50. Nove, *Glasnost in Action*, p. 21.

51. Ibid., p. 25.

52. Ibid., p. 27.

53. Ibid., pp. 26, 29.

CHAPTER FIVE: "*BORN* AGAIN!"

1. Metropolitan Alexy, "Looking Back After a Millennium," in *Perestroika 1989*, pp. 309–12.

2. Ibid.

3. Riasanovsky, *History of Russia*, pp. 34–36.

4. Ibid., p. 49.

5. Nove, *Glasnost in Action*, pp. 116–17.

6. Ibid., pp. 311–12.

7. Ibid.

8. Ada B. Bozeman, *Human Rights and World Order* (Praeger Publishers, 1978), pp. 148–150.

9. Ibid.

10. Associated Press, June 2, 1969.

11. Gorbachev, *Perestroika*, pp. 25–51.

12. Dusko Doder and Louise Branson, *Gorbachev: Heretic in the Kremlin* (New York: Viking, 1990), pp. 290–91.

13. Ibid.

14. Ibid.

15. Fred Coleman, *The Decline and Fall of the Soviet Empire*, St. Martin's Press, 1996, pp. 320, 321.

16. Ibid., p. 428.

17. Ibid., p. 321.

18. *U.S. News and World Report*, December 11, 1989.

19. *U.S. News and World Report*, "A New Chill in the Air?", April 16, 1990.

20. Coleman p. 295.

21. *Los Angeles Times News Service*, October 3, 1990.

22. Marshall I. Goldman, "Moscow's Money Troubles", *World Monitor*, October, 1990.

23. *Associated Press*, January 27, 1991.

24. Coleman, p. 295.

25. Ibid., pp. 274, 275

26. *Associated Press*, December 6, 1990.

27. *U.S. News & World Report*, March 25, 1991.

28. *Associated Press*, April 1, 1991.

29. Marshall I. Goldman, "The Hunt for Red Enterprise," *World Monitor*, December 1990.

30. Ibid.

31. *Associated Press*.

32. *Associated Press*.

33. *Associated Press*, June 15, 1991.

34. *U.S. News and World Report*, "The Last Big Summit", by Robin Knight with Douglas Stanglin in Moscow; Julie Corwin and Kenneth T. Walsh, August 1991.

35. Ibid.

36. *U.S. News and World Report*, "The True Believer", by Kenneth T. Walsh with Carla Anne Robbins, Robin Knight in Moscow and Louise Lief in Berlin, July 1, 1991.

37. Ibid.

38. *Bloomberg News Service*, July 30, 1997.

39. From Wire Reports, August 21, 1991.

40. Ibid.

41. Michael Parks, *Los Angeles Times News Service*, August 22, 1991.

42. From Wire Reports, August 22, 1991.

43. John M. Broder, *Los Angeles Times News Service*, August 21, 1991.

44. *U.S. News & World Report*, May 13, 1991.

45. *U.S. News & World Report*, December 23, 1991.

46. Coleman, pp. 354, 355.

47. Ibid.

48. Robin Knight in Moscow with Julie Corwin, *U.S. News & World Report*, January 13, 1992.

49. Ibid.

50. *The Baltimore Sun*, October 5, 1991.

51. Ibid.

52. Colin Powell, interview on *McNeil/Lehrer News Hour* in March 1992.

CHAPTER SIX: IN PURSUIT OF PEACE

1. *A Search for God* (Virginia Beach, VA: A.R.E. Press), Book I, Chapter One.

2. Robert Alden, New York Times News Service, September 13, 1973.

3. Ibid.

4. Ibid.

5. Associated Press, June 9, 1978.

6. *The New American*, November 5, 1990.

7. *A Search for God*.

8. Brian Duffy and Kenneth T. Walsh, "The Gulf War's Final Curtain," *U.S. News & World Report*, March 4, 1991.

9. Ibid.

0. Ibid.

1. Frank P. Chambers, Christina Phelps Harris, and Charles C. Bayley, *This Age of Conflict: A Contemporary World History, 1914 to the Present* (New York: Harcourt, 1950).

2. Wire reports, February 24, 1991.

3. *U.S. News & World Report,* November 19, 1990.

4. Carla Anne Robbins, *U.S. News & World Report,* November 19, 1991.

5. Javier Pérez de Cuéllar, interview with Charlayne Hunter-Gault, *MacNeil/Lehrer NewsHour,* March 1991.

6. Ibid.

7. Leland M. Goodrich, *The United Nations in a Changing World* (New York: Columbia University Press, 1974), pp. 6, 7.

8. Ibid.

9. Ibid., pp. 12, 13.

20. Ibid., p. 41.

21. Ibid.

22. *United Nations Chronicle,* September 1990.

23. Ibid.

24. Ibid.

25. Ibid.

26. Ibid.

27. Ibid.

28. Ibid.

29. Ibid.

30. Jeffrey Laurenti, lecture at Virginia Wesleyan College, Virginia Beach, Virginia, April 1991.

31. Ibid.

32. Bruce Babbitt, "The New and Improved South America," *World Monitor,* February 1991.

33–45. (Notes deleted.)

CHAPTER SEVEN: BULLETS AND DIPLOMACY

1. *U.S. News & World Report,* November 25, 1985.

2. Charles J. Hanley, "Nuclear-Free Zones Spreading Across the World," Associated Press, August 25, 1985.

3. Ibid.

4. David Gergen, *U.S. News and World Report,* December 2, 1985.

5. *U.S. News & World Report,* Worldgram, December 2, 1985.

6. Peter Ross Range, Maureen Santini, Robert A. Kittle, and Nicholas Daniloff, *U.S. News & World Report,* August 4, 1986.

7. Kenneth T. Walsh and Robert J. Shapiro, *U.S. News and World Report,* June 8, 1987.

8. Associated Press, December 11, 1987.

9. Ibid.

10. Robert C. Toth, Los Angeles Times News Service, November 25, 1987.

11. Associated Press, June 3, 1988.

12. Donald Kaul, Associated Press, July 27, 1990.

13. *Parade Magazine,* August 12, 1990.

14. Associated Press, July 28, 1990.

15. Ibid.

16. James Wallace, "The Forgotten War," *U.S. News & World Report,* June 25, 1990.

17. Ibid.

18. Ibid.

19. Associated Press, December 11, 1988.

20. Ibid.

21. Associated Press, July 21, 1990.

22. Associated Press, July 27, 1990.

23. Associated Press, October 4, 1991.

24. Los Angeles Times News Service, April 10, 1990.

25. Associated Press, July 27, 1988.

26. Keith R. Richberg, Washington Post News Service, September 27, 1988.

27. *Parade Magazine,* July 10, 1988.

28. Ibid.

29. Ibid.

30. Ibid.

31. Associated Press, January 17, 1990.

32. Ibid.

33. Ibid.

34. *Chicago Tribune,* August 19, 1990.

35–37. (Notes deleted.)

38. Wire reports.

39. Knight-Ridder News Service, April 23, 1988.

40. Eloy O. Aaguilar, Associated Press, January 4, 1990.

41. Michael Norton, Associated Press, September 20, 1988.

42. Associated Press, October 4, 1991.

43. Associated Press, October 1, 1991.

44. Associated Press, November 23, 1991.

45–47. (Notes deleted.)

47a. George Gedda, Associated Press, May 22, 1991.

47b. Ibid.

48. *U.S. News & World Report,* August 27/September 3, 1990; August 20, 1990.

49–52. (Notes deleted.)

52a. *The Middle East in Prophecy* (Pasadena, CA: Worldwide Church of God, 1988).

52b. *U.S. News & World Report,* November 4, 1991.

53. Los Angeles Times News Service, October 4, 1991.

54. James F. Smith, Los Angeles Times News Service, and wire reports, August 18, 1991.

55. Ibid.

56. *Chicago Tribune,* August 19, 1991.

57. Tom Hundley, *Chicago Tribune,* October 29, 1991.

58. Associated Press, November 1, 1991.

59. Ruth Sinai, Associated Press, December 15, 1991.

60. Associated Press, December 19, 1991.

61. Associated Press, January 5, 1992.

62. Wire reports, January 20, 1992.

63. William Ruelman, *Virginian Pilot/Ledger Star,* December 1985.

64. James Wallace, *U.S. News & World Report,* June 24, 1985.

65. Ibid.

66. Tom Wells, Associated Press, August 25, 1985.

67. Tom Wells, Associated Press, August 2, 1985.

68. Ibid.

69. Ibid.

70. Ibid.

71. Ibid.

72. Ibid.

73. Tom Wells, Associated Press, August 25, 1985.

74. Wire reports.

75. Ibid.

76. Wire reports.

77. William Drozdiak and William Branigan, Washington Post News Service, February 7, 1988.

78. Ibid.

79. *Congressional Record*, 100th Congr., 2d sess., June 8, 1988.

80. Ibid.

81. Ibid.

82. Ibid.

83. Ibid.

84. George Gedda, Associated Press, October 3, 1988.

85. William Drozdiak and William Branigan, Washington Post News Service, February 7, 1988.

86. Ibid.

87. Ibid.

88. Tad Szulc, *Parade Magazine*, August 28, 1988.

89. Ibid.

90. Ibid.

91. New York Times News Service, February 13, 1989.

92. Knight-Ridder News Service, November 30, 1989.

93. Linda Robinson, *U.S. News & World Report*, July 2, 1990.

94. Linda Robinson and Ana Arana, *in Bogata, U.S. News & World Report*, July 30, 1990.

95. Ibid.

96. Ibid.

97. U.S. State Department; U.S. Drug Enforcement Agency; National Narcotics Intelligence Consumers Committee; the Department of Health and Human Services; Associated Press, 1990.

98. Ibid.

99. *The Economist,* August 20, 1988.

100. James F. Smith, Los Angeles Times News Service, February 5, 1989; wire reports.

101. James F. Smith, Los Angeles Times News Service, October 7, 1988.

102. Associated Press, October 15, 1991.

103. *Baltimore Sun,* July 30, 1989.

104. Jim Drinkard, Associated Press, November 21, 1989.

105. Dali Lama, interview by Jim Lehrer, *NewsHour,* April 22, 1997.

106. A. K. Reischauer, *The Nature and Truth of the Great Religions* (Rutland, VT: Charles E. Tuttle Company, 1966), pp. 144–46.

107. James Adams, "The Real Lesson of the Gulf War," *The Atlantic,* November 1991.

108. Ibid.

109. Wire reports, March 24, 1997.

110. Barry Schweid, Associated Press, April 8, 1997.

111. Ibid.

112. Ibid.

113. Associated Press, April 9, 1997.

114. Associated Press, April 13, 1997.

115. Ibid.

CHAPTER EIGHT: "HE IS THY BROTHER!"

1. Gary Allen, "War On Poverty—Billions to Finance Revolution," *American Opinion Magazine,* February 1962.

2. Ibid.

3. Ibid.

4. Allen quoting Ruth Montgomery, *Los Angeles Herald Examiner,* September 6, 1965.

5. Allen, "War On Poverty."

6. "Indian Encounter," *World Press Review,* February 1992.

7. Ibid.

8. Samuel Eliot Morison and Henry Steele Commager, *The Growth of*

the American Republic (New York: Oxford University Press, 1942), pp. 5, 12.

9. Ibid., pp. 358, 359.

10. Ibid., pp. 488–90.

11. Virginia Beach Office of Public Information, Historical Records of Virginia Beach.

12. John Howard Griffin, *Black Like Me* (Boston: Houghton Mifflin, 1977).

13. Jacques Maritain, *Scholasticism and Politics* (North Stratford, NH: Ayer Company 1957), Quoted ibid., p. 197.

14. Reynolds Farley, *Blacks and Whites: Narrowing the Gap?* (Cambridge, MA: Harvard University Press, 1984), p. 203.

15. Ibid., p. 50.

16. Ibid.

17. Ibid.

18. Griffin, *Black Like Me.*

19. Clark Cochran, Lawrence C. Mayer, T. R. Carr, and N. Joseph Cayer, *American Public Policy: An Introduction,* 2d ed. (New York: St. Martin's Press, 1986), pp. 410–11.

20. Ibid.

21. Ibid.

22. Jim Carrier, Los Angeles Times/Washington Post Service, October 11, 1985.

23. Ibid.

24. Ibid.

25. Ibid.

26. Richard Manning, *They Cannot Kill Us All* (Boston: Houghton Mifflin, 1987), pp. 62–275.

27. Ibid.

28. Ibid.

29. Ibid.

30. Robin Knight, *U.S. News & World Report,* August 19, 1985.

31. Tom Baldwin, Associated Press, July 1988.

32. Tom Baldwin Associated Press, May 1983.

33. Manning, *They Cannot Kill Us All.*

34. Associated Press, November 3, 1985.

35. *U.S. News & World Report,* August 19, 1985.

36. Ibid.

37. Robin Knight, *U.S. News & World Report,* August 19, 1985.

38. Michael Parks, "South Africa's Ban on Photos of Unrest Draws Criticism," Los Angeles Times News Service, November 3, 1985.

39. Ibid.

40. Alan Cowell, New York Times News Service, November 17, 1985.

41. Don Irwin, Los Angeles Times News Service, 1988.

42. Associated Press, February 27, 1998.

43. Los Angeles Times News Service, September 16, 1988.

44. Blaine Harden, Washington Post News Service, September 6, 1988.

45. Knight-Ridder News Service, November 5, 1989.

46. Associated Press, July 9, 1990.

47. Ibid.

48. Associated Press, September 1989.

49. Associated Press, October 1989.

50. Associated Press, November 17, 1989.

51. Laurinda Keys, Associated Press, July 19, 1988.

52. Ibid.

53. Ibid.

54. Ibid.

55. Ibid.

56. Associated Press, July 18, 1988.

57. Interview with Ted Koppel, June 1990.

58. Tom Kenworthy, Washington Post News Service, June 27, 1990.

59. *USA Today,* June 19, 1990.

60. Ibid.

61. Associated Press, June 28, 1990.

62. Ibid.

63. Ibid.

64. Associated Press, March 20, 1992.

65. Scott Kraft, Los Angeles Times News Service, March 19, 1992.

66. Barry Renfrew, Associated Press, July 1990.

67. Ibid.

CHAPTER NINE: "WHY THEN THE TURMOIL?"

1. Morison and Commager, *Growth of the American Republic*, I: 235.

2. David Gergen, *U.S. News & World Report*, July 30, 1990.

3. Roseann Bentley, quoted in a report from the National Association of State Boards of Education, Associated Press, June 9, 1990.

4. Ibid.

5. *St. Germain on Alchemy*, Book One, Recorded by Mark Prophet and Elizabeth Clare Prophet (Summit University Press, 1985). Originally published by Wesley Bradshaw. Copied from a reprint in the *National Tribune*, Vol. 4, no. 12, December 1980.

6. *U.S. News & World Report*, October 8, 1984.

CHAPTER TEN: ONENESS OF ALL FAITHS

1. Sri Swami Yukteswar, *The Holy Science* (Los Angeles: Self-Realization Fellowship, 1972.)

2. Archbishop Mahoney, *MacNeil/Lehrer Nightly News*, November 12, 1990.

3. Gerson Yalowitz and Neel Patri, "A New Wave of Ethnic Violence Threatens India's Unity," *U.S. News & World Report*, November 12, 1990.

4. Ibid.

5. Dr. Ralf Brinkman, symposium on the fall of the Berlin Wall, Old Dominion University, January 1990.

6. Ibid.

7. Ibid.

8. Karla Goldman, "Pogroms and Perestroika," *World Monitor*, May 1990.

9. Ibid.

10. Ibid.

11. *New York Times*, January 25, 1998.

12. (Note deleted.)

13. Quoted in *Virginian Pilot*, January 19, 1991.

14. *The Koran Interpreted,* trans. Arthur J. Arberry (New York: Macmillan,).

15. Bryon Earhart, *Japanese Religion* (Belmont, CA: Wadsworth Publishing Company, 1982).

16. *A Buddhist Bible,* ed. Dwight Goddard (New York: Dutton, 1938).

CHAPTER ELEVEN: IDEALS AND ECONOMICS

1. Jan Dauman, "The Global Economy in the Year 2000," in *The Global Economy: America's Role in The Decade Ahead,* ed. William E. Brock and Robert D. Hormats (New York: Norton, 1990), pp. 201–04.

2. Raymond Vernon, "Same Planet, Different Worlds," in Brock and Hormats, *Global Economy,* p. 38.

3. Michael B. Smith, "U.S.–Japan Economic Relations," in Brock and Hormats, *Global Economy,* pp. 80–83.

4. Lars Anell and Birgitta Nygren, *The Developing Countries and the World Economic Order* (New York: St. Martin's Press, 1980).

5. Ibid., p. 122.

6. Ibid., p. 87.

7. Dauman, "Global Economy," p. 216.

8. Ibid., p. 204.

9. See Still, *On the Horns of the Beast,* chapter 17.

10. Dave Skidmore, Associated Press, March 3, 1998.

11. D. F. Bromley and Ray Bromley, *South American Development: A Geographical Introduction* (New York: Cambridge University Press, 1982), pp. 60, 61.

12. Ibid., p. 62.

13. Ibid., p. 63.

14. Ibid., p. 88.

15. Ibid., p. 74.

16. David M. Abshire, "The Nature of American Leadership," in Brock and Hormats, *Global Economy,* p. 195.

17. Richard Trumka, interviewed by Bob Schieffer, *Face the Nation,* October 19, 1997.

18. Brock and Hormats, Introduction, *Global Economy,* p. 10.

19. Bruce Babbitt, "The New and Improved South America," *World Monitor*, February 1991.

20. Leonard Sussman, "The Distance to Democracy," *World Monitor*, February 1991.

21. Abshire, "Nature of American Leadership," pp. 175–200.

22. *United Nations Chronicle*, October 1990.

23. Peter W. Ludlow, "Managing Change," Brock and Hormats, *Global Economy*, p. 69.

24. Frederick Merk and Lois Bannister Merk, *Manifest Destiny and Mission in American History* (Westport, CT: Greenwood Press, 1983), pp. 24–34.

CHAPTER TWELVE: "THAT NATURAL EVOLUTION"

1. Sri Yukteswar, *The Holy Science*, p. 26.

2. Ibid., pp. xi, xii.

3. Ibid., p. xx.

4. Vera W. Reid, *Towards Aquarius* (New York: Arco Publishing Company, 1969), p. 85.

5. Ibid., p. 79.

6. Ibid., p. 62.

7. Ibid., pp. 91, 92.

8. Ibid., p. 92.

9. Ibid., p. 107.

10. Joseph F. Goodavage, *Astrology: The Space Age Science* (West Nyack, NY: Parker Publishing Company, 1967), pp. 164, 165.

11. Reid, *Towards Aquarius*, p. 15.

12. Sri Yukteswar, *The Holy Science*, p. xiii.

13. Reid, *Towards Aquarius*, p. 14.

14. Ibid., p. 11.

15. Ibid., p. 92.

16. Rudolf Steiner, *Occult Science: An Outline* (London: Rudolf Steiner Press, 1969), p. 301.

17. Ibid., pp. 301, 302.

18. Reid, *Towards Aquarius*, pp. 60, 61.